WHAT OTHERS HAVE TO SAY

"Erhard F. Freitag has done much for bringing psychosocial medicine and spirituality together at the common ground of each—the lives of each and every one of us. I have seen the power of Freitag's methods when used by people who need the help of a positive approach to their circumstances. This is an inspiring book for everyday living!"

Margot E. Kurtz, Ph.D.
Department of Family & Community Medicine
Michigan State University

"Can you imagine that a business person would seek out and use the power of the subconscious mind to help in resolving everyday ordinary, and sometimes extraordinary, challengers in his or her life? Well, I have used the methods developed by Erhad F. Freitag and I vouch for their helpfulness. May we all become more and better attuned to the power that resides within each of us and that is capable of assisting us in our challenges. Thank you, Mr. Freitag."

Otto K. Dufek
General Manager of an automobile group

"Would you rather be right or happy? Erhard F. Freitag has an uplifting answer to this tricky question: You can be both. His down-to-earth method teaches people who are willing to learn, how to solve their most troubling problems. More power to us, every one!"

Carna Zachoiras

"Our Marriage was almost at an end when I came across the book from Mr. Freitag. After reading it I persuaded my husband to do the same and now we have found new ways to live our lives. We are now much happier and contented together. Even today the book is always nearby to help with any problems we may encounter. The answers to all my problems are within me. I only have to find them."

M. Stoilaz

D1569350

"I was addicted to almost everything you can take...heroin, hash, etc. The books from Mr. Freitag have made me realize what I was really looking for. Slowly but surely I found it—Myself—and I finally managed to start a successful therapy. Thank you very much."

Thomas Prino

I always seemed to make the same mistakes. Whether it be in partnerships, at work or with friends and acquaintances. At regular intervals everything seemed to fall apart around me. Reading this book showed me how to recognize the subconscious mechanisms that cause it to happen. It wasn't the others fault, the blame lay entirely by me, even if I wasn't sure why. Now I have found my dream partner, have a wonderful job I enjoy and much, much more. My life has become full of excitement. I a so grateful that fate allowed this book to come into my possession."

Goetl

"After reading the book I visited a few of Mr. Freitags seminars and my life has totally turned around. My goals and wishes became clear and I managed to realize them with unbelievable ease. I hope the books and seminars from Mr. Freitag can help many other people lead a happy, contented, and positive life. Thank you."

Hillebrand

THE SUBCONSCIOUS MIND

A SOURCE OF UNLIMITED POWER

ERHARD F. FREITAG

Printed in United States of America

For information address:
Personhood Press
"Books for ALL that you are!"
Post Office Box 370
Fawnskin, California 92333
800.662.9662   email: personhoodpress@att.net

Library of Congress Cataloging-in-Publication Data
Erhard F. Freitag, 1940

The Subconscious Mind: A Source of Unlimited Power
by Erhard F. Freitag

ISBN 1-932181-07-5

Visit our Web site at
http://www.personhoodpress.com

Visit Erhard Freitag's Web site at
http://www.efreitag.com

cover:	editing:	interior design & layout by:
Linda J. Thille	Susan Remkus	www.madhof.com

cover photo:
Ron Winch

TABLE OF CONTENTS

A Foreword by Dr. Joseph Murphy

Erhard Freitag is an outstanding spiritual psychologist who gives a forceful and inspiring message on the Laws of Life, and has shown thousands of people how to live life triumphantly and gloriously. He has studied all of my books and lectures frequently on "The Power of Your Subconscious Mind", "Psychic Perception", and many of my other books.

Erhard Freitag is an outstanding teacher. He shows you how to lead a finer, happier, and richer life. I recommend this new book from him, which will bless you in countless ways.

Dr. Joseph Murphy
Laguna Hills, California
March 14, 1981

A Foreword by the Author

We live in a period of radical spiritual changes and shifts in values that has started to transform all areas of society. The path to a higher level of consciousness for all of us has taken an ever-growing dimension in these unique times. Our medicine especially awaits an extensive renewal. Treatment methods, up to now strange to our Western way of thinking, are finding their way into the rather orthodox world of medicine. Eastern philosophy has shown us that if we observe something from a different angle, new and necessary things essential for change will appear.

Even though orthodox psychology has only now started to rediscover the higher value of methods of spiritual therapy, I have been able to help my patients in many, many situations using both the oldest and newest healing methods in order to return them to a healthy life. My teacher, Dr. Joseph Murphy, has been working with hypnosis for decades, reporting on it in his numerous books. The positive thinking that I have learned from him has given me a clear spiritual view, and based on this, I have been able to find very plausible explanations for why psychoanalysts up till now have not been able to make any great breakthrough toward success. Indeed, crowded mental hospitals and prisons are proof of the state of medicine in our society today. Anyone who reads this book carefully will find an explanation, especially in those excerpts where I have examined the way our intellect works.

With this book I want to smooth the way toward spiritual strength that each of us possesses and to try to help you help yourself. Every person has been granted the right in this world to independently connect with the highest power in life. More and more, conscious people are aware of this right. Now, on the threshold of the new millennium, a "new consciousness" has started reforming the lives of us all, filling them with more hope. More and more, people know that anyone who needs help, anyone who is trapped in life's predicaments and is trying to be free can find, within, a way to resolve all problems and overcome illness, and thus literally be their own savior.

I am happy and very thankful for having met Dr. Murphy, who showed me the way to my higher Self. I have built my whole therapeutic work on his teachings of the eternal philosophy. Only thanks to this have I been able to achieve success far above the average for my profession, and have cured myself of an acute form of cancer.

This book has already sold more than 4,500,000 copies in 12 languages. More than 40 editions in only a few years have highlighted this book's extraordinary success, and consequently, I would like to express my thanks to you and to all my supporters. General interest in the applied philosophy of life has increased over the last couple of years and I have attempted to accommodate this growing interest. My further seven books are there for you if you have any worries and troubles.

I hope you derive a lot of pleasure in reading the following text. If you have any questions, do not hesitate to write to me. I will be there for you.

Spiritually connected,
Yours,

Erhard F. Freitag, 2003

1

The Subconcious Mind
A Source of Unlimited Power

Who is blind?
One who cannot see another world!

Who is mute?
One who cannot say anything sweet at the right moment!

Who is poor?
One who cannot give anything to the desperately poor!

Who is rich?
One who can be content to the bottom of his heart!

Indian Proverb

MANIPULATION OF OUR UNDERSTANDING

Do you believe in coincidence? There is no such thing! Our restricted daily consciousness lets us overlook too easily the simple rules determining our destiny. Only rarely do we manage to understand the important overall interconnections, and we often lose the overall view in the real sense of the word when it comes to detection of the real meaning hidden within and behind "things." Thus we control events which at this very moment and at this very point in our destiny present a path of significant importance. Whatever happens, we call it coincidence. Let us explore methods of perception together through this book and we will understand that "things that coincide actually belong together."

In most cases, we actually do not have the overview and we cannot understand the finely coordinated and sensitive mode of operation of the subconscious mind. One who does not observe the puzzle play of his own life with due attention perceives everything that happens unexpectedly as either coincidence or simply as an unexpected gift.

Reading this book is, of course, no coincidence in the usual sense of the word. It is something that happened to you at the moment of your life when you were open to new ideas, or it came to you to help you because you were crying out for it, and it will lead you to a "turning point" in all your crises.

For over a thousand years, we have been accustomed to paying attention mainly to the visible things in our world. The adventures of the real world that you can perceive through your senses often seem to be more interesting than sinking into deeper states of consciousness. This would imply us having to sort through an endless train of thought flowing through us from early morning till bedtime.

Are you aware that almost all problems are attributable to the fact that we do not use the power of our subconscious mind to bring about wanted results? We have not yet begun to use our "subconscious mind as a source of unlimited power" for our own purposes and causes.

If you are lucky enough to enjoy the experience of unexpected professional acknowledgement, do not consider it as mere coincidence or sudden attention paid to you by your superior. It is almost certainly your own personal effort that has caused it. You have identified yourself, both consciously and unconsciously, so completely with your task that your intellectual forces have brought about unstoppable success.

In a quite natural and easy way, you can learn how to consistently use this source for your important future targets. If you still do not understand the term "coincidence" as a secretly working inner action, it is probably because you entered into past enterprises with the hard and methodical power of your will. We should learn to understand that "the energy we use in order to achieve a goal actually creates an obstacle to the desired goal."

The paradox of this statement can be quickly understood by any Westerner. Intuition has always been deemed superior to the intellect, which is in turn governed by the will. No planning made by an intellectual with all the mental "push-ups" of his versatile educated mind can replace an intuitive brainstorm. The lifetime achievements of all great researchers and poets prove this. Intuitive perception is always worthier than bare rational knowledge. The intellect can never understand what intuition actually is, nor can it possibly do anything to bring it about.

One who does not have confidence in his own infinite intelligence and wants to perceive the sense of the world only through his intellect will certainly remain what he actually is for a long time: a rough material being in an ocean of ignorance. He will be a person constantly complaining about the difficulties and unfairness in his life, seeing himself as a victim of circumstances. If you want to change this in your life, then this book is really no coincidence. Now is the right moment to change what has to be changed and to ascertain what cannot be changed, differentiating one from another.

It is our false attitude toward ourselves and toward the real meaning of life that often makes us have doubts. It is an illness of our time not to accept and not to allow what cannot be explained by our modern human intellect. Consciousness is to most of us a narrow worldly extract which we are able to perceive with our five senses. We fearfully avoid topics like "the life after life" or "rebirth" because we do not want to appear ridiculous before others. However, a sixth sense has started developing and the feeling for the mental world made of fine material, much more important than we are often ready to admit, is on the threshold of awakening. By reading this book you are about to return to the source of all existence, that is to say to your true homeland.

The Subconscious Mind

The Uncontrollable Power of Thoughts

The state of our consciousness keeps changing in some strange way. If we are sad then the whole world appears gray, even if we are in the middle of a beautiful sunny day. However, if high spirits germinate inside us, then the worst downpour cannot spoil this good mood. What is it that constantly shifts our position between the positive and negative poles?

Which thoughts, for example, go through your head in the morning at breakfast? Do you think about everything that you want to complete during the morning? Perhaps you will be in good spirits because of an invitation to some evening event, or annoyed because of some damage to your car.

And there it is, a ray of light! Today you will meet the one you will always love or sign the contract for which you have longed for such a long time, and suddenly, you are in a good mood.

The situation is very different when you are confronted with a difficult task, which in your opinion could place too much pressure on you. It is too much for your nerves if you have to admit to your boss that you made a mistake. This all puts you off and you consequently leave the house with a furrowed brow and the day already seems pre-determined.

Nothing happens before eight o'clock in the morning. However, you set the tempo, polarizing your consciousness with only a few thoughts. Consider this for all time's sake: You have determined your mood by your own thoughts alone! Since you have looked at this matter subjectively, you might well answer: "All this corresponds to the actual facts; my thoughts have merely confronted me with them." Looking objectively, on the other hand, you have determined your feelings for the time to come by picturing what you can expect over the next few hours. Your subconscious mind is designed to arrange your day according to your expectations.

If the external world corresponds to your personal wishes, you are then satisfied. If something does not fit within your preconceptions, you immediately switch your mood and sometimes develop an enormous potential for bad emotions, thus opposing everything you can. Your subconscious mind carries out what your thoughts have pre-determined! Powerful aggression can develop within you, pushing you to uncontrollable actions. They can be the cause of illness and various undesirable mental states, or may even change things for the better.

It is surely a far-reaching statement to make thoughts responsible for both the well-being and suffering of the body and soul. However, conventional medicine concedes this power of the psyche to a much more limited extent. Nonetheless, holistic medicine already attributes eighty percent of all diseases to psychosomatic causes.

How is it that our consciousness, which seems to constitute and determine our lives, plays so little a part in our lives, as Eastern philosophers have pointed out? Is it our purely intellectualized viewpoint that creates such a limitation? Worldly science, with all its indoctrination, has made it very difficult for us to be able to accept any extension of our consciousness outside our present sphere of understanding.

To put it simply, our brain should be understood as a data bank. It has to find an explanation for everything that happens and a solution to every problem. What do we do when we feel ill? We go to see a doctor for help. That is so natural an act that none would have anything to say against it. However, with this act, our intellect has conceded that it is barely able to arrange anything within the body itself. All of us, regardless of our occupation or acquired education, rely too much on the intellect as "the main center" of our information and mode of action. Science is based exclusively on this unique, God-created "computer" which has secured our life in this wild and dangerous world, making it worth living.

How is it that we repeatedly make certain mistakes, not being able to penetrate into many of life's secrets? Did we lose our intellect or did we take it too seriously, giving it the opportunity to appoint itself the ruler? Has our egotistic, superficial form of liberty taken advantage of us, not letting us feel any longer what an illness wants to inform us about? We are apparently not interested in the power driving us, but only in how we can use it. The exploitation we have inflicted on our bodies, souls, and spirits since long ago is reflected today in the way we exploit the earth's resources.

Most of our fellow humans have not yet realized that access to our usually completely unconscious inner "resources" has become a big question in life and that we are able to determine our own fate to a large extent.

Logic is the beginning of all wisdom, but not the target.

Our Mind: A Source of Creative Force

The quality of your life will improve, regardless of whether you have mental or physical problems, after you discover within yourself your innate source of power and begin to live absorbing its power.

After modern brain research found that we really use only about ten percent of our brain capacity, we are easily tempted to assume that any improvement in the quality of life can only be achieved by an increase in knowledge. We believe that a more extensive curriculum and better training methods would lastingly improve our life and increase the percentage of our brain capacity.

By trying to extend our consciousness by means of our intellect, we are using completely inappropriate tools. Not even our greatest geniuses such as Goethe or Einstein exceeded this ten percent limit. Had they actually succeeded in expanding their consciousness to a higher level, it was not achieved by their intellect. Higher levels of consciousness, latently present in all of us, will supply us with large amounts of creative intelligence if we begin to use them via the channel of intuition.

There is no need to hide behind the statement "But they were geniuses!" Our psychological- philosophical journey through consciousness leads each of us to the existence of higher mental forces within ourselves. Each human being is able to exceed his pure intellectual capacities after ceasing to be ruled by them.

Einstein described how most of his most innovative scientific ideas did not result from any particularly careful combination of diverse considerations. He used to encircle a question as closely as possible with his own thoughts in order to submit everything to the subconscious mind, or if you wish, to his creative spirit. It would take days or weeks, sometimes even years, before some great idea cropped up. The infinite intelligence of his higher Self would send him the solution via an intuitive channel.

Each of us has this creative intelligence responsible for special "capabilities." Both theologians and psychologists have realized that something within us awaits revelation and that we are in a constant state of "development." Magic, the occult, parapsychology, as well as extra sensory perception (ESP) find their explanation in this sphere. According to our worldly conceptions, non-sensual events have still found no respectable place in the consciousness of most humans, including scientists themselves.

However, there are some clear paranormal phenomena that obviously cannot be denied.

A schoolboy, brought to my office by his parents because of some psychological weakness, became quite a personal form of proof to me. We had an extremely interesting experience with him during hypnotherapy. Sometimes he was able to tell us exactly where our co-worker was outside the office or what his mother was doing at home at that very moment. We were immediately convinced of the correctness of his visions through telephone calls. Once he even described in detail my own living room outside Munich, which he had never seen before. In a state of trance, he managed to break through the barriers of rational consciousness, sinking into the unconscious depths of his higher clair-voyant Self.

When I speak about the opening of still unconscious regions of the human Self, I have in mind the inner voice which we leave aside to a large extent, usually giving priority to our more rational views. We must dispose of the complete folly of our reason that declares mental impulses, intuition, and sudden spiritual realizations to be mere superstition and everything extra sensory to be hocus-pocus. Whatever cannot be perceived by our five senses we usually negate and fight against. Many of the new religious communities, meditation, and yoga groups constantly experience this. Without any regard to their possibly valuable spiritual content, they are fought against by established religions only because they do not comply with their world concept. Furthermore, scientists point out real proof to the danger visionaries have experienced by the extension of their consciousness after being treated with dangerous drugs or exposed to magical practices. Thus it is probably right to say that "the devil takes the magician." Before someone has mastered the imagination by means of drugs, he has usually ended up in a psychiatric institution.

I remember one particular woman whom I met during my training in the largest psychiatric hospital in Germany. She had tried, by inhaling herb steam usually created by witches, to attain special levels of consciousness. Her confused mind was not able to find a way out of the trance which she had been led to by the plant extracts. She suffered from persecution mania for a long time and I managed to help her only very slowly, accompanying her back to this world.

There are dangerous ways of extending the consciousness. Psychiatrists' and psychotherapists' consulting rooms are full of such examples. I would like to warn you not to try to extend your consciousness with drugs such as heroin or other harmful chemicals. They can bring you away from the normal state of the human mind much quicker than negative thoughts.

If the basis of our health, the harmony between our mind, body, and soul is utterly destroyed, then methods of conventional therapy are also inappropriate.

Love is one of our basic needs and I am going to refer to it again and again in this book. It should be a part of us if we want to master our fate. Consciousness is present in everything and it is constantly being developed. We can enhance it without jeopardizing ourselves. From this we can get our first important realization: Controlled by our instincts, feelings, words, and actions, our thoughts create our world. People experience what they think they do! This fundamental statement made by Dr. Murphy brings us to the beginning of his theory of positive thinking which I have integrated fully into both my practice and my personal life.

How is it that so many new thoughts from the heterogeneous field of modern psychology come mainly from the United States? American psychologists are much more pragmatic than European scientists. They do not ask too much about what actually happens. They concentrate on the answer to the question: How can I help immediately and what is the best way?

While we western Europeans look for the solution of the mystery of the soul by means of analytical research methods using highly complicated models and extremely different explanations, our colleagues from the USA try to re-integrate the patient back into the field of his duties set by society. In a social sense, to be a useful member of society it is first important to regain emotional harmony and balance. It is therefore not that surprising that the most modern psychotherapeutic practices such as psycho-synthesis, Gestalt therapy, body therapy, bio-energy and transpersonal psychotherapy have come to us to a large extent from American research centers.

According to Indian philosophy, unity of the mind, body, and soul is also important to achieve harmonious balance between spiritual levels and physical vitality, thus leading humans back to God- willed perfection.

The highest reality is found in faith.

YOU ARE WHAT YOU THINK

Interestingly, this statement corresponds to my own more Eastern way of thinking. Consequently, I do not simply send a patient to a neurosurgeon or—even simpler—prescribe him medication. Rather I tell him: "You are what you think and believe yourself to be! Think and believe that what you long for most is health and happiness and it will be so according to your thinking and beliefs."

If you really want to live in harmony and inner peace with yourself and your environment, your subconscious mind will turn these thoughts into reality. Whatever you perceive in your world as form, function, or experience is exclusively the result of your own thoughts. Thoughts are to be understood as living entities striving to be applied.

If something does not please you in your everyday life, then you should change your way of thinking! Whatever happens to you, you sent it out and it has come back to you.

It is very easy to be happy if you only implement a very few laws regarding the mind; many things will change for the better.

The Subconscious Mind

If you want, I will help you with the transformation and implementation of these simple spiritual laws. What is described here is neither a dream nor an illusion, but very realistic; it is the effect exercised by your inner spiritual strength. Once you formulate a thought, it is pushed outwards. You formulate it, it forms. You gave your idea the desired form and the idea shapes your world from the sphere of the subconscious mind.

Attempt to do this immediately! Try to find a calm place where you can make yourself comfortable. Close your eyes, trying to empathize with the following sentences:

"I dismiss all my thoughts! They drift in the sky like small white clouds, not knowing where they are going to, but still full of confidence. I am calm and relaxed. Perfect peace prevails in my heart and my mind. I am in harmony with the world. Harmony flows through my whole Self. It is good that it is so."

Try to actually feel this harmony in yourself, try to devote yourself to it. The presence and the depth of this feeling are relevant to the desired success. You will soon experience a marvelous feeling of inner freedom and you will be open to the good that slumbers in you, awaiting its awakening. From now on you will be successful in realizing your desires and you will soon live a happy life.

Your future success depends on your aspirations, by means of which you will bring about the longed for target. Socrates taught this to one of his pupils in a somewhat drastic way during a walk along a riverbank. The pupil asked him: "Master, how can I become like you?" Socrates told him to accompany him into the water. There he dunked the boy's head under the water again and again, until the pupil struggled for air, fearing for his life.

He let him free and asked: "What is it that you desire most?"

"Air, master, air. Nothing but air!"

Then Socrates said: "If you long for knowledge in the same as you longed for air, then you will be as I am!"

Can you recognize the way to the fulfillment of your desires? Your first step in the near future is to clearly see and feel in front of your spiritual eye the direction to desired success and then to feel the great joy of unrestrained happiness after having achieved your target.

If you still think that you can understand and see any reality, that is to say any apparent reality, you have overlooked the fact that you actually create your experiences through your thoughts. Your consciousness will arrange the surroundings according to the way you think.

This means that the intellect should be modest, stop its dominant behavior, and immediately give up its conceited position of being the highest instance in our life. If it is said "I am what I think," then it implies the philosopher's dependence on his own thoughts. If you steadily think of harmony, success, and happiness, then you will make it all happen. If you look forward to each new day, then you will also experience the pleasant and beautiful side of each new day. Problems are reduced by the fact that you evaluate them from a harmonious point of view. The external world and alleged fate in each case mirror the images of our thoughts, and you have decided to think positively— or have you?

Your body and your soul will thank you with good health, peace, and harmony or whatever you so desire.

In the case of 18-year-old Maria, I experienced how negative thoughts and uncontrollable outbreaks of emotions can stop the development of a young girl into an independent personality. Her parents brought her to me as "totally unfit for life." She was not able to thread a needle or wash up. Everything would go wrong.

An intimidated child, who had already apologized twice for stumbling and letting her bag fall from the chair, sat in front of me. I had to interrupt her mother's gush of words by force in order to be able to hear the girl. This picture of acquired immaturity and an inferiority complex could not be more perfect. One often has to free children from their parents in order to give them the ability to live on their own in the real sense of the word. In this particular case, the parents, who exercised some kind of strict control over their daughter with insulting words and unacceptable measures, had to be forced to stop. I was lucky enough to be able to arrange a professional training place for the girl during the therapy period 62 miles away from her parents' place of residence, and the parents agreed.

This young girl's inferiority complex was removed in a relatively simple way. Since her childhood, Maria had been "all too stupid," "behaving foolishly at dinner time," and "a clumsy oaf." After a few sessions and acquaintance with the first principles of positive thinking, she changed fast. The "wallflower" dared to go to the hairdresser's during the very first budding period of her new self- consciousness, which is always the first sign of the mental improvement by female patients, and she returned a pleasant-looking young

lady. For everyday use I gave her the following suggestive formula:

*"I am healthy, full of harmony and love. The infi-
nite intelligence of my subconscious mind makes me safe
and successful in all my actions. I am skillful and I solve
my assignments with love. I feel free and happy transferring my love to my parents and colleagues, with whom I
cooperate gladly and harmoniously."*

Being separated from her parents for several years
will further increase her self-confidence, making her
immune to the devaluing influence of her parents.
Actually, in many cases the parents should undergo
some kind of therapy as well, but it is obviously simpler
to have your children "fixed" than to lay the blame on
yourself. Their negative attitude and lifestyle, influenced by their obsession to rule, and their constant
niggling harm them most. They described their
daughter as mentally handicapped without even in the
slightest noticing the catastrophic influence their
constant criticism and impatience had had on her awakening consciousness. Maria could talk about her luck
at being able to learn about the liberating power of a
positive attitude toward life and about finally maturing
into a lovable young woman.

You, too, will find on these pages ideas that will
help you make a positive change in your life. From this
moment on, learn how to solve your inner problems
on your own.

*My path too, like the way of any other man, will lead
me to higher and higher levels of consciousness.*

The Subconscious Mind

WE ARE AN EXPRESSION OF OUR OWN IDEAS

Try to observe sometimes what goes on within you when you face an unexpected event. Let us imagine that you have just seen the world-famous magician David Copperfield on TV. Your first thought may well be: "Where's the catch?" No one can make your logically functioning intellect believe in the existence of unknown forces in our thoroughly explored world. You can be temporarily deceived by deftness or by finely hidden mechanisms for a short while. However, your intellect is still convinced that there is no magic involved really.

The logical way of thinking is an important prerequisite for coping with the outside world, but has it ever grasped the rules of your spiritual life? We do not speak of our subconscious in vain when we start exploring our inner world. When we turn to ourselves in a positive way, we soon experience a changing positive attitude toward our inner being. The wisdom within opens, due to a positive arrangement of our stream of thought. We were sent to the Earth as perfect beings who only have to confide in their inner leadership in order to be complete, healthy, and themselves.

Our way of thinking and acting is ruled by the spirit that created everything and which does not simply disappear after a certain period. Our body is the temple of the Holy Spirit, which can already be found in the Bible. We should see it as our residence, a means to an end, as the symbiosis between the spirit and matter for the time of our earthly existence. The Eastern teaching about the incarnation cannot be easily understood by either devout Christians or strict scientific theoreticians, although Christ did actually mention the concept in the Bible when he spoke of our development.

The Earth as the temporary kingdom is there for our spiritual development, whose extent cannot even approximately be conceived only by our intellect alone. The intellect is like the keyhole through which we can only observe a small part of the plan of Creation. You can go around logic only if you learn to trust your inner guide. Logic is in all events the beginning of all wisdom. It is, however, not its goal.

For more than 8,000 years, our ancestors and sages have been reporting on our "inner kingdom." The numerous supporters of yoga and meditation schools are not effusive drop-outs, but those searching for lost forces in the depths of their own being. From these depths germinate such wonderful things as if from nothing.

Do you not sometimes say: "This man is very nice, I could immediately trust him." The best inspiration to judge your surroundings is obtained from the unconscious depths of your soul. By means of positive thought you begin to learn about yourself again and by means of positive words and deeds, you create your own world from that moment on.

The biblical words "a new heaven, a new Earth" imply the following: If we have a new and positive thought (heaven), then we can create a new reality (the Earth).

Each day, perfect your ability to get an impression of the person you are talking to at a glance. First impressions are the most important.

You will have made great progress if you can turn toward your fellow men with your heart and soul, accepting them without reservation as your equals and devoting yourself to them. No matter how badly dressed a man may be, he is like you—only appearance makes you different. Look at his divine nature, and knowing this, try to be loving and intelligent.

The process of learning to lead a successful life starts with listening to your inner nature. Our inner, often soft voice, is too easily blocked by our constant train of thought. It is the biggest loss to lose the connection to your inner self, letting superficiality keep you in motion. A person in such a situation listens calmly and with understanding to the possibility of a happier, healthier life, but does not try to change anything. The determining elements of the worldly ego do not even allow self-love, love of the body, and the well-being and in such a way the status quo is retained.

There are people who cannot have a conversation without holding a cigarette in their hand. Others, thinking negative thoughts, create fears which drive them to madness, or they become obsessed with criticism, which brings them into constant conflict with other people. Now make yourself a promise. Say the following: "From this moment on I will think and act only positively. I ask my inner voice to warn me if a negative thought appears. Having done this I will feel calmer and safer."

Try reading newspapers to find out what people do to each other and to the world. Observe the great number of events that torment you and your desire for a healthy world. Put aside newspapers once and for all and start thinking in a positive way. Or would you prefer to believe that God has destined his creatures to carry a burden around for the rest of their lives?

We cause many undesirable situations through our negative thoughts. Those who read newspapers waste their time and strength by absorbing in their minds many events not worthy of reading and reliving them in their hearts.

A thought, a word is a spiritual force that strives to be realized. Every thought is creative in either a good or a bad way! Therefore try to show due respect and observe "the power of your thoughts." Learn to expect positive results from positive thoughts. Do it here and now! The subconscious mind in each of us is the exchange mechanism that understands every word we say and every thought we create as an order, turning it into reality.

Several years ago, I met a poor contemporary in Munich. A series of great misfortunes had destroyed him. His wife had died, his children had left him huge debts and had disappeared, his right arm was crippled after an accident at work, which cost him his job. All this had taken away his vitality, making him a vagabond.

We occasionally met as I used to walk at lunchtime in this peaceful area. I advised him to start loving life and his fellow man again, to respect himself and not neglect his appearance. I explained to him that his idea of not being able to do anything against his poverty was only an illusion by means of which he was using the infinite power of his subconscious mind not only inadequately, but also against himself. His pain made him dull and he did not even care enough to get insurance money from his car accident or any compensation.

I gave him this affirmation:

"I am healthy and strong. I turn to life and my fellow man with love. Every day I do a small good deed to help someone. We are all God's children. Positive power keeps flowing toward me from all sides, helping me to lead my life successfully."

After more than a year, I met him on my doorstep again (by chance?). Beaming with delight, he told me that he was still using my suggestions. In the meantime, he had been working at an old paper- recycling center and had his own apartment and a housekeeper. Positive thinking had proved that the lowest level of existence does not have to be an inevitable predicament to a person. His life had completely changed due to the change in his way of thinking. He had learned to use the power of his soul for his own benefit, thus becoming again the master of his own life instead of being its victim.

"If you cannot resolve a problem, get away from it."

A Break for Creative Consideration

You have received sufficient evidence to be able to switch to a different approach if you are ready!

Try to follow your intuition before you start doing something new or important. Take a consideration break every day. At a peaceful moment, which is very important before making a decision, withdraw to make an inner analysis of the situation. This is common sense and there is even a proverb advising you to make big decisions after having a good night's sleep. Examine your deepest impulses and feelings toward your intention using the following pattern:

- ❀ Why would I like to do this?
- ❀ Will it serve any purpose?
- ❀ Will it make my life easier?

- Is it essential for life?
- Does it only imply fulfillment of rather superficial desires?
- Which feelings move me to achieve this?
- Can I see a part of life's happiness in it?
- Will it only improve my image?
- Does it present an important need in my life?
- Is my vanity moving me to do this?
- Does my inner voice support it?
- What is my responsibility in this matter?
- Will I be able to achieve it in an easy and carefree way?
- Will it take me a lot of time and strength to achieve?
- Is the matter worth the effort?

If you are honest with yourself, these consideration breaks will give you more and more access to your intuitive levels, which are normally too easily passed over by making too hasty a decision. You should know that your higher Self always decides what is best for you. Therefore, ally with the spirit within you and your life will be filled with joy.

Positive thinking will start almost without effort if you ask your higher Self for advice.

If you manage to get hold of your hitherto hidden feelings and begin to cooperate with your subconscious mind in a trusting manner, you will be able to influence your destiny. You know more than those making their decisions blindly, that is to say, rationally. You may very well know what will happen to you if you decide to start using all power of your infinite intelligence from your mind. How to do this will be explained in more detail in further chapters.

My destiny is to get from Me to You and finally to Us.

The Art of Positive Living

Getting rid of seemingly inescapable compulsions, refraining from being superstitious, keeping away from old-fashioned orthodox ways of thinking, and being able to maintain the harmony of your being at every moment of your life will make positive thinking possible. From now on, you should live your own life and follow your own longings. By this, I am not arguing for excessive egotism, rather "healthy egotism" as described by Josef Kirchner in his successful books. He says that there is no reason why we should sacrifice our life for the egotism of other people.

You carry the power of liberation and self-realization within you from your birth. It is part of the wisdom of the Far East only to help those who are asking for help. If you change your views positively, you will be able to control your destiny. You have taken your own higher development into your hands. The insight that you need a higher knowledge of others to find your way is a prerequisite for help. If this insight is missing, offers for help are always turned down and everything remains unchanged.

This is not analogous to the Christian Samaritan view of help, where everyone should help everyone else. Very frequently a Christian, especially a Christian missionary, sees that his help is not wanted at all.

According to the Bible, Jesus himself does not help those who want to have his strength because of their own egotism. However, he helps those who kneel down humbly before his supreme power, entrusting their fate to divine providence with his blessing and the words: "Go your way; your faith has made you well" (Mark 10:52).

The lowest level of human existence does not find its counterpart in affluence. Poverty never comes from God; it is based on a wrong view of God and his world. The abundance that worldly life can offer is there for everyone. However, the quality of life of a rich person cannot be equated to happiness. When the harmony between a person and his emotions has been destroyed, all wealth in the world cannot help.

"For what will it profit a man, if he gains the whole world and forfeits his life" (Matthew 16:26).

To be able to afford every material good still does not mean that one has everything. Lacking morality and being spiritually empty often turn a person's best qualities into their exact opposite.

Last year, the manager of a big business asked to see me privately. He did not want to come to my consulting room, to be seen going to a psychotherapist. It was about his son and wife. His son was addicted to drugs and his wife was constantly ill. She forced him to visit her in the sanatorium, where she was being treated once again. Suddenly, and this could be at any time of day and night, she would phone him, demanding that he come immediately. She observed his business life and traveling with jealousy and hatred.

I started asking him questions and soon saw the symptoms of a workaholic who used his work to escape from his family problems. His relationship with his family was, in simple terms, restricted to that of handing out a monthly allowance. His sheer single-minded success orientation had turned him into a slave of his work and the happiness of his family had fallen by the wayside.

After a detailed conversation, he finally asked me for therapy. I tried to unite his mind, body, and soul in a harmonious triple-accord again. In the course of many sessions I was able to help him send his son and his wife loving powerful thoughts and consider their happiness as being more important than making money. The peace and harmony that he achieved by means of positive thoughts brought him overwhelming new experiences. His constant strain caused by stress soon lost its influence over his behavior. He could now easily make decisions that had previously taken him a long time to make.

Not long ago I received a postcard from this manager. There were merry greetings from his wife, too, whose psychosomatic illness had disappeared after the change that her husband had experienced.

I am describing these cases to you in all detail to make you recognize the deeper processes underlying them, which also have an influence on your life and which will help you to eliminate your problems by means of positive thinking. Now you will learn how to make your subconscious, your inner source of power, open to positive suggestion.

Our eyes show us only the surface of reality.

SELF-REALIZATION

Our consciousness processes a huge amount of sensory impressions, classifying them as either pleasant or unpleasant. Our intellect always prefers those impressions and ideas that directly ensure and improve its relationship to the world.

Sayings like "This is not clear to me" and "I cannot grasp this" show how intuitively people realize the limitations of consciousness set by the person alone, i.e. by his thoughts.

Try to revive the ability to feel what you are thinking about. Look at every one of your plans from a positive point of view, asking whether you can realize it yourself by means of your inner harmony. When you put something into motion that does not correspond to your moral standards and appears to be unreasonable to other people, simply refrain from doing it. Dr. Murphy said about this: "If a cucumber is bitter, don't eat it!" Also, if you are stuck in a job contrary to your character and personality, get rid of it. It is much easier to change your job than to do something you don't like for the rest of your life and be disappointed, unsuccessful, ill, and in conflict with your inner self.

Remember the words: "If you cannot solve a problem, get away from it."

One day, a butcher who was becoming increasingly depressed came to see me. He told me that he had neither family nor financial problems. It was his occupation that was taking so much out of him. He wasn't capable of killing animals any more. From an early age, his father had forced him to do this and he did not know how to get out of his predicament. It had been twelve years since he had taken over his father's butcher's shop. His suppressed feelings were making him more and more depressed. In the evenings, he would sit at home empty-headed, having almost nothing to say to his family.

In him, you could observe two subconscious feelings. On the one hand, there was his aversion to his occupation and on the other, there was an increasing fear regarding his life, what would happen if....

While talking to him, I found out that he could speak three foreign languages and that privately he was fond of literature and translating. During his therapy I gave him the following positive suggestion:

"There is calmness and harmony within me. The infinite intelligence of my subconscious mind now shows me the right way to freely choose my occupation. My ardent desire to work with foreign languages is fulfilled. I can see how happy my family is about the fulfillment of my desires regarding my occupation. I can now calmly prepare to change my occupation. I am the only authority in my life and I decide on my own how to live my life. There is complete harmony within me. I can feel this harmony being passed on to my family, too. I have chosen a successful life in harmony. I have chosen happiness."

Three months later, he was attending philological lectures at the university as a part-time student. His wife continued to run the butcher's shop until he took a foothold again and they could sell the shop.

In my therapeutic work I find it very important to ensure that talents and good qualities are developed freely so that people can become inwardly liberated and calm. Positive thinking will bring you inner harmony in your everyday life and at the present moment in time only if you begin now. After all, it's only the present moment that really counts. It leads you to the brighter side of life. All you have to do is start now!

You always experience what you think. Wherever you go, you will run into your own thoughts. It is your ideas that shape external events in either a loving or a critical way. Accept things the way they are and you will consequently be able to accept yourself and the world the way it is.

If the head of the state or the government changes, then this disturbance from the norm may manifest itself in your mind at first as discomfort. And why is that? You are the same person with the same abilities. Your desire to live your life optimally draws its power from the level of your higher Self. With peace of mind, radiate your positive attitude toward life to all people around you. This is your biggest and most important ability that will convincingly make every other person, even your superiors, as well as your political representatives, show consideration for you, your life, and your personality. Only your own consciousness defines how you perceive other people.

Try to keep your calm in every situation in life and rely on the power that created you. You will soon realize why, exactly, this or that happened to you. Your new, changed views will give you a new way of understanding and you will be able to see everything—that you up to now considered to be negative—in a new light.

Your positive attitude will activate good life forces inside of you. Or maybe you could say: "The good forces of heaven are coming to help you." You are superior and safe in all matters. The power that you need comes from your harmonious center of your being. Whatever happens, stay calm. Your new self-confidence is your "staff."

Already, your positively transformed view of the world itself will lead you to liberation from frightening ideas, freeing you from devaluing thoughts, and thus bringing about a wonderful change. Choose several passages from this book for daily reading and everything will soon be different. Express your suggestions in a form that only concerns you and read them three to four times a day. Whenever you try to make contact with your higher Self, or when you want to become aware of the immense wisdom of your subconscious mind, you will be helped in finding your inner peace in order to take the road toward a life full of happiness.

I begin every day with a thanksgiving to the spiritual world. After waking up, I meditate for a couple of minutes thinking of the following:

"A new beautiful day is breaking. I shall take in the positive energy from my surroundings. I am looking forward to all my duties that will enable me to give help and to spread the light. Perfect harmony helps me to succeed as I find peace and myself in it."

It would be bad if, having read this book, you were to let the newspaper headlines at breakfast make you lose your balance. Your struggle against the world will begin as soon as you turn to your daily work. Be as solid as rock in the grind of a new day full of duties and potentially stressful situations.

Life is more than thinking, feeling, and fulfilling one's duties. The power of your thoughts is not just a theory; it is a definite, shaped spiritual energy pressing for fulfillment and realization. Therefore, please be very careful with your thinking in the future. You should check the positive contents of your ideas before sending them into the world as a compact, rounded whole. There is a proverb saying: "Think before you speak!"

Use the recommended pause for thinking and in a very short time it will become your control station, so that no swear word will ever come out of your mouth again and on its way from your mind to your "language output" it will be interpreted as being non-positive and thus intercepted.

Doubt, criticism, and stressful situations will soon be things others have to worry about, since you have switched to your subconscious mind as your source of unlimited power in order to deal with your outward problems.

Maybe it is not possible to define the being. The intellect and the mind, the very way they are made, is a mystery.

POWER FROM THE DEPTHS OF OUR UNCONSCIOUS

As long as you do not "consciously cooperate" with your subconscious mind in a positive sense you will be like a non-swimmer who has fallen overboard. He is trying every trick in the book to keep his head above water, without ever knowing how to make the water become a helping tool.

Ignorance of spiritual laws causes all negative experiences, including physical and mental illnesses, as can be seen in the many examples that follow.

Every doctor in a mental hospital can point to patients who believe themselves to be Napoleon, for example. Hundreds of people have become slaves to this kind of delusion. The thought becomes deeply rooted in their minds, making them the best proof of the power of human imagination. In the same way as you can escape from reality in this irreparable, negative way, you can also use the vital forces of your imagination to achieve more success and make way for positive development. Instead of arousing neurosis and fears with a set of false ideas, you can achieve health and ultimate perfection by means of trust and conscious use of your spiritual energy.

Become the master of the power of your imagination in a positive sense. You are the keeper of that treasure. The key to this lies in the idea that you are what you think! To apply the spiritual laws in a correct manner is a great challenge that will lead you to ultimate happiness. How many positive impulses from your subconscious mind have you already squandered due to the will power of your small worldly ego?

An associate once told me about his intuitively gifted wife. "Two-thirds of the greatest achievements in my life I owe to her intuition," he said to me cheerfully. "The last third could have turned out even better as well, if only I had listened to her more!" In the meantime, he confessed that he also managed to increase his intuitive potential enormously by constantly exposing himself to higher levels of consciousness.

Intuition really can be stimulated. Strong creative powers, infinite intelligence, and higher intelligence latently exist in all humans. All we need to do is let the wisdom of the subconscious mind flow more consciously by using positive thinking and turning to our inner healing powers. The intellect needs to be "persuaded" to keep to its task and find its right place within the mind-body-soul connection. Imagine yourself as the master of the house. You decide on the right to vote regarding the individual levels that make up your personality.

An intellectual finds it hard to believe that he can really change his life only by modifying his negative thoughts into positive ideas. To the educated thinker it seems too easy to be able to change one's life by means of new thoughts and that is why he mostly does not preoccupy himself with the subject.

Let us try to reduce positive thinking to an understandable common denominator. Positive thinking does not mean directing your energy of thoughts against your own vital forces. It also means never using "I cannot" and letting go of self-pity, hate, and envious thoughts. Furthermore, it means from now on carrying out all activities in harmony with your inner voice and your conscience. The result will be a peaceful, happy and beautiful life.

When you start to practice positive thinking, your body will soon react, too. Stress and tension are completely transformed into well-being. All organs function together in harmony; they are supplied with positive energy; they are healthy and lively in harmony with the soul. But our history can deliver proof on how hard it really is to convert this clear, simple train of thought, understandable even to a seven-year-old, into reality. Read Buddha's story. Over the many centuries, his teaching has spread from India to all parts of the world. But in his homeland India, his teachings have always been neglected.

Check your aversion, for instance, to biblical sayings. "Please do stop talking about Jesus and the Good Lord," many might say when someone tries to help with spiritual wisdom.

It is us who are very reluctant to let the truth enter our fortress of rigid ideas about the world and the way it works. In our life we get all kinds of hints informing us of our mistakes. It is easy to see the many mental and physical effects that prove the fact that we are very often anything but in harmony.

We should not be too proud of our scientific understanding of our psyche. Until now, we have not been able to correspondingly use the opportunities it can bring us. We can save ourselves and become better people only if we want to. Our Creator blessed us with all gifts, we only have to make use of them to our benefit as well as the benefit of others. We have to start opening up our spiritual field of vision. By means of fruit-bearing seeds, we can turn the garden within us into a paradise. Deliverance is already there, it is waiting in us for the day when we say "Yes" to ourselves, to God, and to the world. We have to come to the realization that our whole life is a process of creating consciousness, a process of becoming aware of ourselves!

In the morning, go to work in an excellent mood, anticipating that only good things will happen to you that day; it is the best defense, a positive attitude. Even if a bad-tempered boss crosses your path, stay calm and spread your positive mood to him.

People who remain within their harmonious being are often the consoling member of the whole group. Their cheerful disposition determines the atmosphere at work. Provide an uninhibited, cheerful experience for each new day by choosing your own positive thoughts. This yearning has always been a part of you. So, if you really want it, it is very easy to find your own piece of clear blue sky within your soul.

Fill your consciousness with good and positive thoughts, because you are the one deciding on their future.

If you can't stop thinking about a scene or an incident that happened today, or if you are tortured by spiritual turmoil, thus causing you to lose sleep and your appetite, then you should try to get your balance by doing the following exercise. Find a peaceful corner to sit in and think about your day using the questions below.

1. How did it happen? Who and what caused the situation?
2. Why have I taken it so personally? Did my ego want too much?
3. Can I see any opportunity to clear up the incident by using truth, honesty, and sincerity?

If you have answered the third question with a "Yes," you have already solved your problem. Go to sleep, push all your thoughts onto a small white cloud and let them sail away into the next day, to the moment when you will stick to what you have decided.

We believe that the things we cannot see do not exist. This is why the spiritual vision has been slandered.

Living Here & Now

Live now, like the Buddhists say. Let your present become your life's main target. Have you ever grasped the sense of the words "to live here and now"?

The body may be here, but the thoughts are mostly a long way back in the past or in the future, in any case far away. When I pondered about the energy of the thought, this "far awayness" played a special, even crucial, role.

Being perfectly relaxed here and now, a book title by Jörg Andrees Elten, when chosen as an idea becomes a powerful suggestion for meditation. "Being perfectly relaxed here and now."

Try to feel this sentence. You will be overcome by a wonderful feeling of peace, maybe you'll feel warm all over, as well. At that moment you will feel you are "there." Only your thoughts can force you out of this condition. And this is what they do most of the day. One who is continuously trapped in the past or in the future is, just as people used to say, not really there. They avoid the reality of existence floating in the present experience, since it consists of the present moment. Everything else is just an illusion, a product of fantasy, having nothing to do with reality.

Please don't get me wrong. I do not mean to say that you should forget all your past experiences and live carelessly in the future. Tibetan begging monks may view this as ideal. Our Western culture teaches us how to rely on our intellect in order to learn from the past and take care of ourselves and our family in the future.

By this I mean people who keep running away from the present every minute and are wandering around in other "realms." They constantly talk about their plans and intentions, or like old pensioners, about events and heroic deeds from their past, or worse still, about their illnesses.

Living in the past makes you old and cuts you off from the present, the only dimension you really exist in. Living in the future makes us lose all sense of achievement and the peace that enables us to live a normal life. You do not have to believe that people who constantly speak of their intentions will ever come to fulfill any of their plans. Let us use our imagination to project our desires and dreams onto today and then will we find fulfillment.

Our Creator's infinite intelligence has given us all the power necessary to make full use of our abilities and to develop into independent people. We only have to set this power in motion by learning how to use the source of our existence. This means trusting ourselves and our Creator.

The quest for knowledge is therefore always the quest for our Creator.

MY PATH TO SPIRITUAL FREEDOM

I know what I am talking about since I also made a journey through life before getting my hands on Dr. Murphy's book *The Power of Your Subconscious Mind.* On the first pages he wrote, "this book is going to change your life, if you do what I tell you to."

I did what he told me to since there was nothing else left for me to do. Up to that moment I was ill, unsuccessful, discontented, and depressed. The negative influence of my childhood was, in effect, shaping my troublesome reality. In other words, I have always been successful, but at the beginning in a negative sense. Many things I tried just to escape the gloominess my life's "destiny" had pushed me into. I remained what I had always been. Overweight, possessed by feelings of inferiority, and always broke, I started working on myself.

I realized that my constant bad luck originated from the negative programming of my subconscious mind. The destructive and devaluing force of my thoughts had hardened due to the many, many negative suggestions I had received since early childhood. My father brought them about by constantly repeating insults. In order to protect myself I will not repeat the tirade of swear words.

Maybe this sounds more or less familiar to you? Devaluing words falling on a young person for years cannot miss their target. This results in the creation of a narrow-minded, destructive adolescent tortured by feelings of inferiority and yet considered to be a so-called normal person by society.

I had also achieved mediocre success in a positive sense, but in a negative way, successfully. This became very obvious during my large number of hospital stays. I experienced many illnesses, as often and as intensely as I could. All in all, during my youth I spent more than two and a half years in hospitals.

Then came the moment when I realized that I was experiencing the same destiny as the thoughtless magician's apprentice. I could not get rid of the ghosts I had conjured up. Negative thoughts can become independent just like positive ones. It all became clear to me. My transformation began when I decided to change and decided to think positively.

My gastric acid problems and heartburn disappeared a few days after I had started really motivating my subconscious mind with affirmative thoughts.

I stood in front of the mirror telling myself that all past statements and claims were not mine, therefore I am able to renounce their power. From now on, only my opinion counts. I decided to view my life as successful in a positive sense. I wanted to walk the way of positive thinking and believe in myself, trust myself, like our Father in Heaven trusts me.

My subconscious mind made my positive thoughts come true like a trusty friend. In a year I had lost 64 pounds and looked like a new man.

All living creatures are part of an unfinished process unknowing of its own future.

FALSE THINKING IN DISGUISE

You can see how, in the end, we all become slaves to ideas imprinted into our minds since childhood. It is difficult to know what powers are at work in our subconscious mind after so much negativity has rained down on us for such a long period of time. How many people felt any highly spiritual substance when Jesus said: "For behold, the kingdom of God is in the midst of you" (Luke 17:21) or when Lao-Tse put the mysterious effect of the subconscious into words: "Ten thousand creatures were born out of the Being, yet the Being was born out of Nothing."

In positive thinking, each close thought is seized upon with both hands and put straight if it shows any trace of wrong orientation. What you are thinking now will determine your next experience. Even the youngest and most poorly educated person can understand the importance of this moment as preparation for the next. If there is anything to be changed, it has to be done now, since it is the only moment we have.

One of the first practical steps is to become aware of our devaluing thoughts and words. It is not always easy to discover what might have inflicted damage on us over the years. If you think you cannot…you fear… you doubt…this suggests timidity, insecurity, and incompetence to your subconscious mind.

In future statements, try to put special emphasis on direct experience by saying: "I am…I have…I can…this moment is just as I want it to be." Jesus said, "Ask and it will be given you; seek and you will find; knock and it will be opened to you" (Matthew 7:7).

An employee once came into my office. After 30 years of work, his company had gone bankrupt and he was faced either with a porter's job in another company, or with redundancy. He was extremely intimidated about his situation and preferred the idea of taking his life rather than living in such shame. After his apprenticeship, he had been taken on in the technical surveillance department of his company, where he had fulfilled his duties over decades. He never stood out, never came too close to anybody. However, no one ever felt the urge to reward his obvious technical qualities with promotion. And then came the sudden leap from security to insecurity! He only has his wife to thank for having found his way to me.

I rarely had the opportunity to meet such a conformist, servile man. He was totally glum. Since his childhood, he had stood in his younger brother's shadow, who was always privileged and praised for doing everything better than him, even when the "big brother" achieved the same. It seemed he should simply be grateful to be alive. Therefore he was like a shadow of a man, tolerated by the family and later at work. All his life he remained inconspicuous in the background, until his company no longer needed him.

To open the eyes of a person in their mid-fifties to the diversity of life and the infinite power of their subconscious mind can be very demanding, even to a trained therapist. A lot of effort is required just to persuade him to remove his blinkers and not see life only from the perspective of work.

In one of my seminars, he heard, probably for the first time in his life, that you could share your feelings with other people. I made him see that the only way toward security, self-confidence, and success is to re-program the subconscious mind. His problems had been caused by destructive and limited subjective prior experiences. At the end of a three-week course of hypnotherapy he was sent home with the following suggestion:

"There is perfect harmony within me. I know that I am sheltered in the center of my being. The infinite intelligence of my subconscious mind gives me the power to provide for my wife and me in the best possible way.

The love that I give to my fellow man comes back to me through their kindness, readiness to help, and their interest in my person.

I see myself as successful in this new activity knowing that my inner power is making this vision come true. I begin each new day with confidence and peace. Everything is prepared for my success. My inner voice is my guide."

Such goal-oriented thoughts, to be elaborated on in the third chapter, should be read several times a day and meditated upon or spoken out from memory. The appropriate content of the words should be coupled with strong feelings of joy and a vision of "reality." If we put ourselves into a state of trance by means of autogenic training, self-suggestions will penetrate our mind.

The treatment of this intimidated man extended over several weeks, including giving him suggestive formulae. After the first two weeks, we all felt the first positive changes in his self-confidence. He began to open up, believing in himself and his world.

Eight weeks after the treatment, I received a call from his wife. Her husband had got a similar position in another company due to a friend's retirement. "Without your treatment he would never have thought of being so independent," she said.

The best thing you can do for others is to do something for yourself.

THE FOUR GREAT LONGINGS

Did you understand the way the suggestive formulae worked? If you did, then you can start observing your continuous train of thought right away. Believe that what you desire is possible. Banish all negative thoughts and suspicions, because you now know that your very thinking determines your life.

It is nonsense to believe that a cat crossing your path will bring you bad luck. Keep away from superstition and do not depend on your daily horoscope.

The stars only reflect your spiritual constellation. Your mind is closer to you than any cosmic reflection. You will experience what others are looking for in horoscopes. I like comparing astrology with sailing competitions. It's all the same to a good sailor where the wind is coming from since he knows how to steer his (life) boat in order to reach his goal. The Bible also says:

"God's winds are blowing from everywhere, you only have to set your sails." Another source claims that: "The stars don't force anybody, they just make you willing."

A person's desires can be summed up in four basic formulae:

1. We are happy if we are completely healthy. This refers to a healthy mind, body, and soul.
2. We yearn for inner and outward harmony.
3. The third important human desire is success.
4. Positive thinking puts us on the way of fulfilling this longing.

We wish to be recognized and we yearn for self-realization. One of our strongest wishes is to secure good living conditions. This does not only refer to material aspects, which unfortunately we in the Western world view as being synonymous with success. Naturally, success is also reflected in your bank account. People who live in harmony with their spiritual side are given more earthly possessions than they need. Let us open our mind and we will never experience deprivation. People who have a positive attitude toward life comprehend the infinite wealth of their being. Wealth is open to all of us and it lets us take part in the fullness of life.

The most important form of human happiness is love. Physical love is only a small part of the love that encompasses all creatures. In every situation, a human being yearns for such an obliging and protective love, which will give him complete fulfillment, happiness, and joy.

Those who strive for love should also give away their love in abundance. Many wise books say: Giving and taking are one and the same, what we give away comes back to us, give and you will be given. According to Erich Fromm's *The Art of Love*, it is of greatest importance to let love blossom inside ourselves. Self-love is the prerequisite for loving another human being.

You are free to long for unconditional love from the bottom of your heart. Be guided by the following affirmative thoughts:

"There is peace and harmony within me. I love myself just the way I am. The infinite power of my subconscious mind fills all cells of my body, purifying and strengthening me completely. From the harmony that fills me up radiates my love to all creatures in the world. I feel the unity of all souls in God and I am an equal member of this union. I live in harmony, I am full of love, and I am healthy and happy. I am very grateful for it."

Self-love manifests itself clearly in the way we treat our body, our clothes, in our whole social environment. Do we neglect these areas or do we keep our "temple of the living God" clear and pure to express our joy of life? Self-love also means overcoming selfish desires and reaching perfect harmony with our destiny by way of positive thinking. Self-love finally means preserving the harmony between the mind, the body, and the soul. It is the way to our self-realization. Be aware that "our highest Self is identical to the universal Soul."

Kindness is a coin that enriches one who gives it away.

Your Intellect—the Biggest Obstacle in the Way to Your Self

Positive thinking can allow you to realize the fairy tale in which the hero saves himself rather than relying on outside forces. As in every creature in the world, there is the power of a higher consciousness slumbering somewhere inside you. Be sensitive to this kind of energy in order to make your daily life happier, more perfect and carefree. To achieve this, you first have to overcome the biggest obstacle in the way; the dominance of your intellect.

Try to overcome your small worldly ego, which is constantly trying to push you into the spheres of covet and desire. Think big so that big things happen! In our consumerism-oriented society, pleasure has become more important than the search for a purpose in life, harmony, and peace of mind. Have you already noticed how tangled up you are due to this trend in these ever-increasing efficiency- demanding times? The media is full of reports telling us what we are to expect from the new millennium.

Put an end to this now. Stop your willingness to take part in the growth of any self-fulfilling negative prophecy. Live and enjoy the present moment. Gloomy future perspectives have, until now, been proved to be wrong, because nowadays we actually live a better life than we did twenty, fifty, a hundred years ago. Just remember the Jehovah's witnesses who have already predicted the end of the world many times. Believe in the present moment, in the will to live, and in all other human beings. Assume your responsibility to realize only good, positive, and divine aspects of your life. You will shape your own world by your every action, by your every thought.

You should be aware of the range and power of your negative thoughts and try to avoid them. You should make yourself responsible for your own actions. Act from your deepest self-conviction and devotion to your own well-being and the well-being of the whole world.

If you forget something really important at work, you should not blame anybody else. If you damage somebody else's parked car while carelessly driving your own, leave a message on the windshield. Assume responsibility for your actions and you will feel your self-esteem grow. Stop obeying your intellect, because it could, through its innate weakness, deprive you of your truthfulness if you rely on it alone. Your personality is growing from day to day and it is now ready to overcome many of the fears created by the intellect itself and its narrow horizons. You are responsible for yourself. From now on let this responsibility be an easy burden.

A noble attitude will activate your inexhaustible strength, which will solve all your problems, making you independent and free. Fear and striving for safety will disappear if you start believing in yourself. This safety grows from within you. Pretty soon you are going to sense the power of your subconscious mind. The biggest life insurance is to be found within you. Your spiritual energy is your own property and it is the original indestructible power of life.

If hate hungers for love, then this hunger can only be satisfied through love.

HARMONY & LOVE

From this very moment, the inner harmony of your being should have advantage over your intellect. It seems amazing how much you can win without any risk. Everything your intellect, with all its willpower, has vainly striven for will enter your world spontaneously. Health and success, healthy self-confidence, and a lot of happiness are knocking at the door of your spiritual home. Soon enough you will see that you have found all the help you need from within yourself in abundance, although you most usually expect it from outside sources.

Some people are afraid of getting into trouble with their fellow man because of their positive thinking. They think they are going to be singled out as being anti-sociable if they look inwardly at things. Our civilization has developed into a very complicated technical structure where information exchange has become of life importance and where we depend on mutual support. Generally speaking, in our material world, our modes of communication function perfectly. Our intellect has gained control over the correct methods.

What is the use of the most advanced technology, which is meant to make life easier, if ever- increasing additional strain at work makes people's lives a misery. Big offices and factories, with their omnipresent and increasing levels of stress, are the biggest focus of infection for most of the worst psychosomatic illnesses. Envy and malevolence destroy people and their relationship with other fellow creatures.

Learn to recognize your selfish motives and control them. Observe how the energy of your thoughts squanders opportunities and creates worries about things that are of no importance, things that only annoy and weaken you. Unpleasant events especially have a long lasting effect upon a person. Be it just an unpleasant evening's conversation between a couple, one is going to dwell on it for a long, long time.

The purpose of sleep is regeneration and a clear conscience should be your pillow to sleep on. A recovering sleep is as necessary as the air we need to breathe. Leave the past and the irrevocable where they belong. Say to yourself "the past is past!" Thinking about the past will only needlessly agitate you over and over again. Be grateful to your subconscious mind for showing you the solution to a troublesome problem almost certainly caused by a lack of love and understanding on your side. Go to sleep safe in the knowledge that you have made up with your partner and apologized for your lack of understanding. Strike while the iron's hot. Thus you will clear your conscience, which will in turn show its gratitude to your insight through a greater personal persuasiveness that will make you capable of putting everyone around you into higher spirits.

The inner calmness and balance achieved by positive thinking will profusely endow you with a good quality of life. The soothing pole of life, the inner freedom to enjoy this magnificent world happily and cheerfully lies within you. Let the intellect deal with the outside, necessary affairs. That is its task. It should not control your feelings, longings, and desires. Draw strength from the superior higher instance of your conscious being, from the endless wisdom of your divine Self.

Test yourself immediately. Turn to the next problem and sub-divide it into its consisting parts. Why did you recently reproach your husband/wife for having no understanding of your problems? Why did you recently reproach your wife/husband for never having time for your concerns? Go to your partner, show him/her all your love and say "I was rather impatient a short while ago. I took things too seriously that I felt uneasy about. They are not at all worth arguing about. I am really sorry."

If you are getting ready for an important task, be guided by the following model:

In the long term, concern yourself with obtaining all information regarding those areas in which you must be well informed. Do it thoroughly. You want to succeed so you demand the highest standards from yourself. In the third chapter you are going to find out how to seek help from your subconscious mind.

In the short term, concern yourself only with your spiritual balance. Bring yourself into complete harmony within both your physical and spiritual household. Entrust the course of the day to the endless wisdom of your higher intelligence. Let yourself be guided by a higher "power" and be sure of success. Say to yourself that "one with God is always in the majority."

If you follow this model intensively enough you are about to be able to solve your problems even before they reach your consciousness. No matter if your assignment appears easy or difficult, lean back in your chair, saying to yourself:

"I am a complete person, I live in the right way, I have the power to realize all my intentions in harmony with God's providence. I live, I achieve and overcome whatever I decide. The inexhaustible power of life within me has kept me safe to this day of my life, it has strengthened and stimulated me, it is leading me at this very moment to the purpose of my life. I am grateful. I am full of the joy of life and I am good- humoredly enjoying my success from the bottom of my heart. I am in harmony with my spiritual center. I am looking forward to all future events. They will be filled with joy and pleasure."

Thoughts like these spread profound calmness within you. At this very moment you are about to build up your own authority, the only one you should acknowledge. Master your destiny with your own power, ruled and guided by an endless wisdom living within you since your birth, wisdom you can resort to whenever you need it.

Write to me about the occurrences of the following day. I will be glad to know that I have given you the right impulse at the right moment.

Most decisions in our daily life are made with our intellect instead of our heart and soul. Our deeds are mainly guided by the criteria of usefulness. However, those who judge others too easily, using neither their intellect nor their heart, will soon find out that their interpersonal relations, too, are top-heavy. Love and harmony very often fall by the wayside if we think and act according to what our intellect tells us to, instead of listening to our heart as well.

Many ways lead toward the source of power within us. The limitation of a very often uncoordinated train of thought can be achieved through concentration, inner prayer, and meditation. All this leads toward our own spiritual power and the center of our being if we make use of it. Everybody should try to find their own way to self-realization because everyone is the master of their own fate.

Positive thinking is, as far as I am concerned, the quickest way to detach yourself from the negative energy of thoughts. In his book *Having and Being*, Erich Fromm draws a similar parallel between a positive and negative way of life. He makes a difference between people who have and people who are. Those who only want to take from their surroundings and their fellow man are in the majority. Few people are pleased with just "being" themselves. Those that are the ones who are connected with Nature and God, they are the pioneers of a new society, in a new era which is starting right now.

Only those living in harmony with their spiritual power can lead a meaningful life. Activate this center within yourself and make your everyday thinking sensitive to the new qualities of your thoughts.

Free yourself from old burdens, instead of loading yourself down with new ones. Free yourself from the false ideas of orthodox, old-fashioned religious philosophy. If you live in harmony with your unconscious, you will be afforded the greatest protection. To become one with yourself also means becoming one with the Creator. It is the only thing worth living for. If you are with God, who can be against you? The mighty power still awaiting your awakening in your subconscious mind is superior to any selfish aspiration. This power can only hoist you up into those areas of life which make you happy and safe from worry, disease, and misfortune. Maybe there is another way to completely understand the extent of such a statement. Case studies from my practice will surely help.

I can still remember the middle-aged secretary who once asked me to help her out of her bad situation. She was the scapegoat of her company. She was responsible for all the bad things that happened at work. Over the years she had begun to worry that her boss would take all the false accusations seriously and fire her.

I could not explain to her clearly enough that, being a scapegoat, she was exercising a both socially and psychologically vital function in her company. The black sheep of the working team rarely gets fired. Every member of the group, including the boss, needs it to release their own feelings of guilt and aggressiveness that they are not ready to cope with.

Such an explanation was of little use to our secretary. I had to help her change her attitude, which had made her become the scapegoat of her company. Since she could not cope with these unjust accusations, she got used to a half-complaining, half-yelling way of responding, which did nothing for her credibility.

First of all, she had to develop her self-esteem. The following meditation texts helped her build up thoughts about her abilities:

"I am healthy and full of harmony. Profound calmness and self-confidence fill me up inside. I feel safe and successful at work. I feel safe in the endless power of my subconscious mind that directs my life, making me happy and satisfied. I think about all my fellow workers and all other people around me with love and harmony. I am grateful to the Creator for the abundance and wealth of life and the inner and outward happiness I can be a part of."

She should repeat these affirmative thoughts several times a day. If necessary, reading with still devotion was sufficient. I explained to her that the deeper she grasped the meaning of these words and the more vivid and picturesque she depicted the impression of her "vision," the sooner she would recognize the fundamental change within herself.

Three weeks later, at our last meeting, she told me that her associates wanted to know what had happened to her. They wanted to know if she had a lover, because they simply could not get into arguments with her as they used to. Soon enough she became aware of her own value. Blossoming harmony radiated from within her out into her surroundings, preventing in advance further confrontations.

Half a year had passed before she was ready to completely get rid of her Cinderella complex. Her calmness and balance attracted other people who needed advice. Her associates, who used to tease her before, were now seeking her help.

Her colleagues, who to that very moment referred to her as the scapegoat and lightning conductor of the company, now found themselves having to examine themselves.

This negative way of delegating responsibility when something unpleasant happens shatters the accuser more often than the accused. A famous English philosopher, whose home had been broken into, stated in a TV interview on that occasion: "They stole all my money, though there was not much of it, but I am glad to be the victim of the robbery and not perpetrator."

The mental background of a department manager in a big computer company was a special case. He also came to me asking for help. From his description, I could discern that he was a so-called "guilt suppresser." He believed that his associates would let him down and would, being lazy, destroy his life's work. Too much work and the wrong lifestyle had overloaded his efficiency and he had begun to lay the blame upon other people.

What did he expect from me? A hypnotic protective shield for his damaged health? I put him in front of a mirror and asked if he could see a man in his prime and in full possession of his faculties. A moment later, having glanced at my face, he asked me angrily if I was teasing him, since he could not stand the sight of himself. That was what I wanted him to see: He had become his own enemy. I explained that in a short while he would be able to look into the mirror again only if he found the strength to abandon his false ideas and cease his self-destructive accusing. I could show him the road, but he was the one who had to travel.

There is probably nothing harder than trying to explain to a stubborn person that his own will power is the obstacle standing in the way of achieving his goals. My manager who needed help was too weary to rebel against this paradoxical law of the mind in any intellectual way. Above all, he needed treatment for his mind, body, and soul in order to survive his rigorous lifestyle. Agitation would continue to be his companion as long as he resisted gaining a deeper insight.

First of all, I advised him to eat less meat, to reduce his excessive alcohol and coffee consumption, and to follow a rigid bedtime schedule, without the hours of useless sitting in front of the TV set that only caused additional strain.

During hypnosis treatment he had great difficulty in letting go of his consciousness, which had been hardened by his rigid mental attitude. In this case it took 50 sessions more than usual. The first affirmative thoughts he received were:

"There is deep calmness within me. The infinite intelligence of the subconscious overcomes my Being, giving me new vitality. It penetrates each cell, filling my being with harmony and love. I have all the power in me. I radiate love and confidence to my family, my associates and superiors and I am successful at work. I am healthy, I live in harmony with the highest laws of life and love toward all beings. I feel sheltered in the center of my being that gives me the strength, protection and power to solve all problems in a safe and easy way."

After four weeks, the man had changed beyond recognition. Well rested and energetic, he walked into my office. Nevertheless, he admitted missing his evening glass of brandy and the countless cups of coffee he used to drink. His restraint was doing him good.

Day by day he was becoming more powerful and was really flourishing.

When he returned home after a four-week stay at our house, he faced a big surprise and the reactions of his colleagues. His family admired his great looks and composure and even congratulated him, whereas his colleagues were left speechless. They knew nothing of his spiritual treatment and greeted him in the way you would greet someone who had come back from vacation.

Later on he told me that it had been a sobering experience for him. But the theory of the power of repeated suggestions proved correct in the end. He felt his old arrogance and vanity rising within him and he had to face the first test in daily life. He had to submit proof of his change and convince his colleagues into believing in his changed personality by setting an example.

It took him several months of amicable behavior, which caused obvious surprise among his associates, before it was possible to create a friendly atmosphere. Only then did he release his old Self. His new insight gave him a new view of the world. We met again at an exhibition and he confirmed that in the meantime he had come to understand the spiritual law he once found paradoxical. The will power he had used to achieve a goal appeared to have been the largest obstacle in its way. What he could not accomplish earlier with the utmost will power, he now manages to do almost play-fully owing to the harmony he had with his divine inner Self.

We could add that the many changes in his personality certainly played a crucial part. A balanced person does not stick to a fixation so stubbornly, but how many among us are perfectly balanced, anyway?

It is important that now he faced all developments in a more relaxed manner. Resistance irritates him less than ever and he can overcome this easier than before. There is also his broadened consciousness and an awareness of his inner voice that make him more sensitive and goal-oriented than a level of pure understanding could ever manage. Even at the very beginning of the broadening of consciousness, there is a whole range of improvements of life.

One of the most beautiful changes was reported to me by a former patient regarding his marriage. It was almost over at the time I first met him; both partners were already thinking of a divorce. Now, as he has successfully worked on self-improvement, the marriage has also been invigorated, he reported with a smile. Not only was he successful, but also happy as he said: "What else could a man want?"

Who would think that in the turmoil of the power of destiny, we could solve all our problems through harmony and love? "For Behold, the kingdom of God is in the midst of you," said Jesus (Luke 17:21). Sometimes it seems to me that we don't even want to imagine how simple it is to achieve balance and inner peace. Perhaps we could extend the saying to: "Don't you know that there is both heaven and hell in you?"

Do not let obsessions or the one-sided ideas of your ego discourage you. Only a fool thinks that he should die because of an unfulfilled wish. We perceive difficulties that open up before us like abysses, because we look at them from a particular point of view. Very quickly they can turn into favorable opportunities if we look at them through positive thinking. A life situation becomes a situation of conflict if we provoke negative occurrences by way of false expectations.

You can apply this doctrine to your life immediately. If you have the slightest doubt about the success of an intention, you should abandon it right away. First, doubt is a drain on your strength and second, it has the power to get its own way since it operates under the surface.

Why are you giving doubt even more power? Change your ways. You have the choice, so choose wisely.

Review your plans. Make an exact plan for your strength, and decide whether the intention is the right thing for you. If you can hear a loud "Yes," then your pattern of behavior is correct.

Decide if you should trust others or be anxious wearing your Self out with doubts.

Remember the following words:

"My plan is perfect. I will give my all to fulfill it. I am successful in my intention and will receive help from the infinite power source of the subconscious mind. I will finish my task in a short time. Work is good for me! God's love fills my soul and stands by me."

The most beautiful thing for an awakened man to experience is to go to the boarders of consciousness, to find doors there, to open them and enter the freedom of absolute being.

HAPPINESS AS CHOICE

You will experience what you are thinking of! It is so simple to release the negative energy of thoughts that blocks you and to completely switch to positive experiences. You can be reproached for acting rashly or in blind optimism only by absolute pessimists, who do not know anything of your alternatives. You chose happiness, you have considered your choice right, and you know that from that moment on you possess all strength to realize your thoughts. You are the only authority that you recognize. Fundamentally use those affirmations connected with the greatest longings that move every human heart. Tell yourself daily:

- ✹ I am healthy.
- ✹ I live in harmony with my spiritual strength.
- ✹ I am successful.
- ✹ I love myself and my life.
- ✹ In love I feel being connected with all people.
- ✹ I am successful in all my actions.

Vary these positive values of thoughts in such a way as to apply them to your special concerns and you will bring light and joy into your life. Do not use negative words such as "no" and "not" in any of your guiding principles. Suggestions are more accurately named affirmations (and this means approval). An affirmation is therefore an approval or confirmation. Call it what you like. Do not negate the things you do not want when you work with your subconscious mind!

If you have difficulties in communicating and interacting with others, you will notice a surprising recovery. You will suddenly experience pleasant reactions in your surroundings and these are the answers to your own positive charisma. What you send out comes back to you.

To brood over the painful past is a highly potent negative working of thoughts. To turn the problems over in your mind, to ask questions of guilt and responsibility in order to once again blame others creates those surges in your soul over and over again, from which you originally wanted relief. It all belongs to that common train of thought that makes so many people suffer and unnecessarily wears them down. You can be done with it now if you so choose.

Is that what you want?

By measuring blood pressure and hormone release and on the basis of pressure exerted on organs, it has been determined by medical research that a shocking experience and stressful situations experienced over and over again put the body into a constant state of alarm.

You begin to sense how essential it is not to let your subconscious mind be overwhelmed by this wild, often too destructive flood of thoughts.

Let us record another important realization and from here on in be able to identify a serious mistake that you will never make again.

To brood over the past is always a highly potent poison for your present and future well-being. You are living at this moment. Do not let yourself be carried off to the past by your thoughts. It would be as if you voluntarily gave up your life of freedom and went into exile.

Here you can start up an exercise which, the more you use it, the closer it will take you to a completely new self-image! Meditate a few times on the words:

"I am rising in my spirit to such a height where the past, present and future fuse into grand view and I am granted a new insight into things."

Using this meditation you will reach two goals at the same time. During immersion, you are protected from all other thoughts that might storm you. And while you are meditating you are aiming at a new, higher experience. Moreover, the quickly recognized success of this meditation gives you a higher perspective from which you will quickly attain a feeling of safety in all your actions.

You will soon be your own master if you start applying these simple laws of thinking and mind. The first small tests and exercises have made you attentive. The positive thinking helps you to fulfill your longing for harmony, love, success, and health.

In the slow, continuous groping of your way to finding your own most suitable suggestive formulae, choose those which correspond most to your lifestyle and your pre-dispositions. Finally, you should create your own entirely personal suggestive formula. Your goal is clear: health, success, love, and harmony are your vision—less would not be enough.

In the following chapter, I will give you more examples from my practice in order to show you the interconnection of those goals in great variety.

2

Positive Thoughts
A Bastion against the World of
Problems

The smile that you send out shall come back to you.
Indian proverb

MIND ABOVE WILL

It is in itself an astonishing discovery to each person that they can follow the influence of ideas and fantasies in their life and their relationship to their surroundings in detail. Whatever we think of, our mind forms things as they correspond to our mental habits. Positive ideas of life can almost certainly induce a strong transformation if we are able to understand this fact. How successful we will be in learning to appropriately connect with the "strength" within us depends on our spiritual and physical health and how harmonious our interactions are with our fellow man.

To live one's personal ideals means to have and to follow an individual picture of life. All our problems originate from the fact that we do not know that we are free and that we can vary our personal "reality" in a thousand different ways.

"It will be the result of too many different conflicts of political interest," I said to the Prime Minister of a neighboring country, "if we continue to lose our "equilibrium" and therefore become prone to political outbursts." After an especially hot debate, one Member of Parliament suffered a nervous breakdown. The victim admitted to me that he had been suffering from dizziness and blurred vision and fits of migraine for a long period of time, mainly due to the fact that he could not keep his calm.

A politician stands on the front of military-style verbal and intellectual conflict. In his profession he sometimes deals with spiritual energies as if they were confetti. His deepest human requirements are completely lost behind the "interests" he has to represent. If he who has made his own spiritual disharmony too strong learns about positive thinking during his search for help, as in this particular case he did, many things can very quickly turn out for the better. During long conversations, I explained to him that the law of karma gives back that which we have sent out. It quite correctly states: "You are responsible for your life. Your ideas control your subconscious mind! And your unconscious will ultimately control you (if you are not too careful)."

Those who understand that they are able to control their own lives with their will and thus manipulate themselves will give it up if they are clever. They will look for other ways to gain insight into their lives through peaceful methods. If you follow the various debates in the German Parliament, it is no surprise that in a poll, German politicians described their work as sheer murder. They are mercilessly worn down by the merry-go-round of power of intellect and political party manipulation.

My politician was given a wide list of tasks connected with the most rewarding job on this planet: the job of working on himself. A reasonable division of the day limited his workload overload and during regular relaxation breaks he was to make for himself a "household plan" and stick to it! We made a plan for the next two to three months and he prepared himself inwardly for hypnotherapy, and therefore, for his new mentality. From then on, he began making suggestions to himself rather than any opposition party:

"There is deep calmness and balance within me. The eternal wisdom of my subconscious mind intuitively controls my thoughts and actions. I rely on my higher wisdom and live in harmony with my spiritual strength.

I turn to my fellow men with love and sympathy, spreading harmony and satisfaction. I love life, I love myself, I love people and I am successful through the inex-haustible strength of wisdom coming from the very depths of my Self. My oath to serve my people with my very best knowledge and conscience is holy to me. From now on I put the good of all above the good of the party."

For daily use during hot debates, whenever he could withdraw for short moment's relaxation, I made him write out:

"I am completely calm. I am safe in the wisdom of my higher Self that leads and directs me at every moment of my life. If I stand up now and step in front of the plenum, I convincingly represent the law of harmony and

love. All my words are interconnected elements and are to lead to more togetherness. It is very simple, because together we are strong."

The auto-suggestive affirmations in his case had a miraculous effect. Many weeks after his therapy, he reported to me on the telephone with a cheerful calmness in his voice that he had confronted a snarling rival who was about to attack him with only a radiant genuine smile. The rival was left speechless and stood with his mouth open as all he could hear were reconciling arguments. This new approach to life, i.e. that based on a positive formation of his subconscious mind, fundamentally changed this politician.

"What took me days before, I can now complete in hours," he told me happily. "I am not only healthy, my work now really gives me pleasure and I am more convincing than before." In his greatest crisis he experienced at the right moment the difference between appearance and reality.

Remember that you have free will. The ability to realize is in fact the very frontier of free will. However, you must always benefit from your actions. You really need to understand this!

A NEWLY ACQUIRED SELF-CONFIDENCE

I experienced an initially similar stressful situation with a well-known soccer player. A few unsuccessful games in the Bundes league and a scathing judgment in the press of his personal commitment did not damage his reputation, but he was seized by his own vanity. His father had not really encouraged him much since child-hood and even he himself sometimes believed himself to be a loser. His fragile feeling of self-esteem reacted extremely sensitively to even the tiniest of changes in his public reputation. A loveless childhood and his personal view of himself had created an inferiority complex and consequently, an over-exaggerated ambi-tion. If he was not the best, he felt himself to be a total loser, he admitted to me only half-smiling. Psychological pressure and masked egocentricity can lead all people in the public eye to this. The tension to which this footballer was exposed increased because of a knee injury, which was, from a psychological point of view, hardly a "coincidence." He had not believed that he would be able to cope with four weeks just kicking his heels, and already during his first training session back, it had become clear that he might be forced to take an even longer break.

He called me and asked for treatment at his house in order to again gain control of his nerves and high inner tension. Of course, no one was allowed to find out anything about this, because an open show of human weakness could be fatal in his profession. At the very least, his market value would plunge.

A man with so many restrictive ideas is almost certainly more difficult to treat than a psychopath. His ego controls absolutely all passes and passages to the subconscious mind, and above the "goal" he nails up the sign: "Temporarily out of order." He cannot get rid of his restlessness, fearing that he is going to miss out on something important or diminish his physical fitness.

Without hurrying, I had to get the man used to calmness by means of autogenic training. It took him three weeks to get deeply into the treatment. Besides various suggestive formulae designed to take him out of his egocentric view of life, he received a formula particularly for problems tied in with his profession:

"I am completely calm. There is harmony and well-being in me. My look is strong and healthy and my ability to react is faster and safer. Every cell of my body is revitalized and flown through by the eternal life strength in me. I am completely healthy and have made good achievements. I can always rely on myself! I feel secure and safe in the camaraderie of my team mates. We are a successful team and I am a valuable and important part of that success."

In further exercises—through catathymic image perception, which I will refer to in more detail in the fifth chapter—he himself reached the insight that he had pushed too far his egotistic desires connected with outwardly looking good. Thus they had become burden to his real physical needs. It was ultimately the reason for his injury. His body had set a clear limit to the misuse of his strength. The psyche of this football player had confirmed the law of harmony between mind, body, and soul, which our will can never violate.

My client became reasonable, which means that he understood what he could and could not change. He had come to realize his real life needs during what appeared to him to be only a relatively harmless down period. A scene from his therapy had an especially strong impact on him. In this scene, he vainly tried to turn upright a wooden cart on which he had lovingly piled up layers of apples over and over again. An elephant would always come and knock the cart over. When, in the end, he recognized his father in the big animal, the person who had always destroyed the work he had built up so arduously, he welled up with tears and reached an endless fury about his relationship with his father.

Many weeks later, I met his trainer at a sports event. Without being asked, he told me that his star had changed. He had become friendlier and less self-opinionated. His professional achievements were now less hectic, but more intuitive and adapted to the overall success of the team. It was now a pleasure to cooperate with him.

A man freed himself from part of his negative ideas and obstacles. In the period that followed, he was on the front pages again as a recognized athlete, expert, and star.

From birth to death, development always takes place and we cannot oppose it.

New Love in an Old Marriage

One day, a 45-year-old tormented woman sat in front of me. Exhausted and work-worn, she sank into the armchair. She could not stand it anymore, she couldn't do anything anymore: couldn't think, couldn't do anything, nor live anymore. Her greatest fear at that moment was the thought that her husband would find out about her visit to me.

Her husband, a higher state official, treated her as little more than a housecleaner. He let newspapers, garbage, and cigarette ash drop to the floor in the room wherever he was sitting or standing at the time. Mrs. Anna had to sprinkle salt on his eggs and pour milk into his coffee. In their apartment, he did not lift a finger to help in any household chore.

His wife was excluded from any change or pleasure. When acquaintances asked after her, he always said that she was very busy in the house. He traveled to Paris and Istanbul; she had to take care of the house and could at the very best go to her parents for a few days. Her everyday life was not what any of us would at all desire.

It seemed to me during her report that I was hearing about some extinct species. This woman had been living in an anachronism for twenty-five years. Meanwhile, she suffered from stomach and intestinal diseases, had trouble with her thyroid gland and kidneys, and suffered from unpleasant facial twitches.

There can be no better example of how a marriage partner can destroy another through mental pressure and meanness. After so much time, it is difficult to make any fast improvements through any dramatic action. Step by step the poor sufferer had to be given a new, stronger personality structure. She was to use the following suggestions at home:

"There is deep calmness and balance within me. I fulfill my tasks with pleasure and devotion. The love of God fills my soul. The endless strength of my subconscious mind flows through my body, making it healthy and strong. I love myself. I love myself as a complete being in my relationship with my divine core. I am sheltered and safe in the depths of my being that protects me, giving me strength to lead an independent, healthy and happy life. My love flows to my husband, as well, who needs a lot of strength to resolve his inner conflicts, as well as to free his good side.

I have a strong personality. I am successful in all my actions in positively improving my life and in what I am aiming for in full harmony with my spiritual strength. In front of my spiritual eye I can see my husband coming to me, friendly and ready to help me. I am ready for action, fresh, healthy and full of peace."

After four weeks, she had already become a different person. The harmony growing inside her had already left its mark on her facial expressions. One day, she came into my office with a new hairstyle and I had to look at her twice in order to recognize her.

Then one morning her husband, who had just returned from a mountain holiday, stood snorting with rage in my office. Brusquely and loudly he wanted to know what I had done to his wife. I told him: "You were four weeks on a holiday and in spite of that, you give the impression of being up tight. Your wife came to us for treatment and I believe that she is well rested, harmonious and blooming. Is this not a pleasant surprise to you? She realized in this period that a good core lies within you, and she will now believe in it in order to be happy with you."

Rarely have I seen such an amazed, but also naive, face. There was absolutely nothing he could say to this! While departing, he incoherently muttered phrases like "should have asked," "after all my wife…" and in such a way proved beyond a doubt how shaky his tyrannical self-consciousness was. The ice had been broken for his wife. Now she only had to remain strong and not let her new spiritual base be shaken. I gave her something like an "icebreaker" to take with her, perhaps to free her husband from his forced behavior as well.

All my suffering was the sign I needed for my re-orientation and it has led me to the right beliefs.

LEARNING TO LOVE YOURSELF FIRST

Twenty-five-year-old Michelle offered yet another case of mental suffering. She had just attempted suicide for the second time when she came to see me. This time, she had wanted to kill herself because of lovesickness, as her boyfriend had left her. At the end of her hospital treatment, she came to my office, still weak and deeply depressed.

Her fundamental problem was jealousy. In the period of being together with her fiancé, he had not been allowed to pay even the slightest attention to any other woman except her. A friendly comment to a waitress would make her completely lose her self-control. At night, she would test as to whether he was really at home by phoning him endlessly. She would investigate for days every minute he had not spent in his office. The young man must have been frightened when he thought of a future with this girl by his side. He comforted himself with a colleague from his office who had a stronger personality.

Along with hatred, envy, and resentment, jealousy belongs to the four strongest mental poisons we can create. It is a full manifestation of a lack of self-assurance and a boundless striving to possess, and any persecuted victim can be left in no doubt that they are bound to an extremely inadequate person. Jealous people mobilize all their strength in order to bind others to themselves. However, in such a way they mostly achieve the exact opposite.

Something in her childhood must have deprived Michelle of developing a genuine ability to love. Jealousy is only a vague idea of love, as Krishnamurti says, not the real, deep affection we are talking about here. Thus, her self-confidence had been stunted and she was not able to grant pure love to someone else. She wanted to, but could not do it. She looked for proof of love from others in order to feel good. A wish to possess without giving is like wandering up a blind alley. We have to turn back if we want to go any further!

Michelle suggested to herself a few times daily:

"I am open to the eternal power of my subconscious mind, which beams through me from the center of my being. I feel the new power of life flowing through me and strengthening me. I am successful in all that I intend with ease and safety. I listen only to my inner voice that gives me certainty to act in the right and proper way.

I love myself. I am full of harmony. All my feelings are clear and pure and lovingly directed toward my fellow man. I know that every human being possesses a divine core and I feel being connected to other souls. There is deep calmness and harmony within me. I can differentiate between egotistic feelings and spiritual connection to other people. Being safe, I rest in my center. This inner security guides me to a positive, happy and successful life."

After treatment, Michelle settled down into her new life. She thanked me for finally having discovered how to get a grip of herself. Time will tell what she will make out of herself, as relapses are a certainty in life, but we should tirelessly try again, from the beginning if necessary.

OVERCOMING AGGRESSION

Pent up feelings in young people are over and over again the cause of explosive and often life threatening behavior. Lack of love and care in the first formative years of childhood have been shown to be the cause of many failures in children's upbringings, to a frightening and increasing extent. Seemingly blasé cold young people face egotistical grown-ups who are somewhat reluctant to admit to themselves their own weakness of an increasing inability to give love. Their own offspring have to suffer and we are all experiencing a growing uncontrollable aggressiveness.

This is what also led to the cruelty with which 23-year-old metalworker Thomas quite simply threw a hammer at his boss when he made him responsible for some work done badly. It was only luck that made his boss step out of the way at precisely that moment, thus saving his head. However, because of the threat to the team, Thomas was not tolerated in the factory anymore. He had already been allowed too much. Known as a thug, he was considered unpredictable and was thus fired.

He came to us on his own initiative because he could not cope with the world anymore nor spiritually digest the constant offense he was causing. This at least showed he had a soft side to his being. He thought of where his development might lead him. He was sure that he himself was unable to master his fits of rage and therefore had come looking for advice.

Such an aggressive attitude toward one's surroundings and to one's fellow man mostly implies a lack of love toward oneself and almost always has its roots in a lack of care within the family circle. Thomas had, as it has been stated, a hard childhood behind him. His father was an alcoholic who beat the living daylights out of either him or his mother whenever he showed up at home. At school, the young Thomas soon started to unload all that he suffered at home onto his class-mates. He became a pain in class. Every person who approached him was a potential enemy to him.

Taking him for treatment meant having to soften a hardened ego. At one of my seminars, he found out for the first time what a real meeting with people was. Then something happened that no one could have imagined happening so quickly. The intensive, mutual care during the dynamic group exercises evoked tears from Thomas's eyes. Never in his life had he experienced the feeling of being accepted so completely and with such care. At first, he was slightly ashamed "because of his mawkishness." However, then he explained with freeing laughter that he had never been so open to others.

Through suggestions given to him, we initially strove to open his inner self to his surroundings. Whoever can imagine Thomas as a typical rocker type can guess how much patience and caution had to be applied in order not to once again allow his rough exterior to destroy the core of his new self-awareness. At least for the crisis period during his hypnosis treatment, we were prepared for the worst. However, Thomas remained like a rock once he was with it. He knew that he had reached this point; he was aware of the chance to become different and freer.

His suggestion formula for working on himself at home was:

"I am a harmonious, peaceful being like all people in my surroundings. My inner strength makes me ready and reasonable. I contribute to a harmonious life together with others and to the best for all.

I love my parents and I forgive myself for everything, as I do others. I like my colleagues and friends who all, like me, want to lead a beautiful, happy and successful life. I feel good and safe in the community. I feel good and safe in my own being that gives me all the strength I need to lead my life in a good and successful way. I am calm and reasonable, listening to my inner voice that leads me to what is right and good. There is deep calmness and harmony within me. I am strong, self-aware and I have a strong positive personality."

Thomas had a tape recorder. He recorded this text and let it play during his sleep. He infiltrated his subconscious mind with these life-giving patterns of thoughts, so to speak. With us he learned to put himself into a deep state of calmness by means of auto-suggestion where these guiding principles could sink into his subconscious mind when he was also at home.

For a long time he was a difficult case for us. His rough shell that had become hardened and apparently impermeable to every loving stimulus started to soften after a quarter of a year. Positive thoughts slowly reached his subconscious mind and replaced his false ideas of life, helping him to overcome the damage he was making in his milieu. He succeeded in letting himself go more and more during self-hypnosis and in immersing deeper and deeper into himself. When he parted from me, we all had a good feeling that we were letting this young man go toward a bright future.

Recently, I heard from him. Happily, he told me that he had passed his examination for a master craftsman's diploma and that he was again employed at the old factory. His inner transformation had transferred its positive radiance with a logical consistency to the outer world so that he now corresponded to his real self, conscious of his own strength.

RISING ABOVE DEPENDENCE

While metalworker Thomas turned his lack of love into outer aggression, 17-year-old Michael turned inwardly more and more as a reaction to the barrage of abuse from his parents. He withdrew from a world in which he was obviously not loved. His parents hardly left any doubt that he was no good enough in their eyes.

"The clumsy guy never does his homework, always sits day-dreaming at his window and gazes into space. He has not thanked us once for the fact that we made it possible for him to attend high school," cursed and swore his father. "He intentionally acts stupidly in order not to help us in the garden. You cannot even send him to do some shopping because he forgets his task from one moment to another. And then this eye twitching! He constantly has facial twitches when you talk to him. We do not know why the boy is so nervous! It is painful to imagine what the neighbors are saying about us."

Michael was really a dreamy boy, which was all that was left to him when his parents had deprived him of every experience of achievement. While skiing he broke his leg because his father wanted to see him go over a steep slope. He would finally have proved that he was a real man. His mother constantly moaned how dependent and clumsy her son was. He could not even take a cup of coffee from the kitchen without spilling it on his pants.

During our first consultation I handed him a form with a request to note down his name, address, and birthday. As expected, the mother reacted promptly and said to me: "Better give it to me, otherwise you will not be able to read it."

This constant decision-making for him had made Michael deaf to my words. When I asked him something, he would not get it. He turned in on himself. The calmer, pensive inner world to which he withdrew became his safe haven and ultimately more important than anything else. It was now vital to take him out of this self-chosen isolation that kept him out of all outer events.

However, his parents also had to learn to give up their almost sickening decision-making for him if any lasting improvement was to be reached. A person that is always sworn at and reprimanded, to whom not even the smallest slip-up or error is allowed, is ready to accept any form of escape. Michael found his in his inner life, and he withdrew into himself in an autistic way.

To make him open up did require a long time, but in the end was actually relatively simple. He longed for understanding and affection and he quickly acquired confidence after I explained to him in a face-to-face conversation that I completely understood his behavior and that I accepted him the way he was!

The most important thing in hypnotherapy is to let go voluntarily of one's exile step by step, while at the same time having confidence in the therapist.

Michael was given the following suggestions:

"There is calmness and deep peace within me. My subconscious mind is endlessly strong, giving me strength and safety to understand everything that confronts me in my life.

I do my schoolwork with pleasure. At school I am careful and I can concentrate. My growing knowledge makes me strong, successfully preparing me for my life. I feel good in the community of my teachers and schoolmates. From the safety of my inner center of strength I learn to open myself up to others. My new friends will also approach me in a friendly way ready to help me, and I will do the same from now on. Harmony rules between my inner world and the outer world. Based on this harmony I am ready and free to completely fulfill all tasks put in front of me with ease and safety. I can feel deep love within me, passing from me on to my parents and friends. Now I know: What I send out comes back to me. At home I feel happy and safe."

With Michael we also undertook spiritual trips during hypnosis. This was especially interesting since at the beginning he found himself in a deep, dark pine forest, a landscape that can be equated with emotional jungle. At the end of treatment this forest disappeared and Michael saw himself in the middle of a wonderful meadow full of flowers.

Four weeks with us were a great liberating experience for him. His facial twitches had disappeared when he left us. Openly and without blockages he could now talk about his feelings and desires. At one of my seminars, to which I regularly invite all my ex-patients and family members, I realized how successful my experience in the case of Michael had been. I was told that he had brought home a highly satisfactory school report in comparison to the previous one and that all his schoolmates had perceived him as being transformed. For the first time in his school life, he had joined a circle of friends. He was clearly on his way to finding himself, and to a life that all of us would desire.

Your greatest obstacle is delay; therefore, think about unity full of love in your everyday life and start now!

A Woman with a Washing Compulsion

Each of us sometimes feels guilty, believing that he at least once has committed an unjust deed or is tortured by the feeling of not always behaving properly. It is an extremely tricky matter to know whether our feelings have justifiable outer causes or whether we are reacting in a neurotic and therefore unjustifiably strong and excessively exaggerated manner. A neurosis is quite simply an overreaction to a signal, i.e. to certain conditions. A neurotic person loses an objective view of their world. For their suppressed feelings of guilt and fear, they react over-sensitively and to outsiders illogically. The consequences are sometimes compulsive actions and the life of such a patient can be strikingly difficult.

I received a visit from a 50-year-old woman who had to wash her hands numerous times daily. She had a shower at least five times a day and on Sundays, even more often. As an employee at a technical office, she used every free moment to go and wash her hands. It would take her at least five minutes just to lather her hands.

After decades, in spite of her cleanliness, she had suddenly developed an ugly skin rash. The cause was not uncleanness, but irritating soap substances, which in the course of time had completely destroyed the protective function of her skin. None of the doctors could explain her eczema and thus treat it, because there seemed no real cause. The patient was desperate. She reacted more and more hysterically, had strong fits of migraine, and was unable to work for many weeks of the year.

What was the cause of this mania? These are almost always unconscious feelings of guilt that mostly have their origin in sexual taboos, and from which "non-stop washers" want to wash themselves. In the case of this woman, who was single and had had sexual intercourse only two or three times in her entire life—and additionally in unpleasant, loveless conditions—an origin of her problems was her misunderstood sexuality. Even as a schoolgirl, she was warned by her mother not to use her hands to play with her body. When she did this in spite of that warning, during her adolescent "voyage of discovery," the implanted fears regarding punishment appeared. At the age of 14 she was seized by a compulsion to rid herself of her putative guilt by means of washing.

The strong adherence of the subconscious mind to such a reflex action for almost over four decades demands an immense readiness on the part of the patient to free herself. Above all it requires her to look at the reasons and causes of her compulsions, and in many cases neurotics are not even able to summon up the courage to name them. Only additional serious difficulties, like in this case the unpleasant eczema, can make them finally become proactive and put an end to what makes their life a torture. A vigilant doctor gave my patient some advice to look for mental causes for her constant suffering and to come and talk to me. With catathymic image perception, a psychotherapist has at his disposal a miraculous source of letting the most hidden closely interconnected events come to light (see also Chapter 5).

No matter how unbelievable it might sound to the layman, our memory does not lose any event that we once experienced. It often only appears as if we have forgotten certain bad events. In reality, we have only lost access to this department of our "library of life" through suppression mechanisms, because we want to make all that is unpleasant disappear during "immersion."

During self-hypnosis or hypnosis, we can almost always recollect details of the past, i.e. that which has apparently been "forgotten." In the case of this patient the images of life coming from the soul also brought to light the causes from her childhood. With a lot of patience we worked step by step in numerous single sessions on her suppressed emotional spheres that she locked up deeply within herself. She was given the following suggestions:

"There is deep calmness and harmony within me. I am fully relaxed. I am safe in the center of my being, the center of my vitality. All my positive thoughts, feelings and desires are in harmony with my spiritual strength, making my life happy and successful. I can feel the deep truth of my inner voice making me do good and right things. I love myself, I love my body, I am united with my spiritual strength. It gives me strength to live freely and naturally. The endless wisdom of my subconscious mind flows through my whole being, making me healthy and happy. I rest confidently in my divine core of being. My sexuality is natural and God-willed and it makes me happy to be united with a beloved person. Sexuality and love are a part of me and they are one."

Repeated similar sentences and expressions during a suggestion therapy have a goal to form, to impress upon the subconscious mind by the constant renewal of the same thoughts. The spiritual energy of these ideas should be melted down in the memory of the subconscious mind, so to speak. Once the suggestions as reflexes make use of the "workshop of the mind," the goal is achieved and the old bad contents disappear.

After a week, we added a further nuance in the suggestive treatment of the patient. We began to influence her problems more directly:

"I am in deep calmness and harmony. My whole body, my skin gives me a pleasantly good feeling, it is soft, beautiful and completely healthy. My inexhaustible spiritual strength flows through it perceptibly, making it strong and healthy. A pleasant wave of harmony flows through me. I love my body, thanking the Creator for giving me this life in abundance and beauty. I am healthy, feeling a deep connection with and love toward all living beings."

It took a long time before we were able to save this woman from her spiritual blind alley. After sixty hours of therapy, in practice she also participated in numerous seminars on positive thinking. Her skin had already significantly improved during the three months of hypnosis treatment. What injection therapies and sanatorium treatments could not achieve, she got over now through her own strength and power of her thoughts. In such a way her inner doctor and healer began to do its work.

Four months after the treatment, the eczema had completely disappeared. That was the outer proof of her inner transformation. After the third seminar she told me that she began having the thoughts: "I am clean and good. My skin is soft and clean. How happy and satisfied I am now!" every time she entered the bathroom or washroom of her company where she had previously always commenced immediately with washing herself.

Her life was freer, more relaxed, clearer and more balanced: All those who knew her congratulated her since she felt so much better now. Also the men at the company now saw her as a woman, not as a wallflower as before. Her charisma became more erotic and things generally took their course.

Borders are our teachers. They are the product of relative perception; therefore, always strive to increase the radius of your consciousness.

THE GIRL WHO COULD NO LONGER WRITE

A married 27-year-old student with two children came to see me with a rather rare problem. She was very sensitive and had telepathic and clairvoyant experiences—which was later verified under hypnosis in which she, for example, saw things that she actually experienced a few days later at the University. The problem that she brought to me at the time was paralyzing her studies: She could not write anymore. Every time she wanted to make notes or record something, she was seized by an inhibition to write; her hand was frozen.

During our conversation, I suspected that she might have had a recent shocking experience, which we very quickly unearthed during hypnosis. The young woman had strong inhibitions, a large inferiority complex, and had had similar feelings since puberty. Her mother had judged all her achievements at school as either good or bad. There were constant complaints about her writing. After school she carried out her first suicide attempt because she was world-weary and apparently felt inadequate.

Sex had always had an especially shameful shadowy existence in her life. The mother always presented all that was connected with sexuality as being the very embodiment of evil, her birth being also something very bad. Being together with her husband in marriage had always taken place in a darkened bedroom—and recently a fellow student "had taken" her stark naked on a trip into the middle of the free countryside and she had not even shown the slightest inhibition. However, they appeared afterwards in the form of a nervous disorder that now made it impossible for her to write.

We dealt with her trauma, among other things, with the following suggestions:

"I am completely free and calm inside. The inexhaustible wisdom of my subconscious mind makes me self-aware, giving me strength to cope with all life situations in a positive and good manner. There is harmony and love within me. I love my life and my body. I am full of thankfulness for being able to find all strength in me; I rest within it in full harmony with my being and with my whole Self.

My body is healthy and ready for achievement and I am successful and clear in my thoughts and actions through my positive being. Divine wisdom directs and leads me at all times and it will show me how to fulfill my desires."

Inner calmness and harmony helped this woman to quickly restore her balance and peace. Growing self-awareness going hand in hand with it gradually weakened her mental sexual block. Positive thinking brought her to a naturalness and relaxed use of her talents and skills. After six weeks of hypnotherapy and two seminars her inhibition to write had passed.

She had an open conversation with her husband that was to help her overcome her feelings of guilt.

Another problem had also to be resolved between the spouses and her husband therefore also came for a talk. The consequences of an infidelity are, unfortunately, rather rarely taken into consideration in advance; an escapade can in the full sense of the word be charming, but cannot basically be justified in such a way. The wife, as well as the husband, had suffered a trauma for her slip-up, and at this point good advice was very important.

OVERCOMING A LACK OF DRIVE

The huge amount of chaos produced by terrorists and waves of violence is almost always judged by society at large. However, egotism and a growing lack of love in society often lead young people to extreme acts.

Youngsters respond more and more extremely, more and more uncontrollably to the superficial view of life of grown-ups' society, who are mostly interested in material possessions. Instilled feelings of inadequacy also often force some youngsters into the extreme position of a total outsider. Too pressurized, youngsters sometimes do not see any solution other than to oppose the pressures of society with acts of violence.

A young businessman, David, whose parents had let be brought up in a traditional boarding school, belonged to those unwilling to adapt. His high intelligence made him grasp quickly and playfully all that was to be learned. Without knowing much about life, he saw no sense in increasing his aspiration for acquisitions that would ultimately enchain him to mainly material values for the next 30 to 40 years. Constant pressure at school and from his parents to finally be reasonable and become a normal, useful member of society took out the last of his willingness for action and led him only further and further in the opposite direction. Alcohol and drugs helped him to be left alone by this society. One day, he stood in front of me and asked me whether I was slier than him and whether I knew where the causes of his rage lay. Completely astonished, he listened to the simple truth that he now had to accept himself and his life in order to be free to a large extent in this society. His contrariness was always present, and he consistently spread his frustrations to almost anything connected with it or that he disliked. "The world" became his area of projection. Now he saw from the outside what awaited inside unrealized and unbalanced for his consciousness to wake up.

At first against his will, then with growing interest, he studied the philosophy of positive thinking and its very sound ancient psychological background. Especially the theory of the power of suggestion caught his attention and he was excited about all that was possible through hypnosis. Finally, in a few days he came for therapy and we treated him with the following suggestive visions of his future life:

"There is full harmony within me. I am immersed in my subconscious mind, letting my endless wisdom direct and determine my life. With full confidence in my inexhaustible spiritual strength I listen to my inner voice that helps me to accept all outer problems and resolve them. I master my destiny with positive, mental strength and love. With love I realize the source of my vitality, with love I

treat my body, the temple of my life; with love I turn to my surroundings because all beings possess the same life energy as me. We are a part of the same divine strength."

This work on himself took a few weeks under my supervision. His old profession of businessman could no longer stimulate him, and thus he followed his inner voice that drew him to the profession of an artist where he now—married with a child—could follow his vocation. Now he only smiles at his half anti-social, half-anarchic viewpoint of old times. At the right moment, his inner voice made him awaken and discover those real values in his life.

3

The Power of Suggestion

Reason is like the moon. It receives the light of consciousness from the Self, which is similar to the sun. When the Self starts to brighten, when the sun goes down, reason becomes useless.

Maharishi Mahesh Yogi

SEEING THROUGH THE INFLUENCES OF OUR SURROUNDINGS

In the single-case examples of previous chapters you may have noticed the suggestive formulae. Perhaps you thought about how or whether one of the described suggestions could influence you? An affirmation should be able to reshape your spiritual attitude. On the following pages I would like to demonstrate to you that suggestions/affirmations really can open up to us access to our unconscious source of power.

Everyone in our consumerism-oriented society is rather superficially aware that all commercials are based on suggestion.

Whatever it is that I would like to make understandable or sell to others, I have to pack into a suggestive, thus an intrusive, form. Almost everywhere in our everyday life we are exposed to suggestions and we accept them because, as a rule, we never actually notice their existence.

Think of this: Suggestions should stimulate you, they want something precise from you. One might like to make you use a certain toothpaste, another wants to persuade you to buy a much, much better make of car. Of course, you should choose only one product if you want to be happy. However, you will not discover a single suggestion that will help you to resolve your own, deepest personal problems. Reducing your suffering is nowhere near as profitable as selling you something. One who suffers consumes as a substitute much more than one who feels good. To earn money is the motto of our society. In the case of anti-cavity products and painkillers, it is not about your health, but your money. What is recommended to you for your inner peace? Commercials want to sell using all the possible helping aids at their disposal. To consume is good, but only within the framework of the essential, the reasonable.

These suggestions are directing ideas you have to follow. They are signs regarding consuming products that lead from your wallet and straight to the wallet of the "promoter."

If you want some improvements in your life, then you should realize that up until now you have not used your energy from your thoughts for your own benefit and things connected with money never will.

If you want to live a better life, turn the poles of your orientation and concentrate directly on the quality of your life, in the very real sense of the word.

Use suggestions, not negatively, but from now on positively, and tell yourself, as the famous doctor C. W. Hufeland did a hundred years ago: "If there are the imaginary ill (hypochondriacs) then there must be the imaginary healthy people as well!" Take this proverb literally. Our mental strength, activated by suggestions, influences the mind, the body, and soul in exactly the same way as adverts do the wallet. Here in this wide field, affirmations should be used to bring about an improvement of both inner and outer living conditions.

Begin to fulfill yourself. Make a clear space in the household of your subconscious mind using "cleansing" suggestions. It is very simple. When you become more aware of your mental energy it will be as if you ordered the "little people" to do their "job" while you were sleeping.

You should know that there are only two reasons not to be successful. The first one is not to start at all, and the second one is to stop too early. Therefore be persistent in the following two things:

1. Your desire to put yourself on the sunny side of life is powerful and definite. You have made a decision and you must stick to it!
2. You should be ready to discover in yourself a far-reaching scale of suppressed feelings. Change them so that they do not stand in the way of your happiness any longer. Release lovingly, but definitely, all unpleasant thoughts and ideas from your mind.

Well, what do we really mean by the term suggestion? According to the dictionary, it is an inspiration, an arbitrary influence on feelings, ideas, and the will. Auto-suggestion, on the other hand, is an influence that we exert on ourselves.

In itself it is nothing special or mysterious. Every day there are attempts to exert influence on our feelings, ideas, and our will. With every billboard, every commercial, every advertisement, skilful psychologists try suggestively to direct us. An idea can develop a suggestive influence only if it can stimulate a fantasy and emotional change in the subconscious mind.

If specialists in making commercials use your emotional world for their purposes, then you should use this higher value within yourself for your own joie de vivre in the future. Be fully aware now of the jewel at your own center and form your new world using positive picturesque thoughts.

Do not let yourself be persuaded by the will of others to buy something, but determine events in your world by means of positive suggestions. Dedicate yourself to the nourishment of your mental strength. No psychologist could ever have explained this to you before now, since they all work almost exclusively with a rationale that still attaches too little importance to the subconscious mind.

If you want to win a person over, then pledge your heart.

OUR ARBITRARY SETTING OF DESIRES

There is only one tiny difference between an idea, our continual train of thought, and a suggestion, and that is the arbitrary setting of goals. When a coat in the store window catches the eye of a woman, or a man enthusiastic about technology dreams of a new hi-fi system, then the idea of this desirable image has a suggestive influence, making the subconscious mind use its end possibilities to bring about that desire.

It is especially effective to picture a desire in your mind's eye that activates your unconscious more directly than abstract words alone. One who programs "health" surely has more success if he can imagine his goal concretely, i.e. visually.

I remember the case of a woman with stiffness in her neck evoked by the effects of mental shock after an incident. I suggested that she imagine herself happily playing tennis again, twisting and turning in all directions, and explaining to her friends that she was healthy again as part of her daily mental training.

A diabetes patient, as an addition to hypnotherapy, had to imagine all his organs playing perfectly in unison. In his imagination, they all expressed thanks to his pancreas and a deep, relaxing feeling of harmony flowed continually through the body.

Positive suggestions can cast light upon our life, especially if we believe that we have somehow lost contact with our world. Mrs. Sylvia, who came for a conversation suffering from depression and general disgruntlement, at first thought it was impossible. Skeptical as she was, I made her go to the door once again and leave her negative attitude outside in order to be able to continue the conversation. "Come revitalized and open-minded," I asked her, "so that we can start our conversation without any negative pressure."

With a tiny smile, she returned and we at last had a positive starting-point for our conversation.

A smile is an expression of a beautiful, enchanting divine strength. Carry out an experiment at home. Sit in front of a mirror, when you are feeling really grumpy, and keep smiling at yourself. I can guarantee that you will feel better within only two minutes. Whatever made you frown, you will consider irrelevant. Mrs. Sylvia was given daily "sittings" in front of her mirror as her first task. Having lost her husband at the age of 38, she had been lonely and depressed for the last fifteen years without having any contact with society. Mourning after her husband, she buried herself as well.

After the end of the therapy, she continued with the following suggestions:

"I rest in complete harmony. I have confidence in my divine core. The love of God flows through me filling me up. It makes me strong and healthy. I love myself and my life being connected with the inexhaustible source of my existence. With harmony and love I turn to my whole life and experience. All my desires are fulfilled. I ask my higher intelligence to show me a loving partner who understands me, who has the same spiritual vibrations and with whom I can step together into the bright future. I always let the endless wisdom of my higher Self lead and direct me. Freely and clearly I look into the future full of harmony and self-confidence."

The life of this patient had already changed during the period of the treatment. She dedicated herself to social work in the Support Group "Advice of the Wise Men" that I had founded, thus giving her daily contact with people. The renewed sprouting of her "attractive" temperament will surely attract a new life partner in a short period of time.

If it exceeds your imagination that a woman who had nurtured an event from her past and the memory of her husband for fifteen years could again become happy and true-to-life by means of suggestions, then let me explain some important connections to you by way of the following lines.

Do not listen to these words, do not let them go, apply them!

Reflexes & Imagination

I have already mentioned how naively and directly our subconscious mind absorbs all that we think of, even if the strangest tasks are in question. Think, for example, how some women jump on a chair if a mouse appears or how other women in the evening look under their bed to see whether or not there is a man hidden there.

A tiny effort can become a reflex, which at a specific time spontaneously emerges from the subconscious mind, making you look under the bed, for example. Observe yourself and all the reflexes lying dormant within you that make you act promptly without thinking in certain situations.

How do you react if you are grabbed around the head from behind? Do you turn to see what is going on? Or do you first shout: "Well, I wonder what this is all about?" Or have you already reached out to strike back? Each pattern of behavior, i.e. each attitude formed by our emotions, can be reformed by positive suggestions. Would you like to uplift yourself again, putting all your strength into the present, direct, real and happening life? Then the ideal moment has now come.

To use suggestions means to cooperate with your subconscious mind. Constantly repeated statements have, as a consequence, a gradual but lasting effect on the consciousness. It is so simple that a seven-year-old child can make use of this truth.

I had this experience with small David. His mother freed herself from constant fits of migraine through positive thinking in a very short period of time. David went through all of this with his mother, inheriting from her the scheme of positive suggestion that I had used to treat her.

He had two ugly big warts on his right hand and a few on his foot. For days his mother heard him constantly mutter: "The warts really must go. Warts go away! I do not want to have them anymore. The warts are smaller and smaller and they are completely disappearing." Within two weeks, the warts had really shrunk, being reduced to small black buttons. Soon, they had fully disappeared without leaving any scars. David had proved to himself his own power of suggestion and this experience surely gained him an important instrument for achieving great success through his subconscious mind in the future.

Children's imagination can undoubtedly be successful because of their as yet young unspoiled soul, while it often requires some additional helping hand in the case of grown-ups. Grown-ups tend to block access to their subconscious mind mostly through their intellect and their will, with which they try to control their daily routine. Here we can again see an apparently paradoxical law, according to which the will that we use to achieve our objective actually represents the obstacle to it.

The Subconscious Mind

I do not want to teach you anything, but to lead you to the source of your wisdom.

DEEP AUTOGENIC TRAINING

Not the will to suggest it, but letting something happen unnoticed by our intellect leads to success in our life. This happens most simply in the form of self-induced relaxation. All spiritual or physical effort first has to be eliminated if we want to enter into our inner world through auto-suggestion. In a restful, peaceful position in which we have freed our senses from their constant attention to the surroundings, and thus fully being able to turn toward our inner world, we create the ideal, those conditions we need to come closer to the as of yet hidden unconscious depths.

This special form of relaxation can best be described as a turning to an inner world. You can relax reaching a state similar to that of sleep, a trance-like sinking, and then enter into your spiritual home through the door of your subconscious mind. Suggestions given by a therapist or self-generated or simply thought about will have a much better effect than the same suggestions in full daily consciousness.

Correct relaxation is carried out if we take some time and "stick to it." A well-known and easily learned method of relaxation is autogenic training. Its various versions are today used for different psychotherapeutic and health purposes. If you have still not mastered your own particular method of relaxation, then participation in a seminar on autogenic training is highly recommended. It is offered at all elementary schools and at numerous training centers in every city. Autogenic training has become an essential pre-requisite for success in suggestion therapy.

In the first quarter of this century, Western doctors became certain that the autonomous functioning of our organs could not be influenced arbitrarily by our will. However, today we know that with the help of autogenic training, sometimes solely through relaxation you can positively influence many types of pain and disorder without needing any other aid. Through auto-suggestion is in your hands to relieve yourself from fits of migraine, bilious attacks (if there are no big gall-stones), stomach ache, even ulcers, muscle cramps, fits of asthma and much more. In such a way you can also ease, or even heal, exam nerves, flushes, stress, even high blood pressure and heart trouble.

If you would like to help yourself, autogenic training can become your best helper and friend. It is important to realize that the better the degree of relaxation and inner letting-go, the easier it will be for the subconscious mind to absorb corrections that come over the course of time.

Since I consider learning relaxation techniques of primary importance, I shall give here a brief summary of the first, essential exercises that are a precondition for the success of suggestive therapy according to the patterns of the positive thinking.

Relaxation in this context implies staying undisturbed from all outer stimuli. Nothing can disturb you, all outer events have become unimportant. In order to really have peace you should find a pleasant peaceful place for your exercises. Bright light, especially one coming from neon tubes is non-stimulating. If it is in any way possible, avoid at all times those side rays of old lighting tubes that make you nerve-wracked at work and in your living space. For the period of relaxation, the light of a candle is most suitable. The flame of a candle has a calming, illuminating power directly influencing your soul.

Lie flat with slightly spread legs and let your arms lie loosely beside your body. Inhale deeply and feel all your muscles loosening up while you are exhaling.

The first exercise consists of feeling your right arm and how it is becoming lighter and lighter (and thus more and more relaxed). The suggestion is: "My right arm is completely light."

You will probably need a few hours to fully apply this suggestion. Once you are trained, you will need to repeat the formula only a few times to reach the desired state again. This feeling of lightness after some exercise more often than not spreads automatically to the left arm also and then to the legs. If you are not completely sure that this is the case, use the same formula that you did for the right arm for the left one as well, and then for your right and left leg. After some time, the idea "my arms are light," "my legs are light" should be enough.

Repeat each formula until you clearly feel that you have reached the desired state. If the feeling of lightness is completely realized, improve your concentration with the sentence: "I am completely calm!" Now follows the second exercise with the formula: "Warmth is streaming through my right arm."

Think about the following expressions: "My arms are light," "My arms are warm." Never use the words: "will be warm" or "will be light." In such a way you postpone whatever you desire for the future. "Is warm" suggests here and now—and not anytime and anywhere.

The goal of the exercise is reached when you can clearly feel warmth in your whole arm up to the hands. A pleasant side effect is that your hands will be warm in the winter.

If you use this exercise one to three times daily, you will completely succeed within two weeks. To master autogenic training means being able to reach a state of complete relaxation in ten to twenty seconds. If it happens more quickly, be happy with your ability to perfectly let go and deeply relax. If it needs longer, do not be impatient. You need to regularly dedicate yourself to your relaxation exercises more than others. You will surely master it, as the longer you carry out this training, the more your autonomous nervous system will let itself be led by your imagination. One who at the beginning has difficulties with these formulae can support the positive idea of warmth flowing into his arms by imagining a pleasant warm heating body touching him. This idea can make the exercise much easier. Once you feel warmth in all your limbs the training can continue. Absorbed by the feeling of warmth, you then suggest to yourself: "I am completely calm!" Now pay attention to your breathing: "My breath keeps flowing calmly and regularly with the rhythm of my body."

Let your breath flow freely. You will notice that real letting go of one's breath makes it flow to and from the stomach. If you let your current, mostly shallow, breathing through the lungs go freely, then the surface of the stomach begins to go up and down. Only deep and calm breathing through the stomach really implies "releasing breath." Suggest to yourself: "The divine breathes through me!"

Repeating every formula six times should contribute to success. Now you continue again with "I am completely calm," adding this time "my heart beats calmly and regularly with the rhythm of my body."

Exercises for the heart should be learned only under a therapist's safe guidance for safety reasons. Therefore, I will omit them, going immediately to the last important preparation for total relaxation.

Concentrate on the place above your navel. Our biggest network of nerves lies between the spinal column and the stomach surface, and is named the solar plexus. Starting with this exercise, put your hand on your stomach for better orientation imagining the following feeling: "Warmth keeps flowing in my whole solar plexus!"

The goal of the exercise is reached when you can clearly feel this warmth in your center. Many people feel a strong pulsating of blood in the upper part of their stomach. Once the partially trained person has safely and quickly reached this state and has succeeded in this in twenty to thirty seconds, they are able to temporarily remove a chain of disorders from the body. A bilious attack, for example, disappears if you extend the warmth from the middle to the right, thus to the gallbladder and liver. In such a way you relax, easing the gall passage.

Stomach aches and ulcers disappear in the same way. The warmth is sent to the left, upper part of the stomach. Filling the whole abdomen with warmth means easing and relaxing the whole intestinal area. Many symptoms and disorders can disappear in a very simple way. Start learning about yourself while activating your own healer.

Now a soft return back to the normal state should be introduced. The body should be slowly activated. In order to wake up lovingly, stick to the following stages:

1. First clench a fist and stretch the arms.
2. Then tighten and stretch the legs.
3. Stretch the arms above the head and spin the whole body once to the right and then to the left.
4. Inhale deeply and open your eyes.

Get used to a slow return to the normal state. You will feel dizzy if you stand up too quickly, because the heart cannot lead the blood back into circulation so quickly from the relaxed areas.

We always create our own world. However much pleasure we derive determines with how much happiness and satisfaction our future days will be filled.

Training for Using Suggestions

These first apparently gentle and careful steps in exercising autogenic training are an ideal preparation for further action. Complete relaxation is the first stage on the way to fulfilling your desires. Now you have come to your main desire, to begin to exert a suggestive influence on your subconscious mind. With relaxed muscles, with a feeling that all tension has been removed from your body, release all nervous reflexes.

I shall assume that you have already reached the goal of the fourth exercise and that your solar plexus "is overflowing with warmth." Leave your body in this pleasant harmonious state and begin preparing yourself for this positive suggestion:

"I am completely calm. Perfect harmony flows through my body and my whole Self. All noise is irrelevant, it deepens my state of relaxation. I release all my thoughts, letting myself be absorbed by the pleasant feeling of sinking more and more deeply into my Self, reaching my most inner core. I rest in deep peace within myself."

With these preparations, you have brought your state of relaxation to a climax. Over the course of time, you will notice gradual differences that will also depend on your daily physical condition. In this detached state, you can begin to let your planned suggestions flow in. It would be best to prepare your thoughts for whatever you will now imagine and then begin imprinting them into your subconscious mind. Remember the following rules for any interaction with your subconscious mind:

1. The more you relax, the easier it will be for suggestions to enter your subconscious mind.

2. Your subconscious mind responds exactly to your words. Therefore suggest to yourself using the presently experiencing image "I am," even if it is referring to something about goals that are still to be reached (for example getting healthy, having success, learning to love and to live).

3. Suggest yourself fewer details and leave it to the intelligence within you to find the best way and the best solution to your big goal.

4. Transform your suggestions, if possible, into picturesque images. In such a way, you are focusing on the subconscious mind's understanding, to which a picture "says" more than a thousand words.

5. A suggestion repeated only once has a weak effect and only repetition of your suggestion two to three times a day for ten to twenty minutes leads you to your goal. The best time for exercise is before falling asleep, when the gateway to your subconscious mind starts opening. Stick to working on yourself for days and weeks. Patience is all-important, it will help you get over any old ideas.

6. Over the period of exercises refrain from self-criticism in any form and do not watch too closely for progress. Focus on the positive idea, take it as a reality of your life and do not let yourself be irritated. Have confidence in the endless power within you. Every doubt undermines your authority, thus putting obstacles in your way.

7. Do not talk about the work on yourself. Generally speaking, no one will show understanding about the fact that you want to free yourself from the situation to which you have adapted yourself in every respect. Everyone will hold on to their own habits and will at best make your work more difficult through criticism.

These guidelines are the result of experience from numerous individual cases.

Ten percent of people who would really like to realize their longings through suggestion cannot let themselves go as easily as is necessary for effective therapy. They are among those who can only relax slowly, but here it can also be implied that "Patience brings about roses." As long as our daily consciousness is over-present in our suggestion therapy, access to the subconscious mind will be blocked. Suggestions reach their goal to a lesser extent and they remain too weak to induce any lasting change. Therefore place a huge importance on relaxation exercises during your own preparations.

A stressed manager with heart trouble, stomach ulcers, and high blood pressure ended up in a real crisis caused by his impatience and nervousness over the two first weeks of treatment. He did not reach the liberating state of full relaxation until the end of the third week. Radiating happiness, he embraced my prettiest female therapist, Zarah Flaschberger, after this particular session in which for the first time in his life he was able to leave the rational position of observer.

The right choice of words is especially important. In a normal interactive tone we often handle words carelessly and thoughtlessly, developing little feeling for how insensitively we are using our tool, i.e. our language. With passive patience our subconscious mind accepts the words which appear to be completely harmless in everyday life, but which are often the reason for many misunderstandings and problems.

The next guiding principle for suggestions is to follow a large and extensive line. Think in terms of big things in order to make big things happen! Do not bother yourself with small things when it comes to your perfect happiness. One who suggests to himself a new coffee set as a dream will not expand his horizons further than the "edge of his plate" as the old proverb goes. Realize that all you need for your happiness will be given at the right moment. Strive for the most perfect fulfillment of your desires that you can imagine or let the wisdom of your subconscious mind create the greatest possible form of life success for you. Soon you will find out that the most beautiful success is based on the four simplest terms: health, harmony, love, and success. You will be able to encompass all good and bad sides of life with these few terms.

Do not concentrate your desires on any single detail. If you do, you will only put up further barriers to your experience. Life has many sides to it and your true destiny is mostly unknown.

An acquaintance of mine got it into his head that he was going to rapidly reach the position of branch manager in his profession. He diligently worked toward usurping his boss. Healthy ambition is good, but he passed over two opportunities offered to him by his headquarters to further his career by becoming director of other branches. He wanted to stay at the company and the stubborn, obstinate blindness with which he focused on a particular position did not make him see his chance. His higher Self for a long time acted in his favor, but he overheard his inner voice. After numerous dreams in which he moved in order to advance, he got sharp ears. His blinkers and his tenacity cost him too much time.

A picturesque transformation from a suggestion has the same influence as the very newest soap in commercials; namely, it deeply cleanses pores while also being resistant to old and "grubby" values coming from within your soul. The subconscious mind will better understand what you want if you use an already well-recognized term for an object, such as "pores deeply" etc. while giving your assignment. The term "job" will perhaps give rise to a man hacking trees and "freedom" maybe a flying bird. Therefore, create from the outset a picturesque idea of your longing and your subconscious mind will not need an interpreter in order to understand you.

A 15-year-old schoolboy, whose transfer to a lower class after half of the school year had been somewhat dubious, found with my help a good solution. After relaxation training and creative suggestion given for his self-confidence, his ability to learn began to grow again strongly. He enjoyed his life again and was given the following suggestions for daily exercise at home:

"There is harmony and strength within me. I am looking forward to going to school because I really enjoy learning. It is easy for me to receive knowledge and to give it back if asked. My attention is clear and I am interested in what goes on around me. I use all my concentration for my school subjects and I am soon to be the first among equals. All that I have learned stays with me forever in my memory helping me to shape my life successfully."

During a few therapy sessions he envisaged his next school report before his spiritual eye. He saw his teacher praising him for having caught up on his work so quickly and so well. This kind of picturesque idea of an achieved goal is the strongest stimulus to the subconscious mind and a clear instruction of what is to be done!

It will put all its strength into this objective, creating the conditions necessary to turn this image into reality, as happened in the case of this schoolboy.

Through your dreams you will become aware of a symbolic-picturesque experience in your unconscious mental areas. There are moments when long ago forgotten images resurface from our subconscious mind in the form of daydreams. Perhaps you can remember moments in which you seemed to have slipped completely into another dimension by a way of some solitary movement or melody. Recollections from your childhood, especially beautiful experiences from the past, are awakened by small external causes. In the same way you can imprint new contents onto your subconscious mind through suggestions. Now determine which of your visions should be supported by the full strength of your subconscious mind.

Observe successful people who seem to succeed so easily in everything they do. They possess a talent for directing their energy in a positive way, considering their goals achievable.

The word "impossible" should be removed from your vocabulary if you want to learn to use your strength in a positive way. Desires are fulfilled if you learn to translate them to your subconscious mind into its language of images.

This life is unique and you live it only once. Therefore, concentrate on the perfection and overall happiness of the world. Renunciation of spiritual development is stupidity, renunciation of health is madness, and to be poor is akin to mental illness, Dr. Murphy once said to me. The wealth of life is open to you, as it is to any other person. Thus use the power of your subconscious mind to become what you have thought of! Create only those images as suggestive assignments in front of your spiritual eye that come from your heart, that have been "created" by your inner world, so to speak.

One of my older friends once confirmed to me that he always used positive suggestions in his life. Since his childhood, he had dreamed of big journeys. Even as a schoolboy, he had found the walls of his home too claustrophobic and he felt an urge to travel to South America and the South Seas. At that time he was among the first to travel around Southern Europe in the early

50s. Today he knows the world, not just as an idle tourist either. During most of his journeys, he admits happily, he was able to combine his hobby and his profession.

He cannot imagine ever being disappointed by the creative strength of his inexhaustible subconscious mind. Whatever he believed in happened to him!

Happiness outside is an illusion. As with illusion, it must be limited by time.

How to Learn to Use Suggestions Properly

Whatever we want to save in our subconscious mind, patterns of behavior, views of life, motions of the soul, the deciding word is spoken by our feelings. They determine what will happen. Experts say that we should emotionally "occupy" our desires so that they may turn into reality through the enthusiasm of our whole being!

You are standing in front of an important change in your life if you can really be happy, if you can be enthusiastic, if you like something from the bottom of your heart.

Were you up to now rather reserved in your interactions with the opposite sex? Were your inhibitions of a fundamental nature or were they sexually determined? With a positive attitude to yourself, with a love of life and your fellow man, you can create a better view of the people around you.

From now on, you should not experience neglect or solitude the way an employed single woman who came to see me did; she felt excluded from the community of her male and female colleagues, and being lonely scraped together a meager living in solitude. During our first conversation she told me about her problems. "All people consider me egotistic and prudish. However, they always want something from me. Twice in the course of a few years, my colleagues at the office had got too close to me and they were surprised when I did not even look at them anymore. People are so disgusting. I find it difficult to get on with them."

Life is a constant rhythm and flow of energy. The spiritual law of resonance makes us experience what corresponds to our uniqueness. We are what we think. If we have thoughts about rejection, then we also experience rejection. What we have sent out comes back to us. My rather frustrating partner in conversation had withdrawn from life because of her negative attitude toward herself. Everything that she imagined as unpleasant happened to her. The positive suggestion I gave her proved to be her salvation. As if a flower had opened up during the night, displaying its splendor, in just such a way positive thinking affected this woman. I gave her the following suggestions:

"I am in harmony with myself and my world. There is deep calmness and balance within me. Full of love, I feel the endless wisdom that the Creator has put into the core of my being. The inexhaustible strength of my center strengthens and directs me. In love and harmony I turn to my life. With its wisdom I realize my spiritual connection with all people. Love is the strongest form of vitality. I love myself and my fellow man.

I give love to my surroundings, lovingly performing every task given to me.

My heart is wide open to anything that happens in the name of good will. I feel safe in the richness of life. All people are aware of the harmony of my being and I experience harmonious love. All goodness comes unto me. I am now happy and successful, enjoying being myself."

I let the young woman take part in one of my seminars, giving her a picturesque suggestion. Her task was to imagine herself as being the center of attention in her office. She was to imagine that everyone was striding toward her, needing her advice and wanting to have part of her positive charisma. She was also to imagine that men were looking toward her for fun, with a desire to experience her closeness with their full emotions.

All those who begin to reveal their spirituality should welcome new things, confronting them as replacement for old ones. Only a limited and undeveloped spiritual horizon sees chaos and apocalypse.

A Task for the Higher Self

Let your days be inspired by love and harmony. One who feels safe in front of other people only if he opens himself up will soon end up lonely, frustrated, and thus in painful situations. He blocks the flow of the divine within him and all negative, as well as positive, vitality gets exhausted. Stay in with the rhythms of life that demand a constant exchange of power in order to be embedded in the cosmic flow in a natural way and thus be able to participate in life.

Here follows a practical exercise that can be fully matched and modified to your individual needs.

1. Choose a positive idea that is directly opposite to your greatest problems. Use, for example, the formula:

"I open myself up widely to all the positive strength coming from my surroundings. Harmony and love keep flowing from me to my fellow man, coming back to me in increasing quantities."

2. I experience in front of my spiritual eye the situation that I have been longing for most (affection, note of thanks, asking for advice, congratulations, love, sex). By constant exercise, this picture will emerge vividly in all its detail in front of my spiritual eye until it clearly and vividly stands in front of me.

3. This once created image which I am immersing into is part of my daily exercise which will last for many weeks. In such a way I can feel my suggestion start to become a reality (see point 1).

4. Day by day, I feel the strength growing and leading me to the fulfillment of my desires. I emit goodness, understanding, comfort, and helpfulness, seeing the value of my fellow man, recognizing more and more the divine core of their being.

5. At the end of my daily exercise, I gradually withdraw from my spiritual idea. I fully immerse myself into my depths, giving task to my higher Self to give me the "inspiration" to bring about my idea. "I have confidence in my higher Self. All strength is within me. I am beloved of and respected by my friends and everyone turns to me full of confidence."

6. To end my exercise, I return again fully to daily consciousness, counting to ten and waking up with

the following words: "My arms and legs are free and light. Being free and light, I am stretching my whole body. My head is free and light. I open my eyes and I am fully awakened and rejuvenated."

This exercise can be adapted to all possible life situations and problems. Tell yourself that your picturesque imagination must be positive to all those involved, putting you into a perfect present. Any notions of future or words like "I will" result in the subconscious mind remaining untouched. In such a way, it keeps waiting for that future with you. Future and past do not exist in our subconscious mind, it knows only of the infinite present. Therefore you should make it grasp your idea here and now, fully experiencing what you desire at the present moment. Do not bring your problem to your higher Self, let it find a solution for itself. Also imagine yourself happy and satisfied in a state where the goal has already been achieved.

Positive thinking says that there is always a way. If you cannot resolve a problem, then you can quite simply remove a problem!

Suggestions of harmony and love will bring you more quickly into the flow of life. You will see that I am not wrong if your physical condition is soon blooming. All backlogs have been got rid of, disorders stabilized, and your pasty face has given way to a hearty ruddiness. Your heart and circulation work freely and in a lively way because you have chosen a better side to life.

If something comes to an end, it does not mean that everything has come to an end. When a year passes, another one starts.

A Catalogue of Suggestions for Personal Usage

Although life sometimes may appear complicated, many things in the area of emotions can be reduced to a few rules. The most frequent problems and worries in your life can probably be resolved using the following choice of suggestions in an individually adapted form, as well:

1. General Suggestions for Physical and Spiritual Health

⊛ I am strong and free. The infinite intelligence of my subconscious mind makes strength and wisdom flow toward me at every moment of my life, resolving everything that confronts me in the best way possible for me and for my world.

⊛ There is perfect harmony within me. I rest in the source of my existence that protects and strengthens me with its inexhaustible reserves.

⊛ I am full of harmony and love. I love myself, thanking my higher Self for the strength from my center that directs me toward my best, leading me to a perfect life. I love my fellow man and I experience the same affection as an answer. My life proceeds in harmony. I am an emotional and spiritual magnet that attracts goodness.

⊛ I am successful in all my relationships because I get all vitality from my inexhaustible center. Full of humility, I put my will and my intellect under the control of the intelligence within me, letting it lead me.

⊛ There is an eternal light of inexhaustible strength lighting within me. I am protected and strengthened by this strength, resting safely in the hands of God.

⊛ Harmony and love penetrate my whole being and my whole Self. I am healthy and free. I am beamed through by positive vitality that resolves all darkness and all that besets my body and my emotional world.

⊛ I make all decisions in my life based on the harmony of my higher Self. I listen to my inner voice that shows me the best way to fulfill my desires. All desires that my inner voice confirms are fulfilled.

⊛ My body is full of harmony and love. I am perfectly healthy and all my organs, muscles and limbs, all my cells function together harmoniously. The infinite intelligence of my subconscious mind sends fresh vitality to any place where it is needed.

⊛ God's perfection is expressed in my body. The idea of complete health now fills my subconscious mind. God created me according to his perfect picture and my subconscious mind now re-creates my body in full correspondence with the picture of perfection from God's spirit. God thinks, speaks and acts through me!

⊛ The endless healing strength of my subconscious mind flows through my whole being. It takes visible form as harmony, health, peace and happiness.

⊛ From now on I put my destiny into the hands of my Creator, who, through the endless wisdom of my soul, gives me the strength to be aware in my center of the right impulse that is needed to be used for my positive thoughts and actions.

❀ I rest in the center of my being. The inexhaustible vitality of my center flows around me like a stream. Light and love flow through me. I am safe and strong, controlling my destiny with divine inspiration.

Suggestions for Adolescents:

❀ I am harmonious and full of happiness. I thank my parents who help me in all new situations. My schoolmates and my teachers are affectionate and learning with them is wonderful and simple. I like everyone and everyone likes me. At school I can concentrate and am fully attentive. All knowledge flows toward me. Endless strength and safety come from my soul, making me happy and successful in the school of my life.

2. Suggestions for insomnia, feelings of guilt, nervousness

❀ There is deep calmness within me. I can feel the harmony passing through my body and my whole being. I can feel the harmonious connection with all my strength.

❀ My head is free and clear. Every time I go to bed all unnecessary thoughts drift away like small white clouds. Perfect calmness flows into me and I sleep until morning.

⊛ Every evening when I go to bed, all thoughts fall out of me. They have served me during the day; at night I return to the perfect harmony in my Self, to the rendezvous with my subconscious mind. The endless wisdom of my subconscious mind helps me to resolve everything more easily. I am safe in the inexhaustible source of my spiritual energy. When I go to bed all unnecessary thoughts are gone. I am fully relaxed. All external things are now totally irrelevant and I immediately fall asleep. I sleep deeply throughout the whole night. My sleep is magically restful. In the morning, I wake up rested and am rejuvenated and cheerful.

⊛ Today begins a new and beautiful day. I greet it with happiness in my heart. I look forward to performing my tasks and to everything that I will experience with other people. I approach others full of harmony and positive energy.

⊛ I rest in my Self every single moment of my life, sheltered and led by the infinite intelligence of my subconscious mind. Wisdom determines my vitality, teaching me to control my destiny in a positive and successful way. I am an extraordinary success.

3. Suggestions for depression, fears and inferiority complexes

⊛ I am completely calm. Perfect harmony keeps flowing through me. I sense the wonderful balance of my physical and spiritual strength. Harmony keeps flowing through my whole being. Positive energy keeps flowing through my body and my mind. My head is free and clear. My heart beats calmly and regularly. All disturbing thoughts fall off of me. I am healthy, free, and clear. The infinite intelligence of my subconscious mind keeps flowing through me giving me strength and safety.

⊛ Free and relieved, I approach other people. I can look directly into their face and experience their uniqueness with sympathy. I experience them in inner harmony, in perfect harmony. I am safe and full of self-confidence. I live my life based on the inexhaustible vitality of my subconscious mind. I am harmoniously interconnected with my highest spiritual energy that the Creator has given me for this life. God helps me, leading me by way of the infinite intelligence of my divine being. I enjoy being together with other people. I am strong and self-aware. I am full of self-confidence and successful in all my actions.

⊛ I am successful with ease in every task, every job that I have to master. The infinite intelligence that I scoop from my unconscious makes me safe and free. I live with the strength of my center. Wonderful calmness and harmony flow through my whole being.

4. Suggestions for smokers

⊛ There is deep harmony within me. Harmony flows through my body and my whole being. I feel penetrated by deep calmness and harmony.

⊛ Cigarettes have become unimportant to me. They disturb my inner harmony. Clouds of cigarette smoke and the smell of nicotine are not good for me and I avoid places where people smoke. They disturb the harmony of my strength, thus harming my health.

⊛ All tobacco products are unpleasant and therefore I do not want to put a cigarette (cigar, pipe) into my mouth anymore. My whole being rebels against this terrible smell. Tobacco has become meaningless to me. I do not even see it anymore, even if others leave it around within my reach. I feel unspeakably good in my inner harmony. Smoking and cigarettes represent a disturbance to my well-being. My inner balance is much more important than a cigarette. I am completely indifferent to cigarettes.

⊛ I feel free and healthy. I feel deeply satisfied, letting fresh air enter into my lungs. Cigarette smoke is annoying. When I think of smoking, I feel unpleasant and a strong feeling of repugnance arises in me. If I bring a cigarette to my mouth, my stomach retches.

⊛ I rest in deep harmony, happy that nothing disturbs this balance and well-being. Since I do not smoke anymore, I feel better day by day in every respect.

For almost any personal matter of concern, you can choose a stimulus for yourself among some of these examples of suggestions. You can be tortured with jealousy or an inferiority complex, sick with ambition or a physical illness. Being happy and healthy very often depends on appropriate and positive motivation of your subconscious mind.

If you daily make an effort to find out how to make someone happy, I can guarantee that sunshine will return to your life.

GROUP SUGGESTIONS

Many people cannot really imagine a practical usage of suggestions. In the positive thinking friendship circle, and especially in my seminars, we use group suggestions, making use of suggestion methodology in order to become better acquainted with them. A suggestion in a big circle of listeners can also give rise to more simple and sometimes more extensive help than in individual sessions. Suggestion in a group is always stronger because an individual feels safer and less observed. Because of this, group suggestions are used in lavish style in the USA. Healing sessions and mass prayer sessions are in principle exactly the same.

All our problems and suffering actually have the same cause. It is our loss of contact with our higher Self, our center. If we concentrate on the original matter of concern, on our longing for health, harmony, success and love, then all human problems can be neutralized in this way.

Thus suggestion has become a very useful therapeutic tool in group therapy. It is not uncommon for participants to call afterwards, reporting that chronic disorders have disappeared. Very often, headaches are among them. It is little wonder that people who are controlled by their intellect first have to free themselves from huge pressure, relax deeply before they can be led by the consciousness of their higher Self. A lot of tension disappears, sometimes forever if there is the right mood during the session.

The Earth does not know of any suffering that cannot be healed.

A Spiritual Journey through Body

Let us now turn to practical exercises using positive suggestion in order to treat mental/physical disorders. We should know that every auto-suggestive treatment depends on the mental effort and general condition of the individual concerned. Do not bring criticism and doubts about your actions into your auto-suggestions, because they will have the same effect as water does in your car gas tank.

Take authority over your life again. You are absolutely responsible for everything that happens to you. Therefore, first accept yourself the way you are. There are certain situations in an individual's life where a doctor cannot help and that leave one no other choice than to take the bull by the horns in one's life. Therefore, remain courageous and safe. You are always under the best care, that which gives you the strength to overcome even the most difficult situations in your life. If you maintain confidence in your divine core, then you are already halfway there to your goal.

With this attitude, now begin treating your physical weaknesses in the most positive way and without the need for medication or outside intervention. The mind forms the body and in this sense, the body is an expression of your mind. Therefore, every one of your body's reactions depends on your spiritual attitude, on the quality of your thoughts. Your physical "existence" is an expression of your thoughts, or more precisely, is the mirror image of your soul.

Start with a positive cleansing of the functions of your body, returning to health and harmony. No matter what your personal case is, concentrate on the following exercise:

Withdraw to a silent place and make yourself comfortable. Relax as much as possible. Observe your muscles. Let all your thoughts drift away on a small fluffy white cloud. Let yourself go. Let it happen. Freely and happily release everything that might disturb you. All outer noise is unimportant.

Lightness and pleasant warmth enter your arms and legs, filling your whole body. Your breathing and heartbeat are calm and regular. Your consciousness now rests within itself, warmth is flowing through your solar plexus, and you feel good and safe.

Deepen these lasting and rich feelings to the point where you can clearly perceive the warmth in your solar plexus. You will probably not be able to experience all of these states right away. You may need a few days or maybe longer before you learn how to control every single sensation.

Your patience will win you the highest prize you have ever received in your life for being committed to your job. You will again win authority over your life.

For decades, you have been at the mercy of strange suggestions. Perhaps it has cost you your strength and health because you had no inkling of how it could happen. Now learn to change, learning to re- charge your batteries with a quantity of positive energy from the righteous power of the cosmos. Your body is connected to the huge inexhaustible generator of life. You will be connected with it as long as you desire. You should be aware that you have always had this generator within you and at your disposal. Now you can establish contact through your thoughts in order to become strong, free, and healthy.

Let us now continue with our auto-suggestive treatment:

You lie comfortably on a couch, relaxed, full of warmth, safe and in perfect peace. Now follow the concept of distancing yourself more and more from your normal daily consciousness and sinking deeper and deeper into yourself, toward the center of your Self.

Imagine that you are standing on the upper edge of a staircase leading you to your center with its seven steps. Count back very slowly from seven to one, stepping back into your mind. Each step brings you a step closer to your center. Now you can clearly feel that you have arrived at your center, your "homeland."

At this point the main part of the exercise starts. Imagine that you have become a small spot of light in the center of your forehead. If you desire, you can now travel through your whole body taking pleasant warmth with you. You are now on a journey of discovery from organ to organ. You visit the stomach, intestines, pancreas, liver, gallbladder as a small spot of light, exuding life energy into every single organ, beaming light to every dark place until all is bright and pure. You say "Thanks" to the organ where you are at the moment. You express thanks to every cell for their harmonious cooperation, for the organ's selfless love toward the whole body, for their togetherness in the big choir of the community of body cells.

With every repetition of this exercise you will experience more strongly and clearly the feeling of tension and your ailments starting to disappear.

To end this exercise you should now go back along the same path, back to where you began. Travel again as a spot of light to the center of your forehead where your homeland in this world is. Now climb the staircase slowly in the mind from the first to the seventh step. When you have reached the start again, end the exercise with these suggestions:

1. My arms and legs are free and light once more.
2. My body is free and light. I turn it once to the right and then to the left in order to wake up.
3. I inhale deeply, stretch myself, open my eyes again, fully awake in daily consciousness and feeling wonderfully rejuvenated and strengthened.

You will be surprised by the effect of this meditation. The spiritual strength and love that you exude will turn into whatever you need for life. Have you not deprived your body of precisely this for too long? When you go on this "journey" again, stay longest in those organs or parts of the body which need harmony most. Repeat this exercise as often as necessary until you can feel that your "jobs" have been carried out. What you spiritually experience in this way will be manifested in your daily consciousness. Your ailments will ease off. Your mind created your body and now it is healing all your wounds from the past because you have asked it to do so.

The healing effect of this meditation depends on its intensity. The clearer and more positive approach to life you have, the more you will create spiritual and physical harmony in more of a noble and genuine way. Through this work on yourself you will find the way to your inner master again, and everything will be just fine.

One who has nothing to do creates work for others.

DETERMINING YOUR EVERYDAY LIFE

What we can achieve on the physical body level through the previous exercise we would now like to transfer to our surroundings. Are you the master of your own time? Do your daily routine and your daily work bring you the amount of satisfaction that you desire?

We do not depend on outside conditions and are not driven by them. Let us realize that our reality has been created by our own thoughts. Today we experience what we thought of yesterday, and tomorrow we shall experience what we have been thinking about today.

You were born to be free. If others determine what happens in your time, it means that you are dependent on them. Determine what you desire to experience in your life. You have taken into account too many influences that have manipulated you. Assume that you live in this body once and only once and therefore live the full version, your vision of life being in peace with God and the world.

The best way to reach your goals is to have a clear idea on how to do so. Achieving unshakable self-confidence by positive thinking is possible to anyone if they really want it. If you fall under the criticism of others, if a doubt can be implanted very easily, your failure is programmed in advance. Follow only your own aspirations and longings and choose a clear and harmonious life now. Build inner clarity through positive suggestions and create a life in harmony with creation using the inexhaustible energy of your subconscious mind. That is your task!

The greatest assurance for your welfare is the power that created you. This inexhaustible source is always there for you when you need it. Be aware of the great meaning of these words.

Check whether your desire is right for the future. If your inner voice confirms it, you can unconditionally say yes to your life and further envisage your goal through your picturesque idea. Identify yourself with it as fully as if it could not be any other way.

From now on live with the ideal of what you have conjured up in your mind. In colloquial speech, it is said: Imbue yourself with it. Prepare for the birth of what you desire to reveal. It is irrelevant what kind of goal it is. In your vision you can lie on a beach on the South Seas, see yourself together with an ideal partner you have always longed for, or healthy and free, bring about things that you cannot presently bring about because of your present predicament. Whatever happens, you will quickly experience firsthand the success of your always creative subconscious mind.

For centuries, the initiated have used the art of imagination. Medicine men of East Asia, Africa and Native Americans even today use this huge source of power. Each of us has the same ability to initiate these series of mental processes in order to reach a goal. Emile Coue once said: "If I think that I would like to do something, but I do not believe in it myself, the more effort I put in, the less success I will have." The inner feeling of not being capable of doing something is always stronger than the will to achieve it. From the beginning, concentrate your feeling on positive consent and realization and you have already won. Thus when your feelings, thoughts, words, and actions coincide, there are no limits; then, your limits are as boundless as the Creator always wanted them to be.

Do not believe that something will be done if you yourself do nothing.

SPIRITUAL STRENGTH TRANSCENDS MATTER

Thousands of my patients have been successful in positively changing their feelings and in realizing that the infinite intelligence of their unconscious is the highest criterion in their life. Millions of people in the whole world today know of the power of the subconscious mind. The reasons for teaching this secretly disappeared as people in our times are mature enough to devote themselves to their mental energies.

It gives me an especially great pleasure to be able to help skeptical academics with my form of hypnotherapy. These rational thinkers are generally far and away the most distanced from their source of strength. Therefore, even to me it is a worthy success to be able to open the door of their unconscious for them, reconnecting them with the world, as the Creator did for you.

Last year, I helped a student of physics and prospective mathematician not only to pass his exams without any trouble and stress, but also to form a firm and unshakable base for his whole personality. If I had told him before that we would act as voodoo healers in the Brazilian jungle do, he would have almost certainly tried to run away.

He was given a picturesque idea, where he saw his professors and classmates congratulating him for passing his exams. Radiating happiness, he daily relived this scene with an inner feeling of calm, which was later to be tested in his particular field of knowledge for which he was already well prepared. He experienced his exam in his mind the way he wanted to imagine it, and then once more in the same way in reality.

You should also look into activating your imagination. Sit for a peaceful hour in your favorite place and tap into your creative dreams. This basically implies that you should have dreams about your life in order to make these dreams come true afterwards. Through your imagination, follow the path of your longings in order to fulfill your greatest and most treasured desire!

From this inner image that should stand clearly and vividly in front of you, create your new reality with your vision. You "see" yourself in the middle of the desired situation, you experience it spiritually, vividly in front of your inner eye and what you see will soon become reality. What you sweetly "imagine" in your trance, what you imprint onto yourself, is "developed" and then has to be expressed. You should be deeply convinced that your subconscious mind, with its infinite intelligence, is occupied with making real the image of your dreams.

The well-known psychologist Carl Gustav Jung was once asked whether he believed in these human abilities. He answered: "I do not just believe, I know!"

It is important to learn how to activate the subconscious mind in order to reach your goals. This was explained in the early 60s by the father of positive thinking, Dr. Joseph Murphy. He taught me how to transfer suggestive ideas during my lectures so that I could further instruct my therapists. It is a question of concentration and inner knowledge that makes you convincing in the real sense of the word!

Dr. Murphy reports on how he could heal with his "power" at a large distance.

He had his greatest personal experience many years ago with his sister Catherine. When she had to go to the hospital in England for an operation on her gallbladder, she asked for his help in California. Without pausing for thought on the symptoms of her disease, Dr. Murphy imagined the following situation a few times daily, as also described in his book *The Power of Your Subconscious Mind*:

"This prayer is for my sister Catherine. She is relaxed and at peace, poised, balanced, serene and calm. The healing intelligence of her subconscious mind which created her body is now transforming every cell, nerve, tissue, muscle, and bone of her being according to the perfect pattern of all organs lodged in her subconscious mind. Silently, quietly, all distorted thought patterns in her subconscious mind are removed and dissolved, and the vitality, wholeness and beauty of the life principle are made manifest in every atom of her being. She is now open and receptive to the healing currents which are flowing through her like a river, restoring her to perfect health, harmony and peace. All distortions and ugly images are now washed away by the infinite ocean of love and peace flowing through her, and it is so."

Two weeks after this, the doctors were astonished by Catherine's inexplicable recovery. X-ray pictures then showed that there was no longer any reason to operate. To me, this was the most beautiful proof of the power of thought.

What kind of person would be more satisfied with helping a suffering person through rational logic if spiritual ways were to present him with more promising solutions? Our scientists helplessly confront with their thinking many apparently mysterious events that can be very simply explained by suggestive techniques.

One of the most phenomenal examples of the power within us could be recently experienced on television. English doctors made a film in Thailand about a wise man who let himself be bitten by two freshly caught mambas in front of their very eyes. No European could ever survive a single bite of one of these deadly snakes. However, the man fell into a deep trance, in which he remained for hours, dripping with sweat. In approximately six hours, during which the doctors did not leave him out of their sight, he stood up as if nothing had happened. Without serum injections or any other aid, he had actually neutralized the deadly dose of poison and had overcome the tortuous experience, thus remaining healthy.

This was a wonderful demonstration of the power within us, during which the yogi removed, i.e. neutralized, the deadly poisons from his body by way of his spiritual strength alone, thus being left unharmed.

Would you not consider your own problems to be relatively harmless and less life threatening when compared to an "attack" on a person's life, like in this case? Do not try to bring about a miracle, but build up your courage, as well as the irrevocable knowledge that you can turn (almost) anything to your own benefit through positive suggestion. Start off with small steps. You will soon experience an exhilarating awakening of magical abilities within yourself.

Particularly, obese people can speedily achieve visible success through auto-suggestion. Stress and frustration are mostly a background to obesity. If you live as almost half of the population do, then choose the following suggestion:

"I am in complete calmness and harmony. I immediately eat less, feeling good and satiated. My appetite is normal and I am soon full at every meal. After dinner I go to bed satisfied, sleeping deeply and soundly. I see myself in front of my inner eye as slender and supple. I feel good and rejuvenated. Weight loss revitalizes me, easing all my organic functions. I reach my ideal weight without effort and I am a few years younger."

If you allow yourself to experience this thoughtful idea daily, sensing how your body adheres to it, then you will receive the first discernible results within a week. The scales will show one to four pounds less, and you will become continuously slimmer.

I experienced with one male patient during suggestive therapy how important influence feelings can have on the successfulness of our idea. For different heart and kidney disorders, I suggested the Hay's diet to the somewhat overweight man of 265 pounds in addition to the weight loss suggestions.

According to this diet, you separate all carbohydrates (flour, rice, potatoes, noodles) from animal protein. Only vegetables, fruit, and milk protein may be eaten with both types of food. Thus you can eat a steak with vegetables, or potatoes with vegetables. Sugar, coffee, tea and alcohol should be avoided at all costs. This type of diet, which should stretch over a few months, has the advantage that it removes acid from the body without any need for special restrictions. All waste products and flab that we accumulate through our one-dimensional combination of foods can be broken down more simply. Dr. Hay maintains that, through this diet, the body can be cured of many ailments, from rheumatism to atrophy of the kidneys and one's weight should also drop to what one would consider normal.

My patient, who came to me with the notion that he could only reduce his 265 pounds through painfully rigorous discipline, believed that it would need a gargantuan, heroic effort for him to reach his goal. After suggestions had already given him support emotionally, his opinion that weight loss implied suffering meant that I had to resort to stronger methods.

So I put him for short intervals on a null-diet, which to many people presents a favored method of reducing weight. He wanted to suffer, and so it was. The null-diet is simple and pleasant, if correctly used, but he included it under the column of "martyrdom." Thus he suffered, pound by pound, in reaching his target weight and was thus satisfied!

One who steadily looks to the stars will soon fall flat on his face.

SUGGESTIONS OF SOCIETY

One who takes his life into his own hands through positive thinking, as described in this book, can soon distance themselves from the suggestion-intentioned influence of their surroundings.

Let us take politics as an example. It is an immense field for suggestions, for ideas that are sold as desirable by power groups.

In politics and economics, a love of life is replaced by the intellect and by a striving for material gain. The politician always thinks in terms of confrontation and extension of power. However, as you sow, so you shall you reap. If you learn to sow harmony by the end of this book, then you shall reap love. At this point, I must state that I fully agree with Maharishi Mahesh Yogi when he says that if one to two percent of the population of a city meditates, then that will reduce aggression and acts of violence by ten to fifteen percent. Positive thinking creates exactly this change, both within you and within the country at large! One who meditates, one who controls his thoughts, gains all the pre-dispositions needed to be master of his own destiny.

Let the sun shine brighter so that you can be seen in the light of your divine appearance!

Remember once more Coue's sentence that an inner feeling of not being able to do something is always stronger than our will. Therefore give freedom to your longing to search for a better and more harmonious life. Dream of your life's ideal so that it can be fulfilled. Begin first with the idea of being free and harmonious. This idea will give you powerful help in your fight against all negativity. You will soon be free from dependence of any kind, not thinking about who or what has contributed to your bad luck.

Love and harmony bring you into harmony with your higher Self. In such a way, you dedicate yourself to your life's greatest task put in front of all us earthly beings. To be again at one with our existence is comparable to entering paradise. Human success, which you want to gain through the power within you, puts everything that you ever dreamed of before into the shade. To live in harmony with cosmic strength means to be healthy in mind, body and soul and to live in a beautiful world worthy of living in. A burgeoning joy for life replaces your acquired stress and your all-too-strong desire to cling to a materialistic view of the world. Everything essential will fall into place if the strength of your subconscious mind is activated. The richness of life is open to you if you are ready for it. So, are you ready?

If you are now able to observe outside events, participating in them with this newly acquired inner calmness and clarity, you will come to realize how much may have been pulled away by the whirlpool of negative thoughts. How often have you wasted your powers of influence on mere acquaintances? How often have you failed to act on your own behalf, playing victim to a state of not being in full consciousness? Secret seducers, keen for power, have found you an easy target and thus have used you for their own purposes. Suddenly you are able to grasp so much more clearly that the biggest political problems that you hear of daily in the news and that currently appear to be reaching a climax, are in fact "home made." Powerful lobby groups are playing upon the fear stirred up by our political leaders. A person who is afraid is much easier to manipulate. He can be more easily convinced to choose a certain party if it promises to eliminate the threat for him.

We can change our consciousness in order to bring into harmony our own living conditions with those of all around us. Ask any wise man in this world and he will confirm that you can make a big and effective contribution to a peaceful world only if you exude love and harmony toward your surroundings. Very simple positive ideas will forever resolve the difficulty the intellect has become entangled with. Take this realization into your heart. It is in your hands to replace old and fear-obsessed ideas that have brought you only frustration, suffering, and disease with more positive ones. In such a way you will have entrusted the strength of your soul to make your dreams come true and achieve your goals.

People keep only two things to themselves: their age and whatever they do not know.

THE SECRET OF SUCCESS

There are surely some among your acquaintances who have a clear-cut goal they are aiming for. With a really strong determination, they carry out certain tasks and follow their hobbies, achieving something considerable. These people have already unwittingly used their subconscious mind as a source of unlimited power. To them, a certain thoughtful idea has become a suggestion and they will mobilize everything in order to realize it. How often have you admired them for their endurance and patience? Take such people as role models as you can learn from them. Start adapting your personal ideas to your mental potential so that you may fulfill your longings. No matter whether it is recovering from illness or a desire to make your neighbor's dog stop barking, with love, all that is positive will be realized. I really mean everything, if you are able to really understand these eternal truths that I have given you.

Do you desire resonating positiveness for your success in positive thinking? One who is occupied with the effect of positive thinking need only observe his family, his friends, and acquaintances. It will not be long before the first astonishing questions arise. You will very soon experience how you have been judged up to now by your fellow man. Thus, do not hesitate for one minute in starting to develop your more loving, better part. Start with small things, but start here and now. Everyone has time to do this important work on themselves. Think about how much time you dedicated to your old ideas. How much time did you spend in the doctor's waiting room over some "minor complaint"?

Nothing has ever been said against getting together with good friends, but look to a circle of friends with whom you can speak about what is on your mind. Consider the fact that maybe your coffee morning circle, or group of bar regulars is, in a metaphorical sense, a "source of infection" of negative thoughts. Rethink once more how much potential energy you eventually wasted in the process of saying or doing something unnecessary, thus not leaving you enough time for the really important things in life.

You will surely suddenly find new acquaintances and like-minded people if you take a path to yourself immediately. You will acquire so much new-found self-confidence that you will be able to realize by your own choice everything that you consider good and important. At this moment it is not important to change anything except your thoughts. Positive suggestions themselves will soon do their work! Here is the first and most important suggestion that you should use from the very beginning:

"I begin every day with a happy attitude to myself and to everybody I meet. I perform everything with happiness and inner devotion. My thoughts are steadily directed

toward all that is good in the present. I am conscious and I can concentrate on all that I do. There is peace within my heart and my mind. I am a strong, positive personality, successful in my profession within society."

No matter how simple these words may appear, they still contradict our daily reality. By looking at what you desire, what you consider important for yourself, you are taking the first steps toward change. All nervous thoughts disappear when you discover how many unnecessary things you did automatically previously and how from now on you can save almost one-third of your entire lifetime through single- mindedness. Let all old time-consuming habits go and all hecticness in your life will end there where your inner peace begins.

After this successful beginning, over the course of time create for your own personal concerns your own suggestions that may transform your whole life. You will feel stronger and stronger inner "growth," in such a way that you will be up to every challenge.

If you visit a person who has the flu, you will feel how your radiating life energy does not allow such a disease to come near you and how you, instead of being infected by it, have an infectious effect on it, that is to say, you bring about a cure. If you are having an important discussion, then go there in the harmony with your Self and let the truth of your argument speak for itself. Imagine what you desire, decide what you want to achieve through this conversation and in such a way everything will already have been decided. Your inner calmness and balance, together with your subconscious mind as a source of unlimited power within you, will already have arranged everything in your favor. The following suggestive formula is an excellent pillar of strength for your self-confidence in all possible cases:

"There is perfect calmness and harmony within me. I entrust to the infinite intelligence of my subconscious mind at every moment of my life. It will now turn my situation to the better, whatever the best decision is for me. I act safely with the strength of my center.

I radiate calmness and love toward my fellow man. I thank the Creator for making me clear and free. I am healthy and successful on the way to a perfect life."

If one or another word seems strange or unusual to you, then perfect the text fully in accordance with your personal feelings, but do not bring in any negative statements. Distance yourself fully from anything that you do not want to do or experience. Accept new, positive ideas as real events as if you had never thought of anything else, and they will happen!

If you ever come to doubt whether you have chosen positive constructive thoughts and whether you can really resolve your problems through your affirmations, then ask yourself this: "Do my thoughts bring me health, harmony, love, and success?" Your inner voice will surely give you the right answer.

Suggestions that you have used for decades have become fixed values by consistent repetition. Of course, your higher Self uses its potential strength to realize your imagined vision of life. You can reprogram this source of power within you and then be happy about many new and pleasant events. Perhaps you will feel the same way as a participant at one of my seminars who protested, saying: "Up to now, I have been irritated by every fly on the wall, and now you say I should love them?"

Love yourself first. It takes time to get rid of something. What we have got used to for decades cannot be ended in a day. Of course, you cannot eliminate your problems overnight, but you can surely begin by choosing a new direction. Choose that which will serve you! The path is your goal, Buddhists say. What they mean is that you can advance only if you really do take the first step on the path to self- realization. Therefore decide where the path should lead you.

Thinking positively, make a choice and let yourself be led by your subconscious mind. Your life will then change by itself. The Taoists, with their Wu-Wei, say that you should flow along with the energy, learn to use it by not using it. Your inner guide will lead you and will always show you the best way to fulfill your desires. The gradual sifting through of your psyche will be conducted by the subconscious mind itself, because it will surely negate all negativity on the basis of your positive attitude. It is as if you went to another room and turned on the light, with the one in the place you have just left being turned off.

"I just cannot come to grips through my intellect," said a patient who had acquired new-found self-confidence and the courage to live her life in just three weeks, "with the fact that I can change my life with an attitude of love and harmony within me."

"Do not think about it," I replied. "The intellect has kept you away from health and success for long enough. Now live with a positive attitude and let 'problems' remain to a greater extent simply things that you can help others to solve!"

A longing for realization is a must in life.

FRESH PROGRAMMING FOR YOUR SUBCONSCIOUS MIND

The diversity of fascinating opportunities for life improvements by means of working on yourself that I have thus far listed contains not even one reference to any harmful eventuality. Simply put, there are none! Positive suggestions lead you to a positive and harmonious life. Positive thinking leads you to a God-willed level of perfection with respect to your being and self-awareness.

Some orthodox scientists still even today maintain that the underlying forces hiding behind a symptom, e.g. a washing compulsion, a nervous twitch, or asthma, will still find a new way to enter into the body if a suggestion has prevented its further development. We partially owe this false notion to Sigmund Freud, who, during his early period of studying hypnosis, supposed that old ideas nesting within the subconscious mind were suppressed by suggestions. He believed that they would again manifest themselves in other physical or mental fields. This can actually happen, but only if the symptoms have been medically treated in an orthodox manner. Indeed, there are certain unqualified hypnotherapists who go symptomatically with the aid of words. You can read more about this topic in the chapter on hypnosis.

I am accustomed to listening to some of my patients telling me during our initial conversation about their years of wandering from hospital to hospital, from sanatoriums to medical practices. Their outer symptoms were always treated, but the cause, i.e. their fears in the subconscious mind, was of no interest to anyone. Thus the alleged disorder, that is to say the negative idea, was able to wander on. It was suppressed, but never removed.

The dominance of a superior idea is applicable over all the diverse levels of the subconscious mind. The French research scientist in the area of suggestion, Emile Coue, had already come to this conclusion a hundred years ago. According to his theory, every thought strives to be transformed into reality and a stronger impulse will neutralize a weaker one. What we come to experience therefore depends on the type of suggestion. Better, stronger, and more positive suggestions will replace those that weaken us, and that subsequently bring about deficiencies and create maladies. Therefore, my therapists do not suppress anything; they rather develop a new, better quality life for the patient. What was old then disappears, making way to the new.

Try to gauge the diversity of emotional engrams (memory traces) that govern your subconscious mind. Observe the various types of prejudice that have found a steady home within you. Behind those ideals of prime importance presented to the general public at large, there are always well concealed over- generalizations. If you replace a part of them with a positive attitude to life, you will then already have achieved a large amount of inner freedom.

There is only one form of evidence of ability: that is activity.

DAILY EXERCISE

One who uses auto-suggestion should be patient, being aware of the crisis that can be caused after a few weeks by age-old habits that are dear to us. The power

of habits has a strong influence that needs to be overcome. Who will put on a pair of old, heavy boots if
new footwear grants him the miraculous freedom of
being able to walk more freely?

Once you have found your ideal form of relaxation, withdraw three to four times daily, which can be
done even if you are at work in the office. Alternatively,
read a prepared text to yourself. After some time you
will know the suggestive formulae by heart. Repeat
them in your head with your eyes closed. This does not
require more than three to five minutes. The beneficial, revitalizing strength that is transferred to you at
such moments will soon make you envisage this short
interruption of your daily routine as a moment for revi-
talization, and not as a chore.

One who has mastered autogenic training will
probably also want to learn the "coachman position,"
a casual sitting position with the elbows resting on the
knees, in which you will be able to fully relax within
ten seconds (in a tranquil place). Soon you will be independent of outside conditions, setting an example to
others with the inner calmness and concentration that
you will be showing from this point on.

Reserve the most important exercise for home.
The best time would be in the evening before you go
to sleep, when the events of the day are behind you and
the body is preparing for a good night's rest. At this
point you should begin your most intensive "immersion." The gate to your subconscious mind will open
up to take in your suggestions. Suggestions based on
the four longings for health, harmony, love, and success
take on the character of a prayer. In such a way, you
become more in tune with your divine Self, your God-
given core, fulfilling the task that represents the sense

of your life. Our path is to be united with our spiritual center. If you shape yourself according to your thoughts, you will already have arrived there.

One who dedicates himself to this daily training needs less and less help from other people. Even if others run to the doctor and are prescribed medication for their insubstantial everyday troubles, instead you should accumulate energy in your depths, expelling with your own strength everything undesirable. The deeper you penetrate into my philosophy of positive thinking, the more clearly you will become aware of all the strength you have to master your own life from within you. What now happens by itself is a process of becoming self-aware. The Eastern masters describe it as being the highest level of human maturity, also known as enlightenment.

Positive thinking is as vital a part of a happy life as much as the air you breathe. Positive thoughts are a revitalizing source of strength sprouting up like seedlings from our own Garden of Eden. Everything depends on you. Therefore create a new paradise with new thoughts and you will create a new earth!

If you allow yourself to have a laid back attitude toward your most important concerns, your striving for happiness and success, your subconscious mind will turn itself toward saving energy, following the impulses of your thoughts.

For this kind of persistence, positive thinking is important. This is not some game of hide-and-seek; you can see by the look on someone's face whether their subconscious mind is filled with enough positive suggestions or not. After a short period of training, you will be empowered, that is to say more sensitive. You will be able to sense mental stirrings in all other beings much clearer than others. Not only have you chosen a perfect life, you are also experiencing a new quality in your surroundings. The methods employed in this book enable your subconscious mind to serve your goals. Success is based on maintaining a steady and unerring interest in everything that turns your life to the better.

4

Hypnosis as an Enhancer of Suggestion

INTRODUCTION

History:

Hypnosis is one of the world's oldest healing methods. Descriptions of a hypnosis session were recorded in Egypt and Babylon some 6,000 years before we began to measure time, and the first written report is already 4,000 years old. Hypnosis techniques have always played a role in the art of healing.

Idea and explanation of the effect:

To hypnotize means to induce a specific change in the state of consciousness using sensory stimuli. In order to achieve this, simple techniques are employed that can be learned. During hypnosis, blood pressure, the functioning of heart, circulation and metabolism, and autonomous nervous system are all normalized. Breathing and the functioning of the intestines slow down. After hypnosis, time seems to have passed like in slow motion photography.

In hypnosis, one's attention is captivated in the same way as while listening to good music or reading an exciting book. The state of hypnosis is not one of sleep, but a special form of waking state. In this trance state, one's readiness and ability to absorb suggestions are particularly high.

By means of hypnosis, filtering and evaluating processes from within the brain can be intentionally reached and directed. Suggestions can create thoughts and actions, influencing certain physical conditions.

Actually, the will of a hypnotized subject cannot be turned off and no one can be forced to perform actions that he would not actually do in a normal state.

Method:

The requirements for success are, firstly, an unconditional confidence of the patient in the therapist and secondly, the therapist's emotional involvement. The effectiveness of a method of hypnosis lies in its ability to resolve the patient's condition.

I remember those first few years after the establishment of my practice for hypnotherapy in Munich with a great deal of pleasure. From that moment on, through my spiritual form of hypnotherapy, I was given the opportunity to introduce a new impulse into the field of health care and healing. From my own example and from the example of many thousands of my patients, I have come to realize that a desire for health, harmony and more insight into the way our mind functions is always the first step on the path to our personal life goal.

People from all social classes and ages have visited me in order to make a recovery, to experience healing as well as to realize other personal objectives.

To make the body function again is fine. However, to realize the cause, or more precisely, the psychological background of a particular physical disorder and resolve it is of fundamental importance and is the only way to attain a lasting positive change in life.

In order to reach humanity's goal, or to use another word, enlightenment, we should reach such a level of consciousness that we would always have at our disposal the existing healing power of our mind, body, and soul. A healthy soul and a healthy mind produce a healthy body.

Whatever might be your problem, your "illness" is only a symptom and merely the tip of the iceberg. The psychological background is actually more important in hypnotherapy and we have to look for it in order to trace and resolve any causes.

One who carries anger and resentment within himself and cannot forgive any suffered injustices will allow this disharmony to manifest itself on the physical level sooner or later. On the contrary, if we are in harmony, we experience a life full of happiness and wealth. With the help of professionally conducted hypnotherapy, you will be able to gain access to your true Self and the inexhaustible treasure trove of your "subconscious mind as a source of unlimited power."

My objective is to mentally support you, strengthening you and helping you to stabilize your emotional/mental balance. During therapy, you will realize that you are actively involved in the events of your life and that you can very much contribute to your own healing.

A Relaxed Person Is a Healthy Person

The basis of hypnotherapy is deep relaxation. During this special state, you are generally more open to new realizations and insights than in an awakened state. To begin with, a state of deep relaxation/trance often results in an initial relief of symptoms. However, the way to a cure leads you to the domain of what lies behind the symptoms. It demands openness on the part of the patient to also look at what might at first seem unpleasant, and what is normally fought against and suppressed. Only if "recollections" are released and accepted is reconciliation possible and health achieved!

In our hectic and consumption-oriented times, many people have come to realize that outer success can only be superficially and temporarily satisfactory if there is any suffering of the soul. Thus, it is understandable that more and more people would like to give their life deeper meaning. They are looking for a spiritual and internalized path in order to experience a deeper meaning in life and the true values of human existence.

I have been following this path too for over twenty-five years. I have learned that only a readiness for constant change, as in the law of evolution, will bring into view new perspectives and makes possible further development. Meeting my teacher, Dr. Joseph Murphy, was of decisive importance. I learned together with him, discovering each day wonderful possibilities that are open to us all. My life fundamentally changed when I learned to cross my self-made limits, to experience new dimensions of life.

Happy as well as sad events have made me aware over and over again of other aspects of life. I have never stopped believing in what has not yet been brought into existence, so that it might actually happen. I experienced ups and downs, but I succeeded in curing my own acute form of cancer in its final stages using the method described here. Thus, I also passed through moments of ultimate fulfillment and phases of painful experience on the way to finding a solution. However, I am thankful for every experience, if only because I was able to learn and develop further.

Each of us desires a healthy, happy life. The potential to completely shape our life in accordance with a creative strength exists in everyone. Yes, it is waiting for us to use it!

In two and a half decades of practice, in many seminars and in thousands of personal conversations, a form of therapy was created that can bring into balance the mind, body and soul. To develop your individual personality in order to make it correspond to the highest meaning of your life is not only possible, it actually represents deeper meaning in your life. Experiencing your own being leaves more room for new, more desirable perspectives. If you so desire it, the path to fulfillment and inner peace lies within your grasp. I welcome you with best wishes if you decide to follow this path of self-realization and love.

As therapists, we try to awaken patients' own abilities for helping themselves to transform everything into what is best and stimulating for them by way of their own talents. A really self-aware therapist can help anyone who asks for help to attain autonomy and independence. A spiritual therapist is, for the period of their mutual path, a friend, father, mother, oracle, and beloved, giving a helping hand to his patient; a person who listens here and there, a friend who clearly and lovingly asks questions and gives answers. Within this closeness, during the intensive exchange of thoughts and feelings, therapist and patient are secret allies. At the moment when the inner "master" and the life-long friend awakens within the patient, they begin to act with genuine confidence and awareness, being what they were meant to be all along.

My goal is to help one try to regain authority over events in their life. A self-aware person is aware of his abilities and an end to fear is within sight.

We are often asked about the real effects of hypnotherapy and seminars. This is a very difficult question to answer, because there is no one particular goal. Everyone learns what they have to in order to be what they really are deep down.

However, we must emphasize that there is only one thing that can be measured as being success: that you learn to allow yourself to be happy. If you can achieve this, the events that make you happy will simply follow on.

What Is Hypnosis?

The suggestive influence of the subconscious mind with the aid of a therapist is, according to my experience, the best way of improving your life. In the same way a force field can be strengthened in physics, so too can spiritual energy. Also, two heads are always far better than one. Hypnosis makes suggestions much stronger. A well-trained hypno-therapist can put us into a deep state of trance where different phenomena can come up spontaneously or as a reaction to outside stimuli in increased amounts. Words, once recollected, can cause an unpredictable movement of muscles, music can induce a picturesque transformation full of fantasy. Combinations of words often unknown to the hypnotized person can surface in their usual state of mind. During a hypnosis session, they are, so to speak, directly connected with the holy and eternally true source of their higher spiritual strength. In this state, healing can take place. Since connections are better grasped and can be better integrated, hypnosis almost always leads more continuously to healing than is the case with other methods.

It is a well-known fact that outside suggestions, that is to say influences from other people, have a much higher level of effectiveness than training through auto-suggestion.

If positive suggestions are transferred by a qualified hypno-therapist, the shaping of your subconscious mind will be far more intensive than if you yourself induced it. The result is a higher rate of success in a shorter period.

Hypnosis cannot in the least be equated with a suggestion. Proper hypnotherapy induces a temporary withdrawal from the normal activity of the nervous system to a state of higher consciousness where the gates of the subconscious mind are open wide. The effectiveness of suggestive/hypnotic influence can be attributed to by anyone who, for example, after years and years of being bombarded with suggestive commercials has given in to the urge of habit as well as the urge to imitate and has grabbed hold of another cigarette, even though they decided long ago that they would never smoke again. One who falls victim to this "commercial hypnosis" ends up paying me a visit to have their desire to change strengthened by my energy.

We all undertake many things in our life mostly within groups of like-minded people. In being like this, you feel strengthened and safe. During a hypnosis session, something similar happens. You are more intensively at a higher mental level and you are able to concentrate more. In such a way you attain positive support during the realization of your desires.

Most of the patients who visit me have strange and fear-obsessed preconceptions about hypnosis. One young woman, who I could help in a particularly short period, told me recently that she had postponed her visit to my office for months until an acquaintance laughed at her before informing her of modern research into hypnosis. They had read the nonsense of the magician Cagliostro, who allegedly made a beautiful young woman obedient for years during the period of the French Revolution by keeping her steadily under hypnosis.

In this age of information, it seems like the most natural thing in the world to learn about even the most intricate goings on at the cellular level in our body by way of popular science. On the other hand, psychology has found it difficult up till now to be able to report on things such as our "special" states of consciousness and from thereon work toward educating people about them. This is because we still do not know very much about this, leaving the extremely fascinating area of suggestion therapy and its possibilities mostly unheard of.

Please first disregard everything that you may have heard or read about hypnosis and try to formulate a new opinion by the end of this chapter. First of all, forget those spectacular demonstrations of hypnosis on the vaudeville theatre stage, or at fairs or on sensational television programs.

During hypnosis, control of your own body or intellect is not taken away from you at all. Hypnosis by way of irresistible eyes mesmerizing you can often be read about in oriental fairy tales. However, the modern hypnotherapy that we are talking about in this book uses a wonderful form of access to higher levels of consciousness exclusively for the beneficial purpose of healing.

Let me show you in this chapter what hypnosis really is and how it can serve humanity. This question has been the linchpin of my psychological and therapeutic career. In thousands of single experiences in my practice, I have found a valid and satisfactory answer. Hypnosis can be an endless blessing in the hands of any therapist aware of his own responsibilities. It offers access, often seemingly wonderful, to our unconscious mental areas. To the experienced hypno-therapist it is a unique method of positively influencing a patient's mental "field."

During hypnosis, you are led into a state of concentration and selective perception, and thus into a deeper mental level. Your consciousness concentrates on a point using suggestive phrases, which becomes especially clear.

If people scream at the cinema or if football fans are out of control in their enthusiasm, they are temporarily within that same selective state of consciousness. Being engrossed in an exciting novel that temporarily causes you to forget your world is a quasi-hypnotic state of consciousness.

The selective contents of consciousness imply great concentration and a stronger attention to the momentous and really most important single area of sensory perception. During hypnosis, an as of yet unconscious spiritual level opens up, into which suggestions can be taken directly and immediately. If you enter into hypnotherapy, the therapist will formulate suggestions (affirmations) for you. However, you are the programmer who frees great strength within your subconscious mind for the purpose of fulfilling the greatest goals in your life. You are and always will remain the most important factor in hypnotherapy. It is up to you how quickly you can get rid of "ideas" that often frighten you and how quickly you will learn to bring peace into your soul. Hypnosis is an extraordinary tool for realizing your ideal of a happy life in only a short time.

Your intellect is in many cases the greatest obstacle in the way of achieving this goal. Learn to let yourself fall into your depths and you will be happy. Learn to use your energy. You have the power and the right in your inexhaustible inner world to instantly resolve all the suffering and problems created by both your intellect and outside influence. Perhaps you have known nothing about this strength for decades. You most likely "successfully" negated your mental depths by living your life exclusively in the outer sensory world. While reading these lines, you can start to mobilize your great strength within your subconscious mind through suggestion. The wisdom within you will soon do its "work."

You are already in the process of carrying out this "work." If you find out that you need outside help, then hypnotherapy is right for you. Within the power of your subconscious mind lies a path leading away from a life of depression and that leads to those heights you have envisaged through the power of your thoughts.

The Subconscious Mind

People who are looking for help come to consult me for different reasons. The greatest problems where patients believe hypnosis treatment can be successful in resolving deeply rooted worries and disorders can be summed up as follows.

Hypnosis can be successfully applied to the following symptoms and conditions:

- stuttering
- loss of voice
- speech disorders, generally
- some forms of paralysis
- impotence (impotentia psychica)
- tics
- difficulties in swallowing
- facial twitches
- nightly teeth gnashing
- bed-wetting
- insomnia
- nail biting
- nightmares
- states of exhaustion
- loss of concentration
- phobias
- persecution mania
- depression
- alcohol—nicotine—other drugs
- psychosomatic/vegetative diseases
- psychological dependence
- chronic pain
- stomach and intestine constipation
- behavioral disorders

- stress (too much pressure)
- loss of self-confidence
- almost all psycho-vegetative symptoms
- ulcers
- different forms of neuralgia
- problems at school
- compulsive neurosis (washing compulsion)
- diseases of the urinal tract
- migraine
- personality activation
- chronic bronchitis
- some allergies
- obesity
- cancer
- asthma
- vegetative dystonia

Further opportunities to induce a positive change in your life through hypnosis:

- to build a stronger personality
- to be successful in your life
- to be more self-confident
- to further develop spiritually
- to be more creative
- to discover and develop hidden talents and strengths
- to learn self-hypnosis
- to realize yourself
- to better understand yourself and others
- self-development in your relationship and profession
- improvement of concentration
- improvement of memory
- to learn the "art of living"
- to extraordinarily improve your ability to learn

This overview is not at all complete. In practice, sometimes one comes across the most unusual situations and combinations of problems. Not even the human imagination is strong enough to be able to contemplate all the complicated situations in which some people can end up. Life is the most creative screenplay writer imaginable.

WHO CAN BE HYPNOTIZED AND EXPECT HELP FROM HYPNOTHERAPY?

I characterize as "normal" those patients who possess intuition and feeling, who can in effect let go. Those are also the most important preconditions to actually be able to confide in someone else. To an intellectual, it is almost certainly more difficult to succeed in this; they hang on to their knowledge, to their strictly formulated ideas of themselves and the world. Their worldly ego does not want to release them so easily from preconceived opinions and they sometimes suffer more than others!

One who informs himself in detail about hypnosis learns about the unique possibilities of achievement through suggestive influence of the subconscious mind. Hypnosis has an up to five times quicker effect than often very difficult conversational therapy. Orthodox psychotherapy needs two to three years to be able to slowly touch the mental state of a patient. With hypnosis, I can succeed in this often within twenty to thirty double periods. This period of time has proved to be sufficient for most worries and problems where there is some promise of improvement. In some "exceptional cases," some sixty double periods may be necessary, whereas in the case of young people, less than twenty sessions are often enough.

With psychotherapy, there is not only a significant prolonging of the period of suffering, but also a less than sure chance of being cured. In our times of money shortages, it is also a question of finance for the patient, if a psychotherapist has to count on taking up huge quantities of time in order to achieve success compared to a hypno-therapist.

Professor Losanov, a well-known expert in suggestion research from Sofia, discovered that successful outcomes are more speedily achieved through hypnosis with his experimental subjects. Indeed, to the family of the mentally ill, it can sometimes appear like a miracle when extremely rapid success is achieved through hypnosis.

Doctors and psychotherapists often send me patients when they have perceived that their treatment using medication or psychotherapy has gone on for too long. Their insight saves these patients a lot of time, directing them toward therapy that really treats the causes. This often improves their life in a matter of a few months, which is what they have sometimes been vainly longing for for decades.

An important advantage is that you are able to abandon medication totally. Psychopharmacological drugs used in psychiatry with their often serious side effects significantly prolong the treatment rather than have any great effect. The prevailing majority of these drugs, which include almost all tranquilizers and sedatives, serve only to suppress the symptoms.

It is among my first measures to liberate new patients from the physical poisoning caused by medications that suppress their symptoms if they want to come under my treatment with any promising success. Some types of health insurance already partially support the more reasonable hypnosis treatment of patients. Others still have to overcome the strict idea of our medical tradition that even today does not officially teach about hypnotherapy.

Some doctors have indeed spoken of mental influences in the case of many illnesses. However, in most cases this remains only a theory. Hypnosis offers wonderful access to our mental depths never reached by a surgeon's knife or medication. The impression that in traditional medicine the proverb of the great surgeon Dr. Virchow still rings true in people's minds is an often undeniable fact that. He said: "The soul? I have not been able to discover it during any operation!"

It is very satisfying to be able to observe a widespread steady growth in confidence in this almost eight-thousand-year-old but only recently discovered form of therapy, whose revival has started. A general shift in consciousness that has been for years observable in transpersonal psychotherapy has led to the point where the unique method of hypnosis, just like after Sleeping Beauty's long sleep, has been given its rightful place again.

The Indian spiritual teacher and philosopher Osho developed an extraordinary activity in this area. Here are some of his words regarding this topic:

"WORK WITH THE BODY OR TO BE PRECISE—WITH FIVE BODIES."

Even the body is not completely understood, not yet. Our whole understanding is fragmentary. The science of man does not exist yet. Patanjali's yoga is the closest effort ever made. He divides the body into five layers, or into five bodies. You don't have one body, you have five bodies; and behind the five bodies, there is your being.

The same as what has happened in psychology has happened in medicine.

Allopathy believes only in the physical body, the gross body. Allopathy is the largest medicine. That's why it has become scientific, because scientific instrumentation is only yet capable of very gross things. Go deeper.

Acupuncture, the Chinese medicine, enters one layer more. It works on the vital body. It tries to work on the bioenergy, the bioplasma. It settles something there, and immediately the gross body starts functioning well.

If something goes wrong in your vital body, allopathy functions on the body, the gross body. Of course, for allopathy, this is an uphill struggle.

For acupuncture, this is a downhill task. It is easier because the vital body is a little higher than the physical body. If the vital body is set right, the physical body simply follows on from it because our blueprint exists in the vital body. The physical body is just an implementation of the vital.

Homeopathy goes a little deeper still. It works on the mental body. The founder of homeopathy, Hahnemann, discovered one of the greatest things ever discovered, and that was: The smaller the quantity of medicine, the deeper it goes. He called the method of making homeopathic medicine "potentizing." One goes on reducing the quantity of medicine.

The bigger the potency, the smaller the amount needed. With a potency of ten thousand, a millionth of the original medicine remained, that is, almost none. It has almost disappeared, but then it enters the most deep core of manomaya. It enters into your mind body. It goes deeper than acupuncture. It is almost as if you have reached an atomic, or even sub-atomic, level.

Then it does not touch your body. Then it does not touch your vital body; it simply enters. It is so subtle and so small that it comes across no barriers. It can simply slip into the mental body, and from there it starts working. Ayurved, the Indian medicine, is a synthesis of all three. It is one of the most synthetic of all medicines.

Hypnotherapy goes deeper still. It touches the fourth body, the body of consciousness. It does not use medicine. It does not use anything. It simply uses suggestion, that's all. It simply plants a suggestion in your mind. Call it animal magnetism, mesmerism, hypnosis or whatever you want, but it works through the power of thought, not the power of matter.

Even homeopathy is still the power of matter to a very subtle extent.

Hypnotherapy gets rid of matter altogether, because howsoever subtle, it is still matter. It simply jumps to the energy of thought: the consciousness of the body.

If your consciousness is able to just accept a certain idea, it starts functioning.

Hypnotherapy has a great future. It is going to become the future medicine, because if by just changing your thought pattern your mind can be changed, through the mind your vital body and through the vital body your gross body, then why bother with poisons, why bother with gross medicines? Why not just work on it through thought power? Have you ever watched a hypnotist working on a medium? If you have not, it is indeed worth watching. It will give you a certain insight.

Trust is everything in hypnotherapy. Without trust, you cannot enter into the subtle parts of your being, because just one small doubt, and you are thrown back to the gross.

Science works with doubt. Doubt is a method in science because science works with the gross. Whether you doubt or not, an allopath is not bothered. He does not ask you to trust in his medicine; he simply gives you the medicine. But a homeopath will ask whether you believe, because without your belief it will be more difficult for a homeopath to work upon you. And a hypnotherapist will ask for total surrender. Otherwise, nothing can be done.

Religion is surrender. Religion is a form of hypnotherapy. But, there is still one more body. That is the bliss body. Hypnotherapy goes up to the fourth. Meditation goes up to the fifth. "'MEDITATION'— the very word is beautiful because its root is the same as 'Medicine.' Both come from the same root word. Medicine and meditation are off-shoots of one word: that which heals, that which makes you healthy and whole is medicine; and on the deepest level, that is meditation" (from "Yoga: The Alpha and Omega," Volume 10, Chapter 7. 1978 Osho International Foundation)

WHAT HAPPENS UNDER HYPNOSIS?

What actually did happen when an asthmatic, like Walter A., after visiting me for two weeks and lying twice daily on a couch for hypnosis, rejuvenated and free of symptoms stated: "You have made a new man out of me"?

An ill person had given up all physical and pharmaceutical treatments. He had given up his yearly stay at a sanatorium, which had always brought him only temporary relief. He surrendered to my spiritual guidance, which dug out the roots of his psychosomatic suffering.

Hypnosis is a relatively simple method that works on our sometimes rather complicated mind. It is less harmful than any form of medication and more effective than any other psychotherapeutic method. Osho said: "Hypnosis is at the top of the list of therapy alternatives." It induces pure healing when introduced through professional hypnotherapy (more about this topic in another book).

Walter A. was ready in the depths of his soul to give up his "rigid" ideas of life full of fears, which had led him up a blind alley when it came to his health. My positive suggestive motivations on the subject of confidence, harmony, and health, which were also among his greatest longings, were ideas welcomed by his subconscious mind. Besides this, these suggestions corresponded to his conviction that it was much better to serve one's physical health and experience a harmonious everyday life than to be the victim of one's own anger.

His rather unbalanced mental state made him welcome the idea of all things positive and he could regain his health that he had unnecessarily given up long ago. Another asthmatic would have perhaps reacted in yet another way, needing maybe more time to change and become healthy. In causal therapy it is not about asthma, but about all those mental layers leading to the problems and to those up till now standing in the way of healing. The soul of my patient was given a creative and positive vitality and his convulsive bronchial tubes could be "saved."

Imagine the state of consciousness, which you will experience in hypnosis, as a state between waking and sleeping.

Access to mental layers and the unconscious depths of our being open up. Positive suggestions can cause real miracles in this area where our conscience and our creative strengths can be reached. In the depths of our mind our human goodness and truth are at home; there is the divine source of our vitality.

The most important goal of my therapy is to make the patient aware of his own strength and depth, which will ultimately help him to resolve his problems.

It will all depend on the contents and inner strength of every single word which flows to you under hypnosis as to whether you will make health, success, and happiness your natural attributes again. Positive thoughts strengthen your mental potency, which can in turn correct almost any mental aberration. I will further discuss this topic later. At this moment I would like to record the fact that suggestions accepted by our subconscious mind under hypnosis can be directly turned into reality if we abandon inhibiting, critical, or even doubtful observations. If we cannot manage to positively "shape" our faithful and still mostly unconscious servant called the subconscious mind alone, then the presence of a hypno-therapist will give us important assistance on the path to a desirable life.

THE THREE PHASES OF HYPNOSIS

If you are slightly sensitive, the slow slipping into a pleasant state of trance can be experienced in three phases. In the first and second phases with which hypnosis treatment is basically carried out, the patient somewhat gets the impression that they are consciously experiencing everything happening in and around them. Although they cannot completely gain influence over their motor nervous system, e.g. lifting their arm or opening their eyelids, in the first few sessions, they often believe themselves not to be in a trance.

In this state, their memory and their mental strengths are free of restriction and various distractions caused by so-called daily consciousness. Suppressed mental layers are accessible again and they can remember apparently forgotten events, even if they go back years. Since all experience takes place in a picturesque form in the depths of our soul, one can once again vividly recall scenes that happened long ago in front of one's inner eye.

A diamond dealer under hypnosis suddenly "saw" the place in his apartment where he had hidden an especially important jewel that he had for months been looking for. A female patient remembered her mother's dress which she had worn on her first day at school and which she had blotted an ink stain onto. What appears to be inaccessible, completely forgotten in daily consciousness can be recalled in the hypnotic state. Hypnotherapy opens up that inexhaustible storage of information that we had already become aware of in the womb.

Many things are not so important as to be steadily at our memory's disposal. Nature has equipped us with a short-term memory. If visually or acoustically absorbed information is not recalled within a few days, it sinks into the depths of our memory. These memories are never totally erased, even if we sometimes cannot access them.

The inkblot on the mother's dress can be easily forgotten. However, if feelings of being hurt are suppressed, this process of suppression requires energy input. The more you suppress the pain, the higher the tension is to which you are exposed. Apparently, even a faint memory can often provide an escape into superficiality for the over-pressurized person.

Suppressed fears, feelings of guilt, or traumatic experiences are the causes of almost all types of neuroses and phobias. Their treatment requires a readiness on the patient's part to release his inner tensions and give his acceptance.

The third and deepest level of hypnosis is a somnambular state reached only by a very small number of people. To be somnambular means to be able to fall so deeply into a trance that almost every sensory perception is cancelled out. Earlier, people believed that they could exert an effective influence on the subconscious mind only in this state. For therapy, this state is inappropriate because the patient can hardly be spoken to. His sensory perception is temporarily turned off. Such a suggestive treatment induced by a hypno-therapist thus remains ineffective.

Siegmund Freud, the founder of psychoanalysis, believed that he could give patients effective suggestions only in this deepest state of hypnosis. Of course, he experienced many difficulties. Naturally, he found out that he could put only a small number of his patients into a deep somnambular state. His faulty starting points, inhibitions and uncertainties in his initial attempts and an introduction to the correct management of hypnosis soon made him look out for other methods. He turned to the free association of thoughts that heralded in the era of psychoanalysis. This was the path that enabled Siegmund Freud to achieve better personal results.

HALLUCINATIONS

The selected state of consciousness under hypnosis represents our daily or waking state of consciousness, only it is temporarily less active. Since information from the eye, ear, nose, taste buds and sense of touch conveyed to us is partially modified, i.e. turned off, we can remember details from the past much better. A female patient once reported that she perceived the smell of roses in her trance-like state. Another completely lost his sense of time and after an hour and a half thought that he had only laid down.

Under hypnosis, our acoustic perception is limited. The therapist suggests for example: "You are fully relaxed, all noise is unimportant; everything you hear only leads you more and more deeply into a pleasant state of relaxation. You can hear my voice only and you feel very, very good!"

A newcomer is always surprised about the precision the subconscious mind works with in turning a suggestion into reality.

My admired teacher, Dr. Joseph Murphy said: "The subconscious mind transforms a suggestion into form, function and experience."

The generally known experiment of making person under hypnosis bite onto what they think is a tasty sweet apple with gusto, when in reality it is lemon, clearly proves that the suggestion of the sweet apple put into the subconscious mind is stronger than the taste buds' sensory perception.

People can get sweaty because a warm room has been suggested, or sensory hallucinations are driven so far that they produce a burn on the skin that had allegedly been caused by a non-existent cigarette. These are wondrous pieces of evidence that subliminal powers are often stronger than the acrobatics of our intellect.

I have listed these experiments in order to make it clearer that the strength within your unconscious is great and at your disposal whenever you desire it. Of course, they have nothing to do with spiritual hypnotherapy. An opposition politician had to be shown the adverse affects his constant negative suggestions had on the quality of our life. Year by year, there are squabbles and quarrels in public. People obsessed with power, the representatives of trade unions and other interest associations sew the seeds of discord, fear, and hatred. Now we wonder why we are standing on the verge of almost inevitable ecological-economic crisis. Fight completely and decisively against such destructive negativity in your personal sphere. Think positively, making all people in your surroundings feel the harmony within your life.

This is to be applied within your intimate family circle, as well as to your outer appearance in public. You will soon notice love, care, and cooperation getting stronger and stronger, and that they always win out in the end. Love is a divine feature and we know that God's mill wheels grind slowly, but finely!

Everything is possible for your subconscious mind and your higher Self. Simply realize that you yourself can become a positive factor in your surroundings through your own positive thoughts. Your positive suggestions will bring you many good fruits if you convincingly stand behind them.

The Experience of Hypnosis

To sink into subconscious layers, in the deep layers of your own Self, means to turn your back to the noisy everyday world. Lie in a calm and slightly darkened place that limits all sensory stimuli from the outside world. Peaceful and meditative music helps you concentrate on your inner life. Slowly but surely, your whole being calms down and peace returns where strife once ruled.

At this stage, suggestions are given in three steps. First, you are given calming instructions in order to relax you. According to the type of autogenic training you are carrying out, the initially introduced relaxation exercises are for creating pleasant lightness and warmth in the limbs in order to regulate your breathing. At this point, the primary functions of organs in the body may need to be calmed through relaxation of the solar plexus. As already mentioned, your eyes and your ears, which are generally used to maintain your attention, even during the process of falling asleep, are encouraged through calming suggestions to abandon their guarded state. Everything becomes pleasantly tiring and light and you feel as if you want to fall asleep.

This is now prevented by special suggestions that create a waking state of consciousness. You more and more clearly feel a deep sense of calmness and harmony within your inner world. As soon as outside sensory stimuli start becoming unimportant, you let yourself go, feeling good and slipping deeper into a pleasant trance. You are in a state of suspension between a waking and a sleeping state. You are in a pleasant way connected to the outside world only through your ear and through the therapist's voice. You find it easy to follow his instructions.

Did you notice that strange feeling already created while reading these lines? Hypnosis does not always have to happen on the spot. Even within these lines there is a healing spirit.

You may be able to conclude from my explanation that hypnosis is not at all a state of being unconscious. You remain "in the present" with a certain selected restriction on your outside senses. At this moment, you have the important task of simply letting go of all outer perception, meaning abandonment of all thought activity.

At the beginning, the intellect sometimes defends itself with a flood of thoughts against this evoked state of trance. Being predominant, it is not willing to let its observing instrumentation ignore even the smallest amount of present occurrences. This threshold now has to be crossed. A continuous train of thought will oppose your intention to sink into your unconscious depths. Even if the therapist suggests that you finally and fully let yourself go, you will reach deeper calmness somewhat slowly. Here the following apparently paradoxical sentence can also be applied: "The energy that you use to reach your goal is the obstacle in the way of your goal."

You should therefore not desire it, but let it happen. One who succeeds in letting his thoughts go, while no longer paying any particular attention to them and thus opening themselves fully to inner perception, will get closest to their goal. They will find the gate of their subconscious mind and open it, letting the suggestions slip directly into the depths of their soul.

HIGH DEMANDS ON THE THERAPIST

The ethical view and "pure" attitude of the therapist are of primary importance in the form of hypnotherapy developed by Dr. Murphy and me. A therapist in my team has to be in it with his heart and soul, making the patient's problems his own. This demands a lot of love of oneself, one's job, and one's patients. The necessary ethical-human pre-dispositions are among the most important conditions for the success of the treatment, whereas their importance is not so significant in other forms of medicine. Only through loving dedication and emotional balance can a suffering and often closed-up patient open up to a therapist. Essentially positive vibrations between them demand carefulness on the side of the therapist in order to avoid any slipping into undesirable areas.

The responsibility that an ethical hypno-therapist has toward another emotional being requires such a high level of self-confidence in order to be up to any conceivable situation. A subtle ability to feel is demanded. His feeling for every patient's special features requires a deep knowledge of human nature.

Hypnotherapy is not an unwinding of an already created text. It demands a lot of care and attention to be able to inspire a patient's subconscious mind with a positive new content.

Suggestion therapy is sometimes also a source of strength to the therapist. The love and harmony that he lets flow from himself to his patient naturally releases a positive resonance within him, too. After the end of a session, he can also feel fulfilled and energized. I have personally observed over and over again my associates going home completely inspired and elated on days when they have had particularly satisfactory results with their patients.

A good hypno-therapist should be a master of language. One false word can have undesirable side effects. Every false word drives the patient from their trance into a state of intellectual attention. This implies that high concentration, deep sympathy, and intuitive understanding of events occurring within the patient all together lead to a new and desirable harmony, both inwardly and outwardly.

Hypnotherapy can achieve the best results during the transition from the first to second level of hypnosis. No one should be afraid of not being suitable for therapy due to not being able to slip into a somnambular state. Only a few people (approximately three percent) are actually suitable for this. I am among them. With one of my female therapists, I become somnambular and I cannot be spoken to temporarily. Then I do not take in any more suggestions for a while until I wake up.

Even for those who can be hypnotized without knowing of this predisposition, hypnosis is always totally harmless when in the hands of an experienced therapist who, based on the experience of hundreds of cases, knows how the subconscious mind reacts. In my long period of practice it happened only once that the so-called rapport was broken. He was lost in his unconscious depths temporarily, not following my suggestions in his somnambular state. In such a way, the hypno- therapist is prevented from reaching the patient and he finally has to end the hypnosis session. That is not difficult or in any way dangerous, because the patient himself will wake up from this deep somnambular state even if it lasts a half an hour.

Waking up from a state of hypnosis may be induced by the following words: "Now you sink deeper and deeper into a pleasant state of nice relaxation, stepping through the wide open gate of your most inner being directly into your subconscious mind. After having made yourself independent for some time, you can now hear my voice again. Everything is good, you can hear my voice and follow my words again. You were in a deep and very pleasant state and now you want to wake up. Give yourself some time and wake up rested, cheerful and in a good mood."

With this roundabout way of avoiding any further deepening of the hypnosis, a trained therapist can easily introduce the return into the normal state of consciousness. A rapport, the relationship between therapist and patient is established once again.

Laymen and those curious and up for experimentation are really not qualified to deal with any such or similar situations. They are liable to put the circulation and heart functioning into imbalance due to their lack of understanding as to the workings of the subconscious mind. In such a way, a thoughtlessly used play on words, an ambiguity, or misunderstandings can lead to irritation.

I have already described the often purely literal direct transformation of the "value of words" in the subconscious mind, which can provide a basis for many harmful behavioral reactions within the psyche and the body. This is also a topic in my other books.

If a child is constantly made out to be stupid, given time, they will create an inferiority complex in their subconscious mind even without needing to be hypnotized. A therapist therefore has to act cautiously if he really wants to transmit simply "pure" positive and creative thoughts.

The intention of therapy mentioned above weakens the fear which I frequently come up against when dealing with a laymen who has so far never experienced hypnosis. The often expressed fear of perhaps being led into actions and self-expression, of being in a state in which they believe themselves not to be in control of their own senses, which thus contradict their desires. Silly fairground experiments may well have reinforced this fear.

There are two reasons why these fears are completely superfluous. First of all, even in a state of deepest hypnosis, it is impossible to extract a person's "secret" that he does not want to betray. Any such attempt immediately halts the hypnosis, putting the patient into a wakened state of alarm. Second, modern hypnotherapy operates exclusively through positive suggestion and there is no intention to manipulate anyone.

In this state a hypnotized person is not ready for any behavior or betrayal of information that he would not otherwise agree to in an awakened state or normal state of consciousness. This also means that he will accept only those positive suggestions that his inner "wisdom" has accepted, i.e. that he desires most.

Moreover, the therapist is also liable to the spiritual law of truth in the absence of which he could never offer any real help anyhow. The therapist finds access to the depths of another person only to the extent to which his ethics have been developed. Only truth brings about the truth. The law of resonance demands that the therapist is what the patient wants to be, and that is healthy, harmonious, and loving. The most important predisposition for successful treatment is a deep mutual confidence between the therapist and patient.

Hypnotherapy for Offenders

At the beginning of this century, there were trials in which hypnosis was investigated as a possible cause of criminal offenses. Over the last fifty years, science has shown that a person cannot be led to do an unjust deed by means of hypnosis. Do not let yourself be influenced by any other opinion. You always have "tenants rights" over yourself and this will remain so. Any statement to the contrary would undoubtedly have come from a professionally incompetent charlatan.

No one can suggest anybody do anything that is any way contradictory to them and to which their deepest feelings cannot give permission. To give a post-hypnotic task to a hypnotized person to commit a homicide or robbery after waking up is completely sense-less, i.e. without purpose. This can happen only if the person involved already carries this intention within him.

"Through hypnosis, it is easier to turn a confirmed car thief or burglar into the top criminal in the city than into a decent citizen," I once said to an attorney who asked for certain guarantees regarding my hypnotherapy in the case of one "permanent prison inmate." No one can become healthy against their own will, the same way as no one will act against his ethics and become a criminal.

However, in any case it is worth extracting a person from their negative "programming." Hypnosis is an excellent method of creating a balance again, as a divine source is present even in the worst of culprits. Goodness is a basic tendency within us all. It only depends on the level to which the character has hardened as to whether the person is unreachable, as well as how much they really want to change. In other words, it is mostly a question of time as to when deep and bad ideas will be successfully released from the unconscious.

In the case of repeating offenders, a more precise judgment about the effect of hypno-therapeutic treatment can be given when we have learned more about the person's mental pre-dispositions. It is better to help a fallen person with loving human care than to entrust him to the brain-destroying monotony of prison.

Prisons are an expression of an inhuman attitude and lack of love. Punishment only increases suffering. "On the contrary, therapy is an expression of love toward our fellow man and healing is a function of love. Love is the greatest therapy and the world needs therapists because it lacks love," said the philosopher Osho.

If the delinquent fed up with his constant derailments longs to become a better person, the chance of success is great. In cooperation with an inner Self that wants to achieve that goal, the hypno- therapist will always find a way to reach the striven-for goal.

Recently I was assigned two similar legal cases from a court at the same time, which were directed for therapeutic treatment. Daniel K. was 35 years old when he was sent to me fresh from the dock. He had already spent a third of his life behind bars for being a total kleptomaniac. Thirty-five-year- old Carl F. had also spent most of his time in a steady exchange between petty embezzlement and theft and trial and prison. The last time he was released on probation with the judge's approval to undergo hypnotherapy with me.

In both cases, I had to start helping them make a new and stronger personality. Having grown up without love and care in a household of parental neglect, they had both developed into people full of hatred against the human world. Through their criminal activities, they unconsciously saw the only possible way of taking revenge on the world.

Six months later, they both acquired a new self-confidence. They got rid of their old frustrations, finding a way of coping with the world again.

I gave them the following suggestion: "I have a strong positive personality. Life with my family and all my fellow man is from now on harmonious and full of love. I surrender to the inexhaustible strength of my subconscious mind. It makes me strong in all life situations and successful in all my actions. There is perfect calmness and harmony within me. From now on I will listen to my inner voice. It safely leads and directs me, making me always do the right thing. Deep harmony fills me with happiness and confidence. I now live in perfect harmony with God and the world on the bright side of life."

More than three years have passed since the therapy. Daniel K. has remained free of prosecution. Carl F. likewise has not become a repeat offender. Meanwhile, his probation period has expired.

Having frequent contact with prisoners and being an expert witness in court trials involving cases of theft, poisoning, cases involving repeated offenses and so on allows me to meet many strange people.

A Persian arms dealer who wanted to get courage and self-confidence through treatment with me first put his pistol together with his shoes down next to the couch and showed me his portable safe. It was a plastic bag with his business capital of $250,000, all in cash.

For years, I had been visited by the king of the city's underworld. His fear that he would someday be ousted during an internal gang conflict was steadily growing.

A spiritual hypno-therapist does not have the right to criticize their patient's lifestyle. However, he has a calm hope of awakening harmony and a genuine joy of life again through his work.

The hypnotherapy developed by both Dr. Murphy and me generally includes the edict that nothing should ever be "negatively suggested." As a rule, we should always see only that which corresponds most to our longings and that we have missed out on most. This means that under hypnosis I never address any bad character feature or human weakness with such condemning words like: "You do not hate your boss anymore!" or "You will never steal again."

Gradually I replace negative thoughts with positive ones. Suggestions of harmony, love, health, and success lead to the striven-for goal. These four most important pre-dispositions of a happy life have the effect of an ice-pick and the rigid, deeply ingrained pattern disappears.

According to the Bible, "our God is a consuming fire" (Hebrews 12:29) that burns everything not in accordance with him. An intensive and positive suggestion acts in the same way, making disappear all that is not in accordance with your opinion.

A positive suggestion is like light, a negative one like darkness. People from Schilda tried to overcome darkness by painting the walls in a dark room white and by trying to take the darkness out in big bags. Simply create light and everything that is not in accordance with it will be removed by its shining. Dealing with negative things and hoping that you will get rid of them implies that they will only get stronger.

If you equate the positive with God, perhaps you will understand the statement that "in union with God you are always in the majority." Your desire to lead a God-blessed and positive life is always stronger than any destructive negating pattern of behavior from the past.

The conscience acts as an example even within the greatest outsider of a society. Help by means of hypnotherapy should generally more often be offered and used in our daily life.

During a trial of a notorious thief, I remember how Dr. Murphy reacted in a similar situation. He was assigned a laborer who had grown up without love, constantly breaking into cars and driving them until their fuel tank was empty.

The court followed his recommendation. To enable this young man to train as a mechanic, he would, of course, daily deal with cars. Soon he had done up his own "crate" and could drive it. The young man's greatest longing was fulfilled and his troubled past was forgotten. A destiny can often easily turn to something positive. If you want to replace frustrating ideas, from now on there is nothing standing in your way.

Just to repeat it more clearly. No suggestion can influence a person against his will, but with his will, everything is possible! The patient has to approve of the affirmations given to him. If he opens up willingly in order to work on himself, miracles can indeed happen.

THE FRONTIERS OF HYPNOSIS

Only a few cases are unsuitable for hypnotic treatment. In the case of some mental illnesses, it would be extremely wrong to use hypnosis. To a psychotic patient, who would acquire most if they were in harmony with their mental strength, suggestion therapy is unfortunately unsuitable for two reasons.

First, they cannot let go, i.e. access to their subconscious mind is blocked by an almost permanent psychological defect. Second, other dormant conditions might be reactivated. Thus the experienced hypno-therapist looks for signs of mental illnesses immediately during the first consultation. In order not to further increase the patient's suffering, he sometimes has to refuse treatment.

Additionally, there are rare cases when patients decide to come for the therapy still carrying barriers within them. One who generally refuses to be treated can never achieve success, even with the best of therapists.

There are then the so-called apparent or alibi patients. They apply for treatment simply because their friends, relatives, or parents sent them and they now want to prove to them that they cannot be helped. They lie down with the thought: "Oh, come off it! With my case, you will be banging your head against a brick wall!" This somewhat transparent assertion is, of course, perfect proof that they consider it essential to protect their favorite ideas from any outside attack, no matter whether they be harmless or life-endangering.

If the patient is really ill and in danger, as, for example, with anorexic people, it can often be assumed that they do not want to be cured at all, because they need their illness to keep their mental balance. Some learn to manipulate their surroundings with their illness and sometimes that feels good.

A patient from the upper middle class paid me a visit having exactly these difficult pre-dispositions. Basically, he did not want to become healthy and he visited me only under duress from his family. In his case, I first created conditions for positive change through cooperation with his girlfriend. She threatened to leave him if he did not change. In such a "harsh" manner, we were able to make him let go and finally cooperate within two weeks. His suppressed fears and inferiority complex could be released. By means of positive suggestion, it was possible to create a stronger new feeling of self-worth.

In such cases, classical homeopathy has proved to be extraordinarily good support for psycho-therapeutic efforts. It can have an effect on deep mental layers. However, as in hypnotherapy, homeopathy is also very dependent on the qualifications of the homeopath. Contrary to the huge amounts of allopathic medications, there are only a few hundred homeopathic medications. However, through a so-called potentizing (diluting), the homeopath is able to get an immense richness of almost 6,000,000 possible combinations. The possibility that the untrained homeopath will find the right medication is very small. Insiders claim that there are only ten to twenty really good homeopaths in the whole of Germany. In my work, I have been very lucky to be able to fall back on the support of one such highly qualified homeopath when it was necessary. The alternative practitioner Peter Raba in Murnau, Germany is one of those few homeopaths who can offer help if all else fails.

Widespread prejudice against hypnosis includes some laymen's suspicion that they will let out something about their intimate life. This effectively creates a whole series of mental blocks in itself, which one can actually be freed from through hypnosis.

A traditional destructive attitude to one's own sexuality almost always leads to the most serious mental blocks. I often wish that there were many more Margo Anand Naslednikovs (from The Art of Sexual Magic, Putnam NY) and Adam & Eves in our society to finally do away with sexual taboos once and for all. A well-known teacher of wisdom holds the view that a sexuality full of relish makes people quickly reach a normal level of mutual care. Without being pressurized by frustration, they find their moral attitude to life without needing to resort to exaggeration.

In spite of all the openness in our culture, sexuality is still regarded as a secret topic which some people talk about too much and others that are frustrated hide.

The confidence a patient has in their helper is based on the secure belief that even in the deepest trance, he will be the master of his own decision as to whether to talk or not to talk about personal matters with his therapist.

THE EFFECT OF HYPNOTHERAPY

You may already have noticed in the described examples that therapeutic use of hypnosis lies in the reconstruction of the mind. Hypnosis has absolutely nothing to do with suppression, violence, or creation of dependence.

A doctor can treat your asthma, skin rash, or migraine with medication. Instead of symptoms, I look at the causes and they are almost always to be found in the psyche. I ask about the symptoms only during the first detailed conversation. Then we generally do not mention them during the whole treatment period until the end, when they have disappeared.

During the therapy period, you are given positive suggestions which are directed at finding a quick solution to your problem. The key to health and happiness always lies within your soul. If you succeed in putting together all your spiritual strength in order to unite mind, body, and soul, all disorders will disappear. Your whole task consists of letting your old ideas go. In such a way, the shift in your thinking has already taken place leading to the realization of our four greatest longings, those of love, health, harmony, and success, which are waiting within to be realized.

It would not be an empty statement if I were to say that spiritual hypnotherapy will provide you with a solution for all that burdens you. In any case, read this book a few times. You will always discover something new and in such a way you will soon find a way to reach health and happiness.

Eastern philosophy holds the belief that real happiness in our life comes with the harmonious union of mind, body, and soul. I agree with this and perhaps you will also share this opinion. The secret of success in life, if there is one, is to shape our days in divine harmony.

Grasp the outmost importance and promise contained within the realization of this.

Conventional medicine has reluctantly begun to evaluate spiritual principles as being important for success in some areas of life. Stick to your own ideal and free yourself from old ballast through positive suggestion. Come for advice if you feel that you need help. There is only one way to turn your longings that are moving your heart into reality. Feel right, think right, and act right. Or to be more precise, constantly think positively!

THE EXPERIENCE OF YOUR OWN PERSONAL SUCCESS UNDER HYPNOSIS

The years of your life have made you the person you are now. Origin, predisposition, and up-bringing have made you the person that is holding this book in their hands at this very moment. Hypnosis is not a miraculous cure that can eliminate in a few hours what has taken decades to create. Although under hypnosis the multiple effect of fast learning and forgetting takes place, changes happen mostly gradually, but they do happen nonetheless. However, you can immediately skip from minus to plus, from positive to negative.

A patient must be "patient." Patience is essential and we should patiently expect the new injection of positive energy from the subconscious mind to be expressed in the whole body as recovery begins.

Regarding every acute disease, we know that recovery is preceded by crisis. In the case of hypnosis, you can experience a crisis within the first few days when you think that you are not going to make it. Old habits fight against the growing strength. Old patterns of thinking and deeply ingrained faults are stirred up. Prejudice, resentment, an unforgiving nature, as well as other disorders transferred to the body as an illness all rebel, not wanting to disappear so easily.

Actual chemical changes take place when your positive mental strength starts to shake up these physical disorders. A 20-year-old diabetic, dependent on his mother, fell from one organic illness to another. In such a way, he wanted to be further supported by her, thus not having to stand on his feet. He got so muddled up by suggestions of health that he experienced a hormone imbalance. The clash of forces within him was of course reflected by his physical condition. He was experiencing a crisis before the new more positive forces won.

Our "dear" old habits, even if they are unpleasant companions, e.g. phobias or neuralgia, smoking or drinking habits, try to ensure their further existence. The best weapon against these temptations is patience. Nervousness can only bring about further difficulties. Critical thoughts and doubts only give rise to further dubious situations. Your subconscious mind has made the decision to live a better life. Having read this book, you will no longer associate hypnosis with any difficulties. You will know that nothing can disrupt your positive thinking. Living with this conviction means that you have chosen a successful life.

Under these pre-conditions, it is easier for a therapist to put you into a meditative trance. At the beginning of a treatment, there are relaxation exercises to ensure the success of the therapy. Later begins the process of completely letting go and the final taking over of the personalized creative suggestions.

Now you have found out that hypnosis cannot be considered a mechanical treatment that is simply performed on you, after which you can go home cured. Your consciousness is much subtler than that. For the first time in your life your own work is helping you advance. No one can take this away from you, because you have shaped your consciousness and now you are able to transform it. We can help you with this. The job of working on yourself is the best paid work in the world. Your pay is everything that you desire. With a therapist's help, you will put yourself on the sunnier side of life.

KNOWLEDGE & LEARNING UNDER HYPNOSIS

Once you learn of the method of hypnosis, you will learn about a whole chain of further very useful possibilities. The relaxation technique that you learn as a preparation removes everyday stress. You become calmer and more level-headed, which is a good basis for successful action.

You will notice that your memory keeps improving. Having better access to your subconscious mind enables you to make better contact with the global depths of your soul. Every little thing perceived by your senses is stored there. When you think of all that you have perceived and then forgot in the course of your life, it should not make you sad. The treasure-trove of your subconscious mind contains all sorts of stored treasures. They were transferred from your short-term memory into the long-term memory and are now waiting there to be recalled.

Our daily consciousness operates selectively with things that present a focus for attention. After a fulfilling day, in the evening we often have difficulty stringing together all our experienced details when looking back on them.

Of course, that protects us from being overwhelmed by the sheer diversity of events. Under hypnosis, we gain access to our infinite memory where all, even the smallest events are registered. Our senses perceive even seemingly unimportant details so completely that we are amazed when we get a glimpse of the treasure chamber of our mind.

I was once asked by a Viennese newspaper to treat a man who had noticed a car in a forest close to Vienna on the road where a murder had taken place. Of course, months after the event, the man had apparently forgotten every detail of the occurrence. I was supposed to lead him through hypnosis back to that place in the forest in order to make him read the car registration plate. At the time, the car had not once lain within his direct view, but under hypnosis, he was still able to remember it. He clearly gave the number, make of car and its color.

The most important thing in this strange event was not the actual solving of the crime, which was astonishing in itself, rather the capacity of the memory to document in detail every single observed moment of our life.

The already mentioned professor Losanov from Sofia in the sixties began to make more use of the brain's capacity, which is only 10 percent used, for simpler and quicker learning. The hypnosis/trance technique is a good helping aid because it succeeds in keeping the brain away from extrinsic superficial thoughts and in opening up those unconscious layers of the mind. Neuro- physiology has determined that brain functioning in a fully awakened state (beta waves) implies that the intellect is at work. On the other hand, lower frequency alpha waves, controlled by deeper mental layers, are produced in a sleepy semi-conscious state.

From a hypnotized person, we can mostly measure alpha waves, and a small amount of even lower frequency oscillations. Each lower frequency indicates that the hypnotized person is in a deeper unconscious level, which enables direct access to "the forgotten." Learning contents can also be used in place of positive suggestions. The advantage of such learning is that it is faster, but what is more useful is that what is learned is kept in the memory more easily.

A Trick for Sleep

I often use the increased ability to learn and readiness to perceive under hypnosis or while asleep for learning or healing purposes by using tapes as a subliminal technique. If you want to dedicate yourself to this new positive conditioning, even at night, you will find a wide choice of tapes with corresponding suggestive texts that can be played during the day or while you are sleeping.

You only need a tape recorder and a time switch. The best time to switch on is between two and three hours after falling asleep. When the time switch turns the tape on for a ninety-minute session, the sleeper is effectively starting his own private treatment therapy as the suggestive text flows directly into his subconscious mind. The volume should not be set too high. It should be hardly hearable, thus not disturbing your sleep.

One using this technique will wonder how quickly a newly suggested idea will need to take a hold. To become a non-smoker or to program a lasting weight loss in such a way is always amazing. It is irrelevant what type of text is in question. If you want to create your own texts, you can also use English vocabulary or mathematical formulae, for example, which will fall into "fertile ground" in the sleep. Those suffering from a lack of concentration or memory disorders can profit from this nightly period so that they can use their whole day at work effectively.

For example, record as your nightly suggestion the following text on tape: "I can concentrate on all that I do and I am happy about my success. Everything that I do is immediately imprinted onto my subconscious mind and cannot be erased. From now on, I can recall all-important details. The learned matter forever remains within easy reach of my memory. I gain access to all that has been learned from my memory completely and at any time. My concentration is getting stronger day by day. Learning gives me real pleasure."

Repeat this text three times in a row on the tape, and if you like, even create your own, completely personally designed texts. With this suggestion, you will attain a basic predisposition of a good ability to concentrate or whatever it is you really desire. Especially for students, this type of "night work" is the most suitable time to accomplish a lot of learning. Too many fall under the influence of physical stress, simply because they do not take care of their body's biological clock, overdoing things in all their adolescent exuberance. Work, once neglected, cannot be made up for by working non-stop around the clock. Thus, at the beginning of the semester, I sporadically receive applications from such people asking for help.

A law student who had already failed a state exam twice visited me full of desperation. He told me that accumulated rage and an extreme aversion to learning had made him come up against a brick wall. He had already gained a doctorate and could therefore already call himself Dr., but he would never be able to open his own office if he did not pass his exam at the third attempt. In his desperation, he often thought of suicide.

It was only a mental block built up by his anger that had to be released. His knowledge was good enough to make him a successful lawyer. His aversion toward constant learning created in his subconscious mind a mental block which at the time was preventing him from absorbing new knowledge or recalling what he had already memorized.

Through suggestions referring to his state exam, his inner self returned to a state of harmony and to the world in only fourteen days. His old zest, his joy for life and learning returned. The exam that awaited him was now only another thing to look forward to and his great inner high pushed him to perform new deeds. As result of the therapy, the next time he passed the exam with an excellent mark. He used his subconscious mind to create a positive and better quality of life.

5

The Buried Treasure of Mental Images

The rule for success is faith.

WHAT IS A SUPPRESSED COMPLEX?

In the chapter on suggestion, I said that old habits in our subconscious mind simply do not want to disappear. Siegmund Freud supposed that traumas, fear, or blocks were deeply ingrained in the memory because our Ego cannot get rid of unpleasant ideas in any other way. However, they have only been "suppressed" from daily consciousness. Freud further falsely believed that this complex of thoughts cannot be removed, but only shifted by new positive suggestions. In practice this would mean that a psychosomatic disorder (see the chapter on "Hypnosis"), e.g. a migraine, would only be suppressed by suggestive treatment and that it could nonetheless reappear as asthma, for instance.

Many orthodox psychologists still fall victim to this false train of thought, not taking suggestion therapy into account as a treatment method. Many people consider hypnosis or suggestion therapy as not intellectual enough. They juggle about with well-formulated speech and word structures that no layman can understand.

Psychoanalysts try to draw conclusions from emotional reactions. In conversations often lasting over years, based on the patient's hidden symbolical descriptions of their suppressed complexes, they help the patient to work them out. This is a complex task since the patient in daily consciousness does not have the foggiest clue about the contents and background of his emotional expressions and neurotic actions.

A human being can be filled only with one complex of feelings or one notion. If he feels ill, he cannot feel healthy. However, if he feels healthy he cannot feel ill either. A poor person cannot be rich at the same time. If a suggestion is intensive enough, a complex is not suppressed but replaced. According to the Bible, "our God is a consuming fire" (Hebrews 12:29) that burns everything not in accordance with him! Applied to suggestion therapy, this means that a stronger positive suggestion will eliminate a weaker negative suggestion!

We are more preoccupied with our mental activities than we generally believe. Many of our dreams are mirror images of our emotional life, reflecting the processing of both good and bad life experiences. Dreams are sometimes difficult to interpret. Since our inner world has its own language of symbolic images, we sometimes have to become like children in order to understand what they want to tell us.

The whole truth is preserved in your soul.

CATATHYMIC IMAGE PERCEPTION

The psychologist Hanscarl Leuner proved that so-called mental images, which mirror our soul in front of our spiritual eye, explain through their symbolic content the most hidden of our emotions. In order to grasp a person's problems, a hypno-therapist has to let them dip into their catathymic image perception (catathymic: mental effect, effect of extremely emotional, suppressed complexes on the soul). Suppressed and troubling events can rise up again from the depths of the soul, contributing to the solving of a conflict. The patient does not have to be asleep to observe their dreams. They are accessible already in a half-waking, slightly trance-like state during which they can talk to their therapist, as in mild hypnosis.

One who lays themselves down, relaxed and letting their thoughts wander, i.e. sending them in all directions, experiences a changing play of images in front of their spiritual eye. They can direct them, but can only influence their content to a small extent. They can immediately imagine the home of their future desires as either a concrete bunker or a baroque castle. They will do so if they do not pretend that they recognize their own emotions. Fears are surrounded by thick protective walls. Emotional and exuberant people see themselves within splendid surroundings.

Psychologists looking for objective proof see catathymic image perception as vague background information about the patient. In their opinion, the sphere of desire and the intention to attain something are troublesome, making this method unusable for researching into the subconscious mind. Contrary to this rational criticism, in thousands of cases in my practice, I have experienced that a person's fantasy has no choice but to scoop energy from its own emotional sphere. The therapist can accurately grasp through his experience and education the symbolic value of forms and shapes therein, learning how to understand the patient to the very bottom of their soul. Based on this, Hanscarl Leuner developed a handy system that I daily use in my practice.

I first take people who are seeking help to my seminars in order to help them get an insight into their unconscious inner life through intensive self-experience. When the main problem has been focused on and hypnosis recognized as the right form of therapy, catathymic image perception brings light even into the last corner of the soul, giving explanations to motives and background to bad events.

Patients confirm again and again the stereotypical teachings of Carl Gustav Jung. This can be seen in the regularity with which certain symbolic images keep reappearing in people. A pine forest in which in their fantasy the patient first finds themselves is a sign of aggression and mental blocks. A meadow full of flowers stands for positive balance. Mountains or inaccessible rocks refer to problems and immense difficulties. If you want to find out more about this, there are a huge number of good books on this topic.

Whole parental dramas in married life are mirrored in these fantastic images, as was the case with my female patient Sandra.

Mrs. Sandra came to visit me in a deep depression. She was a lonely, docile person living in loveless monotony. After a few days of preparation, she was asked to place herself spiritually in "any" landscape. She reported what she saw: "I can see a big meadow. On the left there is a cow. It is light brown, big and strong. I like it. I am stroking it. It likes what I am doing. I will feed it. The cow likes me too. It has big, full udders."

At the request of the therapist to take milk, she says: "I cannot drink from the udders, but I am taking a pot and I am filling it with milk. Then an elephant comes over the meadow. The cow moves away from it. I am also ever so slightly scared about what the elephant will do."

Mrs. Sandra was then asked to stroke the elephant. She strokes it reluctantly, but then reports: "I strongly believe that it likes the stroking, but it isn't showing it. Shall I feed it? That is not possible. I can't do it. I'll try. It is accepting it. Shall I ride it? Oh yes, it's possible. I am even enjoying it. It is taking me over a deep hole. However, I am now very tired. I cannot ride anymore. I am lying down in the meadow. The whole sky becomes black, like before a storm. The sun is gone. The cow keeps staring at the elephant and suddenly it trots away. Why is it leaving me alone now? I stroke the cow. It still regards the elephant. I cannot see the elephant anymore."

Sad and depressed, Mrs. Sandra returned to her daily consciousness. As we later found out through a set of precise questions, she was afraid of her father, although she still loved him very much. He was the elephant whom she had reluctantly stroked. However, he had sometimes helped her to overcome difficulties that had seemed insurmountable (the deep hole in the meadow). The overcoming of her inner tensions toward her father, in her catathymic image perception this was the elephant, finally made her "dead tired." When she was fourteen years old, her father left her mother after a blazing row that she had had to experience (stormy sky, elephant gets away). Since then Mrs. Sandra had felt lonely and abandoned.

Even little side comments can reveal hidden pieces of information. When she refused to drink from the udder of the cow, the reason for this could be found in her family situation. She had never been breast-fed. Mrs. Sandra's mental images had reflected her mental situation with rare simplicity and clarity.

The experienced psychotherapist can draw many conclusions about mental blocks, traumas, fears as well as existing and future causes of illness solely from the patient's interaction and behavior on the basis of their daydreams. This is one of the big advantages of catathymic image perception. It is a simple and easy technique that provides direct access to suppressed knowledge within the subconscious mind. These images of free associations are created in two different forms.

Mental images can be changed and made to disappear, as opposed to rigid, clear-cut "views" which can exist for weeks and months. Behind these views, the neurotic features of character and defensiveness are hidden. In the case of a concrete bunker, this is an example of a fearful mind that needs protecting.

The results of only a single session are of course not enough to get a deep impression. Practice has proved that there are six to seven standard forms of catathymic image perception, although Hanscarl Leuner has found altogether ten, which show and summarize one's inner mental life. The world of mountains, the meadow, the water from its source to the sea or the entering of a house show where specific blocks or dangerous experiences (shocks, traumas) are hidden within the patient.

One who does not want to be sent to a landscape (inner resistance) can drop to the bottom of the sea, into their deep unconscious. The sea is symbolic of the mind, the depths stand for the unconscious layers of one's own soul. One who goes on a voyage of discovery "thoroughly" searches through their archives, so to speak, through their past and their arsenal of secret desires and abilities. If they come up looking over the surface of the water, they find themselves on the level of daily consciousness, beginning to see and use their acquired "booty."

Everyone has self-limiting thoughts, but a wise person does not express them.

THE DIFFERENT EFFECTS OF THE TWO BRAIN HEMISPHERES

The spiritual trips of 55-year-old industrialist Simon, after long journeys, almost always ended up on the rocks. Suddenly, he would stand in front of crushing walls as he ventured left from the path.

In the relationship between the left and right directions there lies a special feature of catathymic image perception. From a neurological point of view, the intellect with its rational way of thinking acts in the left

Erhard F. Freitag

part of our brain. It controls the nervous system in the right part of our body. The right part of our brain is controlled by our mind, our feelings, and superior forces, directing the left half of our body.

In a mental image, we experience this right-left division of our spiritual strength symbolically. When the patient Simon saw rocks on the left, i.e. in the area controlled by his mind, it meant that his biggest difficulties were to be looked for in emotional areas. And, in fact, he was experiencing these kinds of problems at the office. He was an excessively overzealous organizer. As an employer, he found it more and more difficult to cope emotionally with his employees' human weaknesses and the discussions arising from them. His lack of ability to correctly lead people, along with his daily irritations, was turning his life into a nightmare. For a few years, he had been suffering from chronic bronchitis and fits of asthma, which made this pleasant man's life difficult. He was afraid to go to bed at night and to get up in the morning. I was able to help him, leading him to natural self-confidence, as I will describe later in the excerpt on catathymic possibilities for helping.

Relationships and attitudes to sexuality, with their various causes that create serious problems in life, can be explained using picturesque symbols. In order to better understand a single female patient on this level, in a trance I let her imagine herself going for a walk on an empty street. A car driver stopped by her and wanted to take her for a ride. A normal reaction would have just been to have either accepted or refused the ride. However, in her imagined scene Miss Helena ran away full of horror into the middle of a stubby field in which she pricked her feet with each step. This gave cause to search for the origins of this frantic reaction. In later sessions, we found out that as a 12-year-old child, she had almost been raped by her cousin in a warehouse. In this catathymic vision, her fear of her sexuality stirred up by her mother had now grown out of all proportions.

By means of another symbolic image, I tried to understand which inner image Miss Helena had in mind regarding her view of herself. I made her find the most beautiful female first name that she could imagine. Behind such a preferred name of one's own sex, there is always a person whose features the experimental subject desires most. This turned out to be the case here, as well. Miss Helena very quickly gave the name "Margot." To my question about which person she liked with this name most, she mentioned her grocer's wife. This very slim person, in love with life, greatly appealed to her.

"How she interacts with men, so carefree and relaxed. She is always cheerful and happy," she told me later. Thus it was generally clear how Miss Helena was to be helped with suggestions to acquire new self- confidence. We could help her to reach new awareness of her body by means of self-love. A stronger charisma, a slight gaining of weight and a modern new hair style with the corresponding clothes made her ask the question as to whether she was her own younger sister.

From these examples it can be concluded that a single "image" can give only a partial conclusion about the state of one's character. It is only one mosaic tile in the whole mental picture. Only by a combination of the various symbols that the experienced therapist extracts from the sessions while purposefully guiding the patient can he round up the whole picture, giving information about the types of special suggestion that need to be applied.

Through catathymic image perception, even people who can hardly be hypnotized or even not at all because of their rational mental blocking are able to experience their emotional center. The intellect thus cannot falsify these fantastic images, as some laymen psychologists lead us to believe. In a half- awakened state, one very quickly cedes the intellect's power to the stronger layers of the mind.

In the fourth chapter, I spoke of the responsibility of the therapist and the dependence that can be created between him and his patient. With my patient Jacqueline this dependence was reflected after a longer period of treatment using catathymic image perception. She saw herself standing at a railway station. The train arrived and one of my colleagues got off smiling at her, doffing his hat. She got on to travel to her home city and he was now seated in the same compartment. Then she had to change trains to go to school through a tunnel, and there getting on the next train was my colleague again. On her arrival in Munich, my colleague parted from her. Suddenly she did not know where to go. We informed her that her longing for joie de vivre, well-being and naturalness would now direct her steps. In her fantasy during the final session she went to a huge park full of flowers in which she was surrounded by the brightest colors and most wonderful smells. Very happily she sat in the middle of a flowerbed.

Her therapist had stepped into her mental background as a "positive" factor. This was an unpredictable side effect called transfer that was to be carefully adjusted on her path toward independence.

MENTAL STRENGTH ELIMINATES PROBLEMS

Conventional psychotherapists are starting to become more and more familiar with catathymic image perception because it quickly highlights surprising discoveries about the paradigm of our psyche. However, they have not learned anything about the wonderful possibilities of the suggestive influencing of the subconscious mind. It will take a while before hypnotherapy is recognized. Direct work with the subconscious mind is still a vague matter to orthodox scientists. What they do not realize is that they actually undermine the power of the subconscious mind through their doubts. One of my successful experiences was to relieve an academic of his inner blocks and troubles using catathymic image perception. There is a further great advantage to mental imaging when compared with very long psychoanalysis. Directed by a therapist, you can often condition the subconscious mind to accept positive ideas. The higher Self represents our spiritual headquarters, which is always ready to create better living conditions if only we desire it.

During catathymic image perception, help can be given in various ways. Fear-provoking symbols such as giant birds or lions are, for example, accepted as equal to us human beings by virtue of the fact that we feed them. It can happen that a monster, if approached in a friendly manner, in a second can suddenly turn into a sheep. The metaphor lies in the realization that the demon represents the patient's own unresolved desires or thoughts, and that they have now been "saved" by friendliness and love. Everything is in the process of eternal transformation, and fear can also be transformed if we realize our misconceptions and correct them.

Adhering to a principle of forgiveness and a friendly approach to all things hostile transforms fear-inducing concepts, causing inner harmony to surface. If hatred is a hunger for love, then this hunger can be satisfied only with love. If a fear symbolizes longing for love, then only love can help.

Even if a problem seems unsolvable, the therapist can issue an order to radically free yourself by chasing the threatening symbol away forever. This happened when one of my patients saw himself seized by a giant octopus. A sword (symbolically) was slipped into his hand, and he was able to push the monster from the rock with one stab.

This was an aggressive but necessary act of liberation which allowed him to get rid of a strong suppressed emotion, as we saw later. After waking up he knew exactly what that huge burden was in his life. Now he felt strong and up to the situation.

A mother of three children ventured into a cave in her symbolic drama. Suddenly she stood in front of a giant spider that wanted to grab her with its numerous legs. The woman screamed in horror, trying to escape, but she could not move from the place. The therapist told her that she too had a magic sword (the strength of her own center) in her hand which she could safely defend herself with against anything that attacked her. With energetic movements of her arms on the couch, she cut off all the spider's legs, finally pushing it into the depths of a dark hole. Shaking and crying, she woke up from her trance. She was scared, but felt relieved after this disgusting deed. She whispered, as white as a sheet: "My God, that was my mother!"

The 50-year-old woman had freed herself in her subconscious mind from the torments and fears of her hard childhood implanted in her by her authoritative and violent mother. In the weeks that followed we experienced this woman's rejuvenation. Three years of psychoanalytic treatment previously could not even begin to touch the problem.

Good is the one who gives from themselves.

The Ability to Move Mountains

Children have the most colorful and beautiful experiences during catathymic image perception. They are surely closer to their subconscious layers than grown-ups, reacting to the images of their fantasy in a much stronger and realistic way. Often they can really move "mountains of problems" with their ideas.

Fourteen-year-old Richard, who had been stuttering since he was four years old, quickly found the origin of his suffering in this form of relaxation. In his mental image, "his" landscape was a big meadow with a lot of blue and yellow flowers (adolescent carefree attitude). Then he entered a forest and went to a hut in its middle. With a magical wand he did some magic, producing bread and water on the table. He ate and then wandered further. Suddenly he came across a dwarf (his inner voice) whom he asked, at the request of the therapist, for the reason for his speech disorder. The dwarf explained to him that at the age of four he had fallen on a stone slab, which had horribly frightened him at the time (shock, trauma). He also told him how he could speak properly again. Richard could now imagine falling into a deep sleep and waking up being able to talk to the dwarf normally. If he were really able to believe in it, everything would soon be all right.

For a while there was silence. Suddenly Richard gave a start, saying that he felt bad and that he wanted to throw up. As we found out later, he had again gone through the experience of falling onto the stone slab, at the time apparently suffering from a serious concussion.

"Listen to the dwarf," the therapist told him, directing him to use the strength of his thoughts in order to calm down and soften this shocking experience. In such a way he should have immediately felt better. And it really did happen. The event with the dwarf continued in the state of trance. Afterwards Richard was surprised that he had not stuttered anymore in his conversation with the dwarf. My assistants and I were also able to ascertain a significant improvement. When his parents took him an hour later, he again had speech problems. It took ten more weeks to analyze all the causes before Richard could speak normally.

The stuttering in his case was not only attributable to his serious fall. Richard had an extremely authoritative father who was steadily putting him under pressure. Before the end of the therapy, I involved his extremely understanding parents in a tactical move during his decommissioning. In the presence of his father I suggested that Richard offer to contract his advice, paying token compensation of one dollar per month for this advice. However, only if Richard actually wanted it. If the father were to interfere without being asked to give "advice," he had to pay a ten-dollar fine!

I was able to make the father understand that he could stimulate and strengthen his son's fragile self-confidence only if he transferred to him a more stable feeling of his own self-worth together with love, tolerance, and a lot of patience. He should also let his son express his own opinion. Stuttering can be a very stubborn disorder, especially if the causes go back decades. Even hypnotherapy cannot always successfully offer help. Sometimes two or even three types of therapy over a period of one to two years are necessary in order to bring about a lasting improvement.

Imagining light can be an especially big mental help in any symbolic drama. The light of "enlightenment" as an idea has been very closely connected with religious mysticism since the very beginning of humanity. The wise man Sant Rajinder Singh conveys in his long traditional chain the path to enlightenment through an extremely effective form of meditation, through the experience of light and sound. Mystics of all periods have spoken of the appearance of light, with the saints being sprayed with a shining light, or in the East with light-filled white lotus flowers. Yoga and meditation disciples always experience the appearance of light while overcoming barriers in their consciousness.

In modern psychology, there is (still) no place for this. I integrated spiritual light into my therapy as it was presented in the teaching of chakras. My likeminded colleagues and I took the symbol of light into our work as a superior higher strength against all dark and pathological things. To awaken the light in a patient means to make them establish contact with their higher Self. In the real sense of the word, it implies awakening their natural divine strength.

One who reaches spiritual maturity, as many followers of meditative prayer and Eastern meditation have experienced, transcends pure rational thinking and non-belief in the afterlife. Not everyone can transcend their narrow egotistic thinking in a short time, but everyone can strive for light. Since it shows the path to truth, all the positive strength of the universe joins it!

One who listens to a patient who has freed himself from various disorders through an inner connection with their wisdom will never be heard to speak about "illusion." They will know what is to be done, following their path to fulfillment. Leading the suffering person to their inner strength, symbolically experienced as light, is in my opinion real psychotherapy.

What up-bringing, school, and religious education classes have kept away from adults, my therapy is not reserved for the latter periods of self-realization. It can help a young person to overcome their complexes and life problems right now.

Healing takes place if love is flowing.

Healing takes place if the therapist forgets their knowledge and the patient their illness.

THE MIRROR OF MARRIED LIFE

Rachel, a young woman married to an Indonesian, showed through catathymic image perception her emotional difficulties which she had been suffering from because of her husband's different mentality. On the edge of a green meadow, where her fantasy placed her, stood a dark pine forest on the right side (mental blocks and aggression). On the left side there was the bright summer sun, distant rocks and a lake. Behind her she felt a gray wall. She was supposed to let the sun-rays fall on it. However, the wall disappeared and the rocks reappeared in the sun behind her.

The lake in front of her was small and shadowed by the forest (her suppressed soul). She was to send the sun and love into the forest. Now it became lighter, brighter. Squirrels appeared. She fed them. The squirrels wanted her to come closer to continue feeding them. She stepped further into the dark forest. A young man appeared, a dark type in a raincoat, approximately 35 years old. His name was Kevin and he greeted her. She was to go with him. She knew that this was about sex. When she refused this he went away.

It got dark. Her task was to send sunlight to her surroundings. It got brighter. Now she saw hills, sand and sea and a white boat with many people on it. She did some magic to put herself on the boat that had come from the East. All the people were dressed in Indonesian style. A dark-haired woman greeted her. She came from New Guinea and asked Rachel whether she wanted to travel to Indonesia. "Yes," she responded. Was she married and did she have children? — She did not want any children, he wanted only sex. It was all very difficult. The old woman nodded full of understanding (a discussion with the higher Self).

In later exercises she found herself underwater in this lake (subconscious mind). Many small red fish appeared. A giant fish came, constantly looking at her. Its name was Gobi and it was fourteen years old. She was scared and wanted to swim away from him. With love and light (which the therapist recommended she use), he became increasingly friendlier. She fed it with grass, which it took, feeling good as she stroked it.

Now she wanted to position rocks at the bottom of the lake with the help of fish (still dependent). Everything was to become green, covered with water plants.

It took Mrs. Rachel weeks to harmonize through hypnotherapy her three main problems: professional and emotional confidence, sexual frustration, and difficulties in adapting to her husband. Gradual change freed her from the many shadows of her past. Only because she felt that she had to do something about it did she look for solutions, finally finding a way.

Many could find a way to a happy life if they paid more attention to their inner voice.

It is not good to limp in front of a cripple and consider it friendly.

Fears Disappear in Light & Love

Twenty-eight-year-old Edgar experienced under hypnosis direct contact with his subconscious mind. The dependent and slightly anxious businessman, who was to take over the business of his father, saw at the beginning of his catathymic image perception only a forest from a small clearing. Somewhere in the middle of his treatment he described the situation in the following way:

"On the right side there is a stream with a bridge (possibility of changing profession) close to a meadow with a lot of sheep. On the left side there is a distant meadow in front of the forest and I see myself lying in its middle. High grass almost completely hides me. In front of me there is a huge mountain with a lot of trees. There are birds around me. I feed them. People pass me by, greeting me, friendly."

"Bring in more light," suggested the therapist.

"The whole landscape becomes brighter," he continued. "Everything is clearer. In the background I can see a village. I do not want to go away from here, I would just like to laze around here."

In the days that followed, he told me that he had talked to his father. He explained to him that he was not yet going to take over the business, but that he would first study business management before assuming responsibility for the company. His father was very surprised about his determination. At the end of the treatment, Edgar experienced a direct reaction from his subconscious mind.

"I am climbing the hill lying before me," he reported from the state of his immersion. "It is very easy to reach the top. It is sunny and I have a wonderful overview of the landscape with all its villages. An older man (his higher Self) approaches me with a big Saint Bernard. He says that I have made the right decision, but that I should not rush into anything. Now the old man puts a hand on my shoulder. We eat together (inner harmony). The old man says that I will overcome all future obstacles as easily as I reached the top of the mountain. My future will be as sunny and clear as the view here. My friends also arrive on the mountain. I tell them what the old man has told me. They are happy with me."

My experience with Edgar had become a success by the time we parted in my office. He was well on his way to success in life and we were able to slightly contribute to this.

An Austrian doctor had a somewhat more blocked personality combined with sexual neurosis. Daniel N. already had a Ph.D. and was well on his way to achieving a second Ph.D. His single-minded striving for knowledge and rational achievement had deprived him of all inner calmness and balance. His mental images revealed sharp contrasts. Dr. Daniel N. reported the following:

"On the right side there is a forest with a lot of small pine trees. I can see a long wall made of natural stone. However, it is completely senseless because there are cows grazing somewhere else. On the left side there are dense bushes. I cannot see through them at all. Christ's crucifix is in the way and there are only molehills on the meadow. Far back I can see my home city. In front there is also another city and many roads leading to it." The therapist asked him to let light and love flow into his landscape.

"The grass has become very dense, the trees on the right side are suddenly becoming smaller," he continued. "There is a wonderful little daisy there. I greet it. It looks at me, friendly sending back a smile. Its name is Iris. A bee comes, flies onto the flower, imbues the nectar, flies away (blown opportunity, no relationship).

And the wall? It does not disturb me at all. It is purposeless. I would rather look at my flowers. To build a house from the wall? Oh, no! Or yes? That would not be a bad idea. However, I do not have the will.

A big calf approaches me. It looks at me trustingly with its big brown eyes. It has really soft nostrils and it is swishing its tail. I stroke it reluctantly and now it is running way!" (disturbed relationship with females).

Later on, Daniel N. only wanted to sniff the flowers, ride around or lie in the sun. All restrictions in the landscape, such as walls, fences, strange flowers of mole-hills were not disturbing. He had become too much used to these restrictions because of a strict, loveless up-bringing. He never saw water, the symbol of the unconscious strength of his mind. To an intellectual, it is a particularly common pattern to find valid only rational events in life. He had become a down-to-earth rational type of person that, until the very end of treatment, did not show any readiness to let go, not even temporarily releasing his fixed ideas and rooted emotions. My help mainly consisted of giving him impulses to make his inner life gradually become clearer, of making him read books on this topic and of making him slowly get used to the existence of his still unconscious strength.

You are not bad if you are not good, you may only be unaware of other possibilities.

JOURNEY OF DISCOVERY INTO THE PAST

Catathymic image perception is not limited simply to defining existing mental contents at a particular moment. In deep relaxation and hypnosis, our memory can be better used than in daily consciousness and we can understand again even the most distant past of our life and every experienced scene. This gives us a possibility for re-awaking forgotten or suppressed experiences, which even today subliminally determine our everyday life in various ways. Fears and phobias, generally all types of neurosis, can simply be explained by suppressed feelings of unresolved past experiences.

Generally, causes of every such problem can be identified by a "sifting through" of the subconscious mind. Psychotherapists call this method of tracing past events regression or tracing back.

In a deeply relaxed state, the gate to the subconscious mind opens up, making the presence of our mental strength more conscious. It is a well-known fact that in such a way everyone can be put back into their childhood. For example, they may adopt the way of thinking and writing of an eight-year-old. Memories can be recalled from up to a pre-birth period. Even science has confirmed that a person possesses a consciousness that is already able to register things five months before birth.

Already in the unborn state, the first mental scars can be created, being the cause of many problems in a grown-up. In professionally conducted regression, parents' statements before birth can resurface. If an unwanted child should have been aborted, or the parents had serious life-endangering conflicts, the oncoming human has already emotionally taken part in this. More and more, psychologists are recognizing the power of statements from prenatal periods, integrating these experiences into their therapy.

Individual cases soon make this clear. A northern German patient, Mrs. Stella, came to me as a chronic diabetic. She had been dependent on insulin for twenty-five years, more and more losing her sight. Through hypnosis, she was looking for courage in life to enable her to cope better with her weak body. I will later refer to the possibilities of hypnotherapy in cases of chronic illness such as diabetes (Chapter 8). Only a description of my method is currently of interest. In order to explain the cause of illness in the case of Mrs. Stella, we looked for traumas in her early childhood. She was a typical example of the fact that mental shocks are saved within our memory. Even if we have been dispelling the unresolved feelings from our daily consciousness for decades, they have not really disappeared.

After a sufficient period of preparation, we started regression with Mrs. Stella. In a trance, she was asked to let her life proceed backwards in front of her spiritual eye up to the moment when she was still healthy. She again found herself as a five-year-old girl on the coast with her mother. She played, running back and forth, being gentle to her mother and feeling her loving closeness. She could even remember her pleasant smelling hair. Finally, in flurry of chaos, her mother rushed back to their house… and died! She parted from her daughter, laid herself down, no longer reacting in spite of little Stella's attempts to again make her "live." For hours, the small child waited in vain for her mother to wake up again. Of course, she could not understand what had happened and she cried heartbreakingly until she was found cuddling up to her dead mother.

In this symbolic drama, she now saw herself again playing in the street. "Another girl approaches me saying: I know that your mother is dead, my mum read it in the newspapers."

Stella screamed: "That's not true!" Big fears arise in her. "Other children are very excited. The girl describes it as being a sensation. I am running to my nanny. "Lady" Monika takes me onto her lap comforting me. She says that none of it is true. My mother is in the hospital. However, I know that she is not telling the truth. My father should have told me that my mum was dead. Now he's in Russia."

Stella steadily ran to the telephone. She waited for her mother's phone call. After a year, her father came back home telling her that her mother was in heaven feeling good.

This long tension provoked in Mrs. Stella a feeling of endless loneliness, and a fear of life appeared. Now she knew the cause of her illness. Her strokes of fate, suppressed into the unconscious, will lose their negative influence if they are "saved," i.e. processed, and new order can follow.

6

The Art of Being Perfect

THE SEARCH FOR HAPPINESS

Hardly any term has such a many-sided human interpretation as the word "happiness." Many writers of literature and philosophy have written intellectual essays on happiness. However, what is happiness, what is its real content?

"Someday I would like to be as happy as all other people," said a fifty-year-old widow to me. Was this just thoughtlessness or simply a lack of understanding of the destiny of others? Barely one in every hundred people would consider themselves really happy if asked. Although the search for the "pot of gold at the end of the rainbow" has become a sign of our times, many do not strike it lucky, simply because they are looking in the wrong places.

I will not deal with any artificial descriptive explanations. In my opinion, my happiness lies in the awareness that I carry all the infinite creative strength of this wonderful life within me. What makes us happy exists within us all. Even you carry this jewel within you and it is only a question of when your conscious being will experience this heavenly bliss.

The greatest fallacy that numerous people accept their whole life is the view that they cannot escape their own destiny. They should listen to the wise Indian Osho, who in one of his discourses explained that "All events in life are there because you attracted them. What you will make out of them is only your concern!"

He also rejects the idea that a person's life is forever determined by their character. To the Western intellectual our character is formed under the influence of heritage, up-bringing, and surroundings. Where is the living mind that created the body?

"It has already been knocked out of me by my father," said Arthur M. to me. With this bitter claim, he described what many people sadly still refer to as an up-bringing. However, Arthur M. showed a rare strength of character, opposing his father's constant devaluation since he considered him to be a complete idiot. In the sixties, the young businessman became a competitor to his father in the fashion industry. His company made a name for itself in Europe.

Your life is woven out of thoughts.

FREEDOM FROM FANATICISM & EGOTISM

If Arthur M. were an isolated case, I would not have mentioned him. Every frustrated person can experience that it is never too late to take "destiny" into your own hands. Your age is unimportant if you still want to attain happiness. You have caused all the bad and negative situations in your life, and they have as much power over you as you allow them to have.

The step toward our goals sometimes requires energy and confidence in our inner strength. One who believes themselves to be weak surrenders without any reason to an ominous destiny that in reality only exists in his head. To be more satisfied and balanced, we only need to remove those ideas afflicted by misconceptions. After turning to positive thinking, we are often unable to comprehend how we could have been misled for such a long time by narrow-minded ideas, thus depriving ourselves of happiness.

A woman in her so-called best years told me the turbulent story of her life peppered with constant failures. After recounting all her negative dramas, I was able to convey to her that she should change director in her movie of life. I made her understand that every topic and every problem should be observed from many sides before it is considered predestined. She will experience misfortunes as long as she does not learn what these problems want to tell her. Mrs. S. grasped this and accepted my request. It was a pleasure to hear of her change and her surprise about this within a few weeks. Friends and colleagues complimented her about this change. Never in the past had she heard so many pleasant words. She reported the following: "I was completely ignorant about what I had landed myself in. It seemed that my unhappiness was justified!"

Incitement to strike or to racially discriminate against certain ethnic groups around the world proves how falsely directed fantasies can give the impression of being more real than reality itself. One who is satisfied with himself does not need to get rid of listlessness and aggression. They will not be victims, because the inexhaustible source of their vitality provides them with strength.

In your drama, you should turn from victim to director in your life movie. Contrary to an actor with a prescribed role, you are protagonist, author, and producer with your own direction. Working on yourself is your life task. All that you perceive is a play without an end and without limits, and you can choose what "serves" you best.

The continuation of the comedy called life is in various ways controlled by our control tower. Every thought and every deed originates from the source of our strength, our steadily activated mind united with God.

Enjoy creation, but do not forget the Creator.

Wrong Thinking Shapes & Controls Whole Professions

Once our intellect starts claiming to be able to evaluate spiritual energy, a person loses their connection to the basis of life. Whole profession groups are driven into the narrowness of a dogmatic lifestyle by the dictate of a rational point of view. At the top of the "negative list" of extremely effective professions stand doctors, lawyers, police officers, and teachers. These profession groups are most bound to the negative effects of our falsely directed ideas about life. Without exception, they observe only the material and intellectual side of our life, too easily overlooking the spiritual basis of creation.

Surgeons' often irresponsible statements in the operating room are proof of their lack of connection with their own center and their own spiritual potential. Their skill, patience, and the refinement with which they play a trick on various physical ailments may well be admirable. However, they still remain defeated by the superficiality of their actions. With the strength of their inner intelligence, they would be much more successful.

How self-satisfied and arrogant does the still prevailing doctors' opinion that ulcers can only be treated with surgery sometimes sound. Any psychotherapist with a normal case could make an ulcer disappear within a few weeks without ever having to touch the patient. Our mechanical and materialistic oriented world of healing remains without emotions. The use of expensive medical devices seems to be more valuable than our healing spirit. The power of our subconscious mind can preserve our health better than any medical technique in the world.

In many clinics in the USA and increasingly in Europe, there are special emissaries who take care of the patient's emotional well-being during an operation. A southern German operating room nurse, a reader of my books for five years, through positive thinking got rid of a migraine that had lasted for years. She described to me her strange practices with people to be operated on under general anesthetic.

"Now we will take the first step," she reports to a patient who is under anesthetic. "Your pulse and your breathing are completely normal. The doctor is now operating on you. Everything is clear and well organized. He is full of confidence that you will soon be healthy again. Our indications shows how well and full of confidence you are, cooperating in order to be healthy. We are sure that you will soon be with your family again. ... Now the operation is finished. Everything has been successful. You made it. With your constitution and your belief in yourself, everything will soon be healed. I wish you a speedy recovery!"

Who would not desire to experience the help of such a nurse in their darkest hours. We are all invited to see positive thinking as more than just pure theory. We will suffer most if we classify all that is positive as being lower than what induces suffering.

Stillness will show you your being. You have gone out of it and will return to it.

The Art of Positive Imagination

The intellect is always attached to outside events. One ministerial clerk expressed this very pragmatically. After a therapy session he turned to me asking: "Dr. Murphy says: 'If you have a fever, tell yourself: I am healthy!' However, how can I claim to be healthy when I feel that I have a fever?" He considered it a contradiction that he first had to overcome the fever before he could influence his healing. To him, everything should have its order and this order should correspond to a simple logic. He was so anxious about fulfilling the norm of his intellect that he did not possess any self-initiative to direct his own thoughts.

Did Dr. Murphy take his readers by the hand with advice? Of course not. He meant it the way he said it: One who is ill experiences the consequences of the situation that is weakening the body and is looking for a pathway to health. The body's defense system works flats out and the ill person undermines the process of healing by confirming that they indeed feel ill. Instead of this, they should welcome the fever as the cleansing of the body by mobilizing all subtle energy and by seeing themselves already healthy. Auto-suggestions such as: "I am healthy" manifest a desired state in a speeded-up way. Positive thoughts should redress the balance of the influence of negative states, letting new healthy strength flow through you.

Use the following suggestive formulae:

"There is perfect harmony within me. The mind, body and soul are as one. I love my body, turning to it with loving and creative thoughts that create health.

Infinite vitality flows to me from all sides, now healing and renewing my body fully according to the picture that God has of me. Divine harmony strengthens and purifies me. It washes away everything that is dark. With each breath a new vitality flows into me. Each breath makes me stronger and healthier. Overnight, I will get healthy, becoming the same old person. I am again united with my spiritual center. I am protected and strengthened by the infinite intelligence of my higher Self."

A patient with heart trouble, shaken up to a great extent and full of mental blocks, experienced through hypnosis his own spiritual strength for the first time. In a short time, he learned to recondition his subconscious mind in order to protect himself from his illnesses.

Some critics who waste their energy of thoughts on doubts call positive thinking positivism. They compare it to the land of milk and honey, where everyone would like to be but no one can, since such a reality only exists in fairy tales. Signs of ignorance in our life can be seen from our belief in injustice, death, and the devil. No one should be deprived of their belief. However, everyone should be aware of that fact that it is exclusively their belief, their idea of the world that determines their life. The intellectual thinks that belief is ignorance, but would they care if they were classified as ignorant? However, it is not simple rational logic that determines our life, rather the strength that rules over this world that many call God.

I know from my twenty-five years of experience that positive thinking has helped thousands to extract themselves form serious crises in their destinies.

Of course, it is nonsense to tell yourself: "I am healthy and successful" while thinking within: "Let's see what happens now!" If doubt prevails, everything will remain unchanged. Because I feared in such a way, it happened to me. Only if we are really convinced will a suggestion gain ground in our subconscious mind and the desired state come up. Therefore think about that thing that has not yet come into existence in order to bring it into being!

Love is to perceive another person the way they are. It also means opening the door through which both of you will hear the message that has been reserved only for you.

EVERYDAY HAPPINESS

Positive thinking always means having a new view of things and implies a positive change in personality.

One who starts concentrating on harmony and love will harmoniously participate in the sunny side of life. A positively oriented person does not force themselves to believe, but experiences the world the way it is, full of everything that their heart desires. One who courageously and happily devotes themselves to life will soon experience the truth of the words from the Bible: "heaven is within you." However, what has gone wrong in the two-thousand-year history of Christianity? Christ was obviously a positivist, but he could not permanently connect the anxious human mind with God.

Let us leave this topic aside. We were not born to this world to live in sin and suffering, but to step through a gate rising above the past. Each of us has been granted by the Creator the strength to reach perfection and harmony. We should use it and our life will be fulfilling. Positive thinking is the first step to recognizing this strength, so release it in order to follow our path to freedom.

Do you not think that you will enjoy your breakfast if you let your happiness shine through for the ensuing day? Open your heart to your world, look out into nature and at the trees outside the door. Everything that you perceive will bring you strength and affection. Trees are strongly rooted in reality, but they still lead peaceful and independent lives. Perceive the sun's rays or the purifying rain. Enjoy them today because they are here to make you happy.

Now, at this moment, you really do exist and you can feel joy and happiness. You can feel that life is more than burying yourself in books or machines. Day by day, you will feel a huge strength rising from within you. You will not see everyday life as gray, but you will

experience in your being all the diversity and beauty
that God has created.

Since I have begun every day with a joyful greeting
to the new day, asking for inner guidance and giving
my confidence to the omnipotence within me, I can
conclude with utter satisfaction that my own emotions
are always mirrored in whomever I speak to. A friendly
greeting and an attentive look in the morning provide
the fuel of sympathy for the whole day.

What else can we desire other than to live our
lifetime in joy?

*Try to see the good and the beautiful in everyone and in
such a way you will rise above yourself and above others,
reaching a state of being stronger together.*

EVERYONE IS AS RICH AS THEY IMAGINE THEMSELVES TO BE

Who would let their day be spoiled by an inferiority complex when in a joyful and receptive mood? If
we were to believe that it might be difficult to defend
ourselves against this inferiority complex, then what
this really represents is an attack of negative thoughts.

Everywhere in nature only the inexhaustible diversity, only the infinite richness called life can be seen.
God grants all talents, he is wealth, fullness and joy.
Turning your thoughts to poverty would mean that
you have voluntarily allowed your life's light to just tick
over. There is no guilt-free poverty. A poor person who
considers his poverty to be his karma is the victim of
a destructive illusion.

From observation, no other group appears to have a greater poverty and victimization complex than do the homeless. Many of them seem to have given up, considering the circumstances they find themselves in. It could be made otherwise merely by using the infinite intelligence within each of us.

It is so simple to overcome naveté, not to be imprisoned by self-limiting ideas anymore. You are what you think you are. It is a wonderful experience to follow the path to inner harmony, leaving all narrow-minded ideas in the past.

Everyone can free themselves from the yoke of negative thoughts. If you open your heart to the world, if you make your vitality flow, then there are no limits, everything is open, you can achieve anything, or as Dr. Murphy formulated it: "There is no end to the glory."

Tell yourself daily:

"There is perfect harmony within me. I have confidence in the infinite intelligence of my subconscious mind. All my best desires are fulfilled. My heart is fully open. Love, goodness and fulfillment are within me. I can feel that my good strength has taken my destiny into its hands. Being grateful, I rest in my divine center from which I shape my life in beauty and perfection."

If you let these words become "real" and "alive," you will have the experience that you are the Creator and the Being at the same time. You will sink into a spiritual kingdom, being amazed that the material side of life actually creates itself. The Bible says: "Long for the heavenly kingdom and everything else will be given to you" (Luke 12:31).

Overcoming your intellectual ball and chain will make you a free being because you are born to be free!

Love cannot possess, nor can it be possessed.

FREEDOM FROM GUILT

In our society, the intellect is so dominant that even God has become a term of negativity to many people. The greatest burden on humanity, i.e. a feeling of guilt, is acquired to a greater extent in the very place where normal people are seeking comfort. The picture of God has been so distorted over the course of the past two millennia that Christian teaching has sometimes resulted in one spending one's life in abject mediocrity, fear, and desperation.

I believe that God is pure love, pure forgiveness and giving. God is not angry and since he created us in his image, only out of love and nothing else are we ever in our core as divine as he is.

Preachers of Christianity thoughtlessly push people into dependence, into feelings of guilt and frustration. How can an innocent new-born child be sinful when it has been granted the breath of the highest spiritual strength by its Creator to accompany it into the world he created? The most famous healer in North America in the previous century, Dr. Phineas Parkhurst Quimby, found out that sixty percent of his patients were full of feelings of guilt created by the influence of the church.

Positive thinking recommends that you believe in God's love in the land of all living beings. You should know that the divine presence never punishes and never condemns. We are those who punish ourselves through our negative thoughts. The Son of God is our own spirit and he is within us. Yes, you have read it correctly. The Son of God is our own spirit and we are the Son of God with all other living beings in the real sense of the word. To live means to express divine holy strength. Divine wisdom freely lives in infinite richness for all things and for all of us and we do not have to ask for it.

Go with me on a journey into your holiest inner life. For a while get rid of all notions of guilty feelings which might have occurred to you while reading these lines.

It is not a sin to show the present state of the Christian world, but it is a sin not to follow the order of the Creator and be happy. God wants us to be happy no matter whether we believe it or not. Sin is to miss the goal and if we accept that love is the goal for us all, then not to love is the only sin which we can succumb to.

Now let all thoughts of the past completely fall away and reject all knowledge that would like to creep into us with its criticisms and judgmentalisms. At this moment of turning to your inner world, do not think of the future! What remains for you? You can feel your body. You perceive your surroundings with your senses. You can feel your being breathe and live without any disturbance. You rest in the eternal divine present. That is the moment of true existence. It is heaven on Earth, or what is often called enlightenment. Observe yourself carefully, feeling the still presence of the creative omnipotence that has created all life. If you succeed through prayer or meditation in stepping into this place of stillness, then you are at your goal and your life is fulfilled.

Take the authority immediately and decide which thoughts should appear within you. Gain the authority over your life to be and remain the master of your own house.

All suffering that you perceive in the world is only healing pain. It is the pain of birth and now let love flow where that pain once lived.

Destiny as Task: Harmony in Real Life

You can waste a large part of your life or turn toward real experience through positive thinking.

Many people sell their souls for money in these times. Work is the root of all ugliness, Dr. Murphy once explained to me. He was referring to our misconception of identifying ourselves through our work. Many live for the sake of work and not for their own sake. We should bear it in mind that we work to live and that we do not live to work!

Do not just do things in order to earn money. Your profession should correspond to your vocation and never be something that will only allow you to earn your living. Work should give you pleasure and increase the joy of this world. Work has a low level of effectiveness if you perform it without inner devotion, mechanically as an unpleasant activity, basically if you have sold your soul for money's sake. If you work only for its own sake you will soon lose the will and your life will become a burden. An escape into illness is too often a solution if an unfulfilled everyday life determines your whole life. Your soul will give you signals regarding this "sell-out."

"Your soul is closer to you than the scarf on your skin," says an old Islamic proverb. Absolutely correct, this is our mission. Let us establish contact with our mental depths and we will recognize the causes of or suffering and problems within the increasing mental monotony that often creeps into many people's lives. Positive thinking is a path to your inner Self and your guide if you need one.

Since I started exploring my transcendental layers, fulfilling the longings of my true being, I have become religious, getting closer to God in the real sense of the word. On the path to your true self, you will also realize that the only existing God is within you, it is your Self.

Follow your life path joyously and full of care. Your life was determined for you only and you only live it once.

Make it a habit to immediately fulfill all types of tasks. Let everyone know what you think of their entreaties, their job, their offers, their thoughts, or desires.

You find a matter either important and you approach it, or you say that it does not interest you. One who likes having all their options open does not understand themselves. Their fears control them from the unconscious layers determining their life.

If you want something from others, then watch the tone of their response. "I still don't know… " or "maybe…" or "maybe I can take that into account" etc. all imply "I'm not interested!"

Do not waste your strength on trying to persuade that person. Your will is inferior to the unwillingness of others. Mental pressure scarcely helps, often coming back to you as some difficulty or other.

"I often hear the warning voice within me." said one of my patients, "However, I more often than not am only ever ready to follow it when it's already too late, when everything's hit the fan so to speak."

All of us have made this mistake at some time. That should be a thing of the past now. Our Ego does not have the right to act against our inner knowledge, thus pushing us into unhappiness.

The first step is to turn with confidence to the wisdom of your soul and love yourself. In Chapter 7, which is about fear, I will explain this in more detail. What we normally understand as love is only an egotistic desire, possessiveness. A witty Englishman once expressed through sarcasm how it reaches a climax in our society: "Nothing preserves friendship more than the regular exchange of banknotes."

Intellectuals might find the use of terms such as harmony and love to be an exaggeration and even out-of-date. They should not surround themselves with a false halo by enthusiastically talking about harmony. Positive thinking implies a positive approach to reality.

Now there should be nothing that can shake you. Nothing can shatter you if you begin feeling the eternal fountain of life within you. To rest in God means to know that the river of life always flows bringing you everything that you need. If some outer things are lost, others are immediately found. If one door closes, another two will open. Do not think that your company, your boss, or your insurance policy are a guarantee of survival. Instead of this, pay more attention to your true source of security. A harmonious person connected with their higher Self will not give power to material things. They give neither the sun, the moon nor the stars power over themselves. They give it exclusively to God, and his spirit within them is their closest friend.

Do these words sound too religious to you? If so, you might be acting against your own internal convictions by not realizing yourself. If you want to trace the essence of life in a purely rational way, then you will miss out on its most important part. It was the spiritual aspect that gave you life. There is nothing in our cosmos except divine omnipotence. Do not allow your ego to determine your life without your permission, with its narrow-minded views.

All knowledge is simply an aspect of the whole, giving proof of that part of omnipotence that is God. Knowledge does not lead to wisdom. Once you have ascertained that you know nothing, you are standing on the threshold of your own self-aware mind. Individual knowledge is not real knowledge. It is only a drop in the ocean compared to the wisdom waiting to help you live your life the way you desire it to be.

Albert Einstein once said in one of his discourses on the well-known popular proverb "Faith without science is lame and science without religion is blind": Do not cling to knowledge of details. Think, feel, and act from your center where all knowledge of your being is united. From there you will scoop up the truth, freedom, and other values that will help you lead a perfect life.

One who trusts his inner wisdom will soon see through the methods of those obsessed with power who would like to have you in spiritual tow. If you are united with the creative omnipotence within you, there is only one truth. It is invisible, eternal but still your personal reality. Creation, in its infinite intelligence, has put all power and knowledge into you and you can have confidence that you will be granted everything that you need.

In our society, the term "success" has been given a slightly one-sided materialistic definition. A successful person is to most people associated with financial strength.

Up-bringing, education, and profession almost exclusively concentrate on this one-sided definition.

Success is open to you, as well. If your thoughts are filled with success, its realization will be initiated in the workshop of your mind. Our whole being is set up in order to secure success within the range of human existence. This is manifested by a harmonious relationship as well as by one's profession. A person's development is expressed on many levels as well as in one's bank account. Money is a good help if it is kept within the "river." It is a good means of making our life easier. However, real wealth is based on a fulfilled life, and this is open to everyone. It is the gateway to our destiny.

Light does not attack darkness, it takes it away.

POSITIVE CHANGE IN THREE STEPS

Greedy people speculate for material profit. In the name of progress, they pollute our environment, forcing us to lead a stressful life. They do not know what they are doing. Every type of greed for more than we need makes us pass our greatest spiritual source of strength by without even noticing it. The cosmic strength within us gives us what we demand with a pure heart and a deep inner participation.

One who believes oneself to be neglected by luck should search within for the misconceptions that have led to them being hurt. We should realize that our own (negative) thoughts and our doubts are the obstacle that keeps us imprisoned within our fears and problems. Let us transform our fears and our negative thoughts into positive energy and we will undoubtedly become winners, reaching the goal we desired. Whatever you want to achieve, there is no obstacle to you reaching a fine objective through the omnipotence lying within you.

Tackle your desires in three steps:

1. Do not make any negative statements. Transform your way of thinking through positive suggestions, telling yourself daily:

    "There is love and harmony in my heart and my mind. God thinks, speaks and acts through me. I have confidence in the inexhaustible source of my vitality, which determines my life, turning everything to my advantage. It strengthens my spiritual abilities, making me do the right thing at every moment.

    From the peace in the center of my being, I exude love to all people in the world. I can feel and I know that the more my positive strength radiates, the stronger the stream of positive events is that inevitably come back to me. Everything that I long for comes to me. The harmony of my being fills my life. Everything happens by itself. "

2. One who dedicates more and more attention to love and harmony will not waste his time and energy on outbursts of negative emotion. Eliminate rage, anger, envy and jealousy from your life. None of these feelings will ever be of any advantage to you. Rage is based on a lack of admission of causing our own unpleasant situations or on our own idea of what constitutes an unjust life. Envy comes up if we do not believe we are able to achieve something that others have achieved. Envy weakens our vitality

because it makes us humiliate ourselves. Jealousy is a lack of self-confidence that we transfer to our partner. Jealousy is one of the most destructive mental poisons that ever existed. It is a waste of valuable time and energy, the false side of life that does not advance us any further.

Lovingly, but decisively, drive away the smallest trace of these feelings from your mind. Peace and harmony are sacred from this moment on into the whole of the future.

3. Learn to communicate with your subconscious mind with the help of images. As soon as you are sure about your intentions and your inner voice has confirmed that it is the right way, transform your plan into an image. See yourself in your vision reaching the goal of your desires. If you want to build a house, you should imagine the completed house. If you have a physical weakness, see yourself as healthy and cheerful. If you are aiming for professional promotion, you should imagine yourself in the position that you want to reach.

At least once a day, sink deep into your ideal image through meditation. See the final situation vividly before you. Nothing can resist this creative suggestive strength except your own doubts and your fears that it will turn out to be wrong. Your subconscious mind will use its inexhaustible strength to realize your intentions and you will thus experience what you are thinking of.

Only the weak tell lies.

SYSTEMATIC CONTACT WITH YOUR SUBCONSCIOUS MIND

A successful person does not need any outside help. They know who they are. They know what they want. They rest within themselves and their mind is clear because their inexhaustible source of strength will do everything else.

The secret of an unsuccessful person lies in the fact that they do not know what they want.

A person who does not know what they want also does not know who they are. A person like that is among those who have not found their place in life and who have not put any effort into finding their Self. This implies that life is a process that leads to realization. I would like to tell you that once you start realizing yourself, everything that you refer to as "being on the way" will be initiated. One who does not know who they are and what they want stands in their own way. Solely through their not knowing about their alternatives, they do not make any progress. Thoughts like "It's not really my thing" demonstrate how they have not begun to be aware of their own infinite mental strength. We should carefully approach the consequences of these words in order to grasp what lack of self- awareness really means. If one is not aware of oneself how can they use their inner strength to achieve their goals?

Such a form of self-development follows very simple rules. Our character is created through influences and our reactions to them. The extent to which we realize the sense and position of our being in life decides our level of self-realization and thus our personality.

Ask people who are successful, who have really made it. As a rule, they will all give a similar answer to this: "My success? I knew what I wanted! Even if others laugh at me or consider me crazy, I have total self-confidence and have always remained true to myself. It has been very simple. I have followed the spiritual image of my goals that are vividly in front of my inner eye!"

Take away a rich person's millions. It will not affect them very much. Their mind is programmed on wealth. Without a dime to their name, they would get their millions back within a few years. One who feels rich will be rich!

Observe your colleagues, neighbors, or simply a few street workers. The one cheats with their long breaks and cutting corners in order to save energy till the end of the working day. Another is interested in their job. He completes his job precisely and quickly and even enjoys it. It would be little wonder if he were soon to become the foreman of their group. Their superiors will notice their commitment, effort and quick handling of any accepted task.

You will always be able to recognize that the active person who is aware and determined will attain more success in life. Nothing harms a person's personality more than lethargy. A negative attitude to work and the steady fight for power and a higher income, so prevalent in our economy, turns people into destroyers of their own soul. Inflation and unemployment are the consequences of low quality human ethics. Unemployment is mostly the result of stirred-up fears. It serves political and other interest groups to extend their power. You should realize that one who rests within himself is unassailable and free to follow their path the way they want.

Do not blame past situations. Your reaction to events is the creator of your own problems.

Desires Become Reality

Create clear and precise images that you will give your subconscious mind to be realized. One who says "yeah" today and "nay" tomorrow makes themselves like a rocking horse that cannot make any forward progress.

If you have a special desire, picture it, with your eyes closed, in the most vivid colors. Indulge in this image of the optimal fulfillment of your desire. Indulge in it with your fantasy until you reach the highest levels of your imagination.

Once you reach this point, ask your conscience whether you can eventually influence or harm some other person. If this is not the case, then turn the image of your bringing about your greatest desire into your daily meditation. It will mean that the positive strength of the cosmos is coming to help you if you act for the benefit of all people. Recall what it is you want to achieve during short breaks two to three times daily. Especially in the evening before falling asleep, you can let your desire be created in front of your spiritual eye. Using this image, influence your subconscious mind with the following suggestions:

"I will experience my desire in reality exactly the same way as I see it fulfilled before me. The infinite intelligence of my subconscious mind will use its omnipotent strength to achieve this. I see myself reaching the goal. All that I see now is already reality. Thank you, Father, that it is so."

The additional dimensions of consciousness, referred to nowadays by the commonly used term "extension of the consciousness," cannot be discovered using sensory tools such as our eyes, ears, nose, or sense of touch and taste. We can experience them only through inner contact with our mental layers.

Use your very own knowledge of humanity to your benefit and the benefit of others. Go on a royal path to a perfect life. One who starts using positive thinking in their everyday life should be prepared for momentous, miraculous and blissful experiences. Test the diversity of your alternatives. It is simple. What you create in your thoughts will happen to you.

If you have to get over some failure, do not allow yourself to be depressed. Every failure is telling you something. It is a messenger who has something to give you. Tell yourself: *"Since there is only cause and effect, it had to turn out like this. I was not aware and I shall take this failure as a good reason to observe, being more aware in the future. Failures are a closed door. But two new ones will soon open. I concentrate on my strength and my inner voice. I am clear and safe in all my actions. My goal is clearly before my eyes. I am successful in what I long for from the bottom of my heart. The infinite intelligence within me directs and protects me and it will lead me to the fulfillment of my desires."*

PROTECTION FROM STRANGE INFLUENCES

Do not let yourself be influenced by self-limiting proverbs such as "Seven years of bad luck" or any other type of doubt, for that matter. Even a bad dream about an incident is not a reason to become anxious. Nothing is predetermined if you do not believe it to be.

Of course, there are clairvoyant dreams. One who has these abilities will know whether to understand a dream as a warning. One who believes in being cursed really believes it to be so. No one has the power to spiritually harm us. We can give them this power only if we believe ourselves to be vulnerable. An African medicine man's curse is effective only if the cursed person is informed of it. Their belief makes fear rise up within them and this finally kills them. What they believed happened to them.

Do you feel beset by some unknown power? Then shake it off! Deny access to such alarming thoughts. You are free if you feel free and you are not free if you believe yourself not to be free. The curse "Go to hell!" most affects its user. It produces the energy of hatred, which is the power that weakens them most.

It is very simple to protect yourself from negative energy. If you are overcome by an anxious impulse, pray. Put yourself under the protection of the highest intelligence within you. Let yourself be guided by God. There are many stories where a doubting Thomas in great trouble finally experienced admittance to his divine core. Follow your insight, sinking into your depths to the source of your life. The strength of God surrounds and protects you. If you feel safe through this connection, no power can harm you. There is only God and nothing else can touch you.

For this purpose use the following words, enunciating shrilly as if you were on the stage: *"Harmony and love keep flowing through me, through my whole being. I can feel the power of my center strengthening me and determining my life. I am safe in this source of my vitality. I rest in the inexhaustible strength of my highest intelligence. It surrounds and protects me day and night. I am strong and free. One who searches ultimately finds, one who knocks gains access. Thanks to God, I searched and thus found."*

After this, meditate on the meaning of these words. One who lets himself sink into the stillness of their innermost being, followers of yoga and meditation call it immersion, will find the answer to their questions. One who looks for protection will find it. The indescribable feeling of happiness connected with an invulnerable safety makes every meditator a rock in a storm. Negative and outside events will soon lose their power and everything will be fine.

To make it more understandable to the intellect, and to transcend the threshold of my daily consciousness, I say: "I am rising in my mind to a height where past, present and future fuse into one grand view and I am granted a new insight into things." When you withdraw spiritually from the outside world imagine this: "I am at one with everything! I am in everything, everything is within me."

Today there is the possibility of taking part in meditation groups in almost every small city. Try it if you feel a longing for spiritual depth.

Everything within and around us is energy, movement. Every atom of even every stone moves in its own way. You also have your individual being, your individual frequency. It is our revolutionary goal to achieve union with divine omnipotence once again, that which was once lost by Adam and Eve.

In this book, let us stay on the practical level of our surroundings. We should not immediately desire the highest goal of life, but start with our superficial reality. Positive thinking is the way to free yourself from your daily difficulties. The more consequentially you call your mind to order within you, the more successful you will become and your life will soon be problem-free. The key to your life happiness at the end of this book obviously lies in your own hands.

"Heaven is within you," said Jesus. It is just for you to open it up.

7

Defeating the World's No.1 Enemy - Fear

Man was created free,
He is free,
Even if he was born in chains.

THE THOUSAND FACES OF FEAR

Fear is among the biggest mental burdens on humanity. Ever since Adam and Eve departed the paradise of harmony with their spiritual guide, thus having to find their own way in the material world, fear and insecurity have grown to visibly become a sign of our times. It is said that fear has a thousand faces. Fear is the excise people have to pay for being the only humans who really understand the world. Many views of the world are based on the fact that we are the pride of creation. Have we become self-satisfied? Do we live under the illusion that we can intrude into the inner world of nature?

As a harmonious part of the whole, we are welcome. However, if we are troublemakers, Mother Earth will call us to order. Everyone who rests within themselves, keeping contact with their divine source of life through positive thinking, has nothing to fear. They have been integrated into the cycle of the cosmic round dance, being stimulated and stimulating at the same time.

The paradox in our world is that the very institution that should actually be helping us overcome our material philosophy of life is using its clerical power to spread deep fears within its believers. Its pretensions of being the mediator of God has been underpinned by threats of an angry God, through torture in the Middle Ages, to today through less than convincing arguments.

The most shocking example in my previous practice was the story of a now older lady, whose fears, induced by Christian teaching, had deprived her of being able to lead a free natural life for half a century. Mrs. Katharina A. was a district forester's respected daughter. She fell in love with a young "holidaymaker," as he was called at the time, and a few months later she fell pregnant. Her holy world was shattered because of the horror that she had sinned, bringing disgrace on herself. Her student was still unable to marry and they found a doctor who "took away" their child. Before that, Katharina swore to the Virgin Mary that she would never give herself to any man if she were able to get rid of this disgrace as well as the child without the neighbors noticing. In her endless despair, she swore with all that was holy to her that the worst illness should strike her down if she were ever to break this oath. She did not want to have pre-marital sexual intercourse ever again.

However, her love grew stronger the next summer as the lover was once again on vacation in the village. Soon Katharina's 55-year-long period of suffering began. Serious stomach and intestinal disorders appeared. She steadily had to reach for painkillers. A circulatory disorder and hot flushes also came up. She experienced a whole range of psychosomatic disorders. She profoundly suffered although no doctor could help her. The promise given to the Virgin Mary under the shock that later eased had become a forcing suggestion to her subconscious mind, and this was hellish for Katharina.

She now lived her life without opening up to men because of her sworn oath and her fear of confession. Thus, her punishment was suppressed from her waking state of consciousness, but was still constantly being administered by her subconscious mind.

Katharina A. was never given any insight into connecting her constant illnesses by these events. The redemption that was to come to her through her new experience of the love of God could not have been foreseen at the time.

I knew that God does not forgive once nor seven times, but always and for eternity. He is the strength that moves us. We are divine beings created in accordance with his image. Whatever we do, he does not condemn us and he never accuses us of anything. We can walk our way in freedom, shaping it the way we desire it. However, how was I to transfer this confidence to my female patient? How was I to make her understand that it was her who had condemned herself in her despair to a life full of pain and suffering?

This background knowledge about the endless suffering that is spread in the name of God, and the fact that many people are oppressed by the church, was the main reason why I turned my back on the church, disappointed with its insufficient management of Christianity. In my early years, without any official help, I started looking for myself for the core of my being and I met God. The opposite can also be applied. As I was looking for God, I found myself. It is rightly said that the Father and I are ONE. I found him within myself. Today many priests look for my advice if they have spiritual problems. If they have to keep a tight rein on their sexuality, sometimes I manage to convey to them that the Creator does not want them not to use his gifts. They should not give up their joy of life for God's sake!

It is said that "love is the greatest life energy." How can an institution appoint itself as mediator of God's order if it spreads fear and horror, threatening us with punishment if we do not obey it? The Creator's omnipotence is a life-enhancing and creative strength. It does not punish anyone. We do this with our negative ideas of God and the world.

To love God means to respect the divinity within us, i.e. that spiritual strength that created us. What you think about yourself you also think about God. Base your confidence neither on dogmas nor institutions, but on the only real basis for life and that is the omnipresent living spirit within you.

If you have a healthy relationship with your divinity, with your life partner, and with all other people, then you feel safe. Only a loss of confidence originating from the intellect creates fears.

You are the herald of something new. You appear and the old goes away.

SELF-LOVE

"Love your fellow man as you do yourself." Who understands the meaning of these words in our everyday life? One who does not love themselves cannot love anyone else. They distance themselves from their holy center. One who does not love themselves can be simply described as "crazy." Is our world, with all its chaos, not living proof of this?

According to one study, 95 percent of Western civilization is considered neurotic.

In everyday jargon, we always call people crazy who, in our view, dance to a different tune. One who acts outside the norms of society is considered mad. Society is, in many cases, not even aware of the fact that it pushes some of its number into isolation.

Let us take a widespread illness as an example. Schizophrenia has become symbolic of our time with its various latent, active forms. According to the opinion of psychosomatic science, it is not innate but acquired. A susceptibility to schizophrenic states is latently present in every person. It can be activated by loneliness or some other cause, such as tension in the family, as in the case of adolescent schizophrenia.

Conventional medicine considers schizophrenia an anomaly of the metabolism of the brain. This corresponds to the exclusively materialistic attitude of science, which has not been granted the privilege of finding the soul as of yet.

"Pure fact is in itself inaccessible to us because we can only get close to it in perspective," once wrote Immanuel Kant. This attitude toward both soul and faith that has prevailed to the present day serves to satisfy a society that believes itself to be at the pinnacle of an old culture. Anomalies of metabolism can certainly be determined in some mental illnesses, but they are symptoms of this illness rather than its cause. I have often tried to follow the fantasy of schizophrenics, achieving interesting insights. A mentally unstable person does not find it easy to live under the almost inhuman pressure of order within our society. Sometimes they can only save themselves by distancing themselves in order to avoid further reprisals.

If a mental patient feels themselves to be dissatisfied with their therapist prescribing them tranquilizers for their psyche, claiming that they are still suffering from their mental illness, there is a high probability that the doctor who is treating them will refer their case to a psychiatrist. When medical practitioners speak of a case, they often subliminally demonstrate that they have depersonalized the case. The person as an individual has once again fallen by the wayside. At the clinic, fits are treated with pharmaceutical drugs. Even to the psychiatrist, the physical level is unfortunately the only accessible "opening" for reaching the patient.

What actually is a mental illness such as schizophrenia? If psychiatry only recognizes a problem of metabolism in the brain as the cause of illness, then it is really difficult to prove anything else.

If a lunatic finds their way again, putting themselves on the straight and narrow, we are often unaware of how it happened. We assume the reasons they got ill, we assume why they got healthy again. However, the fact that the healing actually took place is of the utmost importance.

"A madman does not need a doctor, but a friend," said an Indian sage. He does not want to be treated as an object, but to be loved and taken care of, because his distancing from the world is often only a form of escapism. His subconscious mind discovers that in such a way he can live far more comfortably. At some point he was not able to cope with the world anymore. He withdrew and saw other people looking after him. He transferred the responsibility for his life to the psychiatrist.

"If you can tell a madman that not only is he crazy, but that you are too, links will immediately be forged. Then he is reachable," said Osho to his disciples.

Our intellect sometimes cannot follow the intellectual flights of a schizophrenic. All around the world scientists confirm that the enhanced perception of such patients overlaps to a great extent with psychedelic experiences in experiments with drugs. The schizophrenic has become a master of imagination. With the power of their imagination, they create a "place" where they can find peace. They cannot become the masters of their "multiple dimension" again, because they have pursued their illusion too far, not finding a way back to reality.

The different areas of psychology and psychiatry should pay more attention to the possible causes of these "illnesses," to the surroundings, to the eccentricity and anomalies of society. We can learn to understand to a far greater extent what was needed to remain hidden.

However, we will return to the main point of this book and that is to shaping our lives and our character in such a way as to be able to cope with the world and not go mad. In cooperation with both the discovered and undiscovered spirit within us, we can reach self-realization while at the same time staving off the possibilities of pathological withdrawal.

Awaken the desire for God in others.

EXTRAORDINARY WAYS TO A HIGHER CONSCIOUSNESS

Years ago, I undertook my own experiments searching for self-realization. Once I generously bribed the guard of the Pyramid of Cheops to lock me up inside the pyramid overnight after the end of a tour. I spent seventeen hours together with the alternative practitioner Stefanie Merges in the complete stillness and darkness of the royal chamber close to the sarcophagus. The English Yogi and writer Paul Brunton experienced here a schizophrenia which he reported on in detail in his book Secret Egypt. Many small copies of the pyramid are today used for energetic experiments in different places.

During these mystical hours, we experienced the incomprehensible mysterious powers of the Pyramid of Cheops on our body and soul with their prototypical force. An hour after turning off the lamps, darkness was lost and I believed I could see everything in the soft glow of an unfathomable source of light. I felt beamed through, illuminated and investigated, as if I had been connected to a huge generator. The longer I sat in the meditation position with my eyes closed, the brighter it was within me. I perceived my whole body and my head as being brightly beamed through and vibrating with this incomprehensible energy. I could now understand why people with negative attitudes and fears are not able to stand this concentration of energy. In the deathly hush of this pitch-black night, their fears and insecurities would become immense and reach a climax. Such extreme states can lead to madness and are also the reason why for years no one has been allowed to stay overnight in the royal burial chamber.

The sensitive Melanie Merges described it in a similar way: "I was surprised that it was so light in the passageways, although I knew that the lighting had been turned off ages ago. After fifteen minutes, I sensed a loud singing (humming) in my head. Erhard Freitag also heard it. Did it come from outside, from the Sphinx? Was it possible? Was that a wind in the ventilation shafts? We could not explain what it was. It seemed as if women were singing. We were exactly in the middle of the burial chamber. I immediately get a strange taste on my tongue when I talk about that night. We were in a state of high tension, just like foehn [a warm, dry wind descending a mountain]. It was wonderful to meditate and we felt as if we were without a body, only pure spirit.

Twenty minutes before midnight, a deep humming-like droning began to sing an eternal "OM." It must have been our heads vibrating, because the pressure in our heads continued to rise for the next two days. Never have I experienced such an extraordinary atmosphere in my life!

When, fully dazed after seventeen hours, we staggered into the warm sun again, we thanked Ra, the old Egyptian god of sun into whose kingdom we were allowed to return, for the mysterious clarity with which we had experienced this. Over the next two days, we could not close our eyes at night, our soul was fully awake and our intellect simply could not comprehend it."

The American researcher John C. Lilly put himself into a special mental state in a different way. He let himself be closed into a big tank filled with salty water where he floated on the surface without moving in absolute stillness and darkness. Today there are such tanks for self-experience experiments at the disposal of the general public for those looking for something extraordinary. In perfect stillness and without any sensory perception, we try to find access to higher levels of consciousness. So far, only mystics and saints have reported what awaits to be discovered beyond reality. It is high time this level was revealed to us all.

I have especially been fascinated by Eastern cultures that try to reach the light, the final goal in life through yoga and meditation. In such a way I have received strong impulses from Indian wisdom. In my view, one of the deepest "insights" was born in Indian philosophy. Most Europeans, who have hardly read anything about this, are unaware that it can provide the essence of both Eastern and Western wisdom.

The intellect can recognize problems, but the level of change lies deeper.

I Sense God with My Center

Sometimes the followers of different spiritual paths come to my office seeing me as a stop off on their search for effective techniques for faster "advancement." They all have the same motive. They are looking for freedom from this world, but they are mostly looking for it within this world. However, they can find it if they put together heaven and earth, if God and the world are reunited.

Even the effort of trying to attain a perfect state of being presents an obstacle in the way to enlightenment. We should learn to let it just happen and we then will be guided. However, if we intend using our will, we should be aware that "we can have what we desire only if we do not desire it anymore."

Begin right away when you wake up in the morning. No matter which thoughts come up, tell yourself: "I can feel God in my center!"

Whatever happens, do not let yourself be distanced from your center. Always turn to the only power that has given you life, making you overcome all superficiality, guiding you and giving you safety.

The fear that makes us feel lost and confused acquires as much power as we give it. We are the ones who over and over again determine our destiny through our fear. Fear has the ability to magically attract the very situations that have brought it about in the first place. The law of resonance draws like toward like. I can well understand that anyone really imprisoned within their fear will see this almost statement as irony.

A few days ago, I was visited by a woman who for years had been living in angst of her fears. Infuriated, she said: "How can you fob people with deep mental problems off with such useless advice. Fear is within me! Or are you claiming that I'm imagining it?" I answered her with a counter-question: "Do you think that you approach life with confidence, taking strength and safety from such an attitude? Or do you believe that someone or something outside is always responsible for your situation?"

Of course, she did not have any self-confidence with respect to her life and she was thus imprisoned within her world, where she played the victim. Something else somewhere else was always to blame.

A lack of contact with our own self, with God at our center, is to blame for many petty fears in our everyday life and the eventual ensuing madness. Isolation and imprisonment are the causes if we become unbalanced. Our negative thoughts are the cause if we lose our grip. Positive thinking is the pathway to awakening. It is based on the realization that we were neither created by some abstract force nor a product of fantasy. That force is fully comprehensible only if we have confidence in it. To look for this realization means to knock at the door which is then opened for us. At some point, the presence of God at our center is no longer just a question of belief. It becomes knowledge of our own nature, which is God itself.

If you have turned toward positive thinking, you have not done it out of boredom, but because of an inner guidance from the (un-)discovered God within you. How can you still be afraid of having this knowledge of a creative force within you? How can you be depressed? How can you have fears knowing that God within you guides you and that the divine principle lying within you is ready to help you whenever you need it? Fear has no place in a person who has confidence in their creative force. I want to show you the way to your God. You will find him anyway, even without me.

If someone is suffering, sympathy is the most useless form of care. Sympathy only strengthens the bond with a negative experience of "destiny." A wise person will speak of the necessity to break the Ego if it fights against the higher consciousness, which is its usual reaction.

This can really sound harsh, but the best way to help another person is to show them the cause of their suffering. To fulfill the desires of an egoist implies actually feeding their egotism. One who recognizes positive thinking as the solution to their problems already has their goal within their sights. With the aim of offering help to those who feel caught up in the net of their own thoughts, circles of friends have been founded that, on my initiative, try to cultivate positive thinking. With each meeting, the number of participants is growing. Many of these self-help groups have already created new circles for new interested people.

If you give nothing, you will receive nothing.

REMOVING FEAR FROM EVERY CELL IN THE BODY

Psychologists long ago realized that there is a hidden fear behind almost every symptom of illness. Fears are created in our childhood because this is the period when we cannot defend ourselves from excessive negativity. Fears can influence the unborn child even five months before birth. If there are additional difficulties during the birth, because of the mother's fears, the young human child can come into the world with a much higher potential for developing fear than a child from a harmonious relationship after a normal birth.

We collect experiences from our earliest child-hood. Traumas, shocks, and aversions suppressed into the unconscious make you suffer all your life, and should be discovered and eliminated. It has already become a part of everyday life that adolescents increasingly have to confront harshness, not knowing how to proceed. No fear or suppressed complex has the right to last-ingly exist in our subconscious mind. It is never too late to become aware of your strength, and in so doing, release the "burden" of impressions within our uncon-scious memory. Positive mental energy is the strongest power in the cosmos. Nothing dares and nothing can contradict it. Our higher Self awaits our undertaking to free ourselves from this narrow-mindedness.

If we want to control our life only through our intellect, we will be able to master the growing list of demands only through some kind of compensatory measure. For example, smoking, alcohol, bulimia or sex without love present attempts to divert the mind in an attempt to blind yourself from your problems. Positive thoughts relieve you of these suppressed complexes wherever they might be hidden in the subconscious mind.

A female patient, who was visiting me due to her lack of self-confidence, her fear of exams and as a way of giving up smoking, was suddenly found dripping with sweat in our treatment room in the middle of her therapy. In the short time the therapist was absent from the room, the female patient must have experienced something very disturbing. My therapist woke her up and she stood up wheezing. She told us that she had suddenly experienced extremely painful cramps in the back area of her kidneys and in the upper part of the pelvis. Years ago, she had been injured in a car accident on the right side of her spinal column. After particular activities, such as driving a car or studying for days on end, she always needed treatment from her doctor. Under hypnosis, she tried to relax and remove the pain but could not.

During our conversation, another problem came up. She found it absolutely abhorrent, as she reported, to be considered hysterical or a hypochondriac. Since her childhood, she had had a firm sense of self-control and a certain front. Her family would say: "How you feel inside is of no one's concern." This "attitude" became her second nature.

Surprised, she observed my female colleague laughing happily. "Today we have untied two knots in you," we explained to her. "By letting yourself go, you have relaxed for the first time. If you steadily tense your muscle and then suddenly relax, this relaxing hurts. Your pulse can quicken and a breathing disorder can appear. In your case, the back cramps are caused by the fear that you will experience again the pain that you suffered after the car incident. The second knot was the idea from your childhood that you had to hide your inner self. Now you have opened up, telling us everything and you will experience this new-found freedom from your mental troubles as freedom from your physical pain as well."

During the final consultation, she thankfully reported that she had not had back pain since that strange session when she succeeded in completely letting herself go. It was a sign that a traumatic block had been released. "Loss of mental blocks" and elimination of her problems resulted in a better understanding of her fellow man. Her unconscious strength kept flowing in order to help her finally cope with her studies. "Thanks to you, my life has become deeper, more colorful and harmonious," she wrote a few months later.

Followers of classical psychology would never consider it possible to resolve these problems through suggestion. This is in no way an argument against positive thinking, rather a lack of ability to rid themselves of ideas drummed in by years of education. Although there are hardly any statistics on the subject, according to estimates, the processing of suppressed complexes in orthodox psychotherapy is at most around 25 percent successful.

One who can let themselves go, replacing negative ideas with positive suggestions, will be successful in eliminating their inner tensions, fears and traumas, as I described it in the chapter on catathymic image perception. All by themselves, the patient will later find an explanation of their adventurous journeys into their own depth. They will overcome their old fears solely through understanding that these fears can only exert their tormenting power if left buried.

If we can just once see through them in clear consciousness, these ideas will lose their burdening content, thus sinking into unimportance. This means that positive thinking will have reached its goal.

Do not believe in magic, but in yourself. In such a way magic can take place, assisting you.

The Behavior of Trying to Impress in Politics

One who rests within themselves is full of harmony of the mind, body, and soul. The symbolic fairy tale of the Brothers Grimm "about one who set out to learn about fear" aims to convince the majority of people that fears are a part of being.

This is mirrored everywhere in our public life. A possibility for compensating for fear is reflected in a striving for power. One who wants to be worth something has to loudly demonstrate their superiority in public. They become a victim of their own behavior of trying to impress in an attempt to extend their power. The noisiest troublemakers in politics hit the headlines most. Driven by their own insecurity and fears, they preach hatred, stirring up trouble within the business sector.

All politicians and trade unionists are, almost without exception, falsifiers of the sense of life. They do advocate development, perfection and a harmonious life, but what they actually mean can only be read between the lines. There is only one guarantee for a better life. That is to change one's consciousness to correspond with a natural, God-willed life.

Any positive thinker will sooner or later succeed in eliminating mental blocks that consist of fears and frustrations, with or without help. They do not only free themselves from their burdens, but through their growing harmony, they become a calming influence in a global sense.

Try telling this to a politician! He cannot even comprehend that the contents of his consciousness determine his energetic and mental constitution and that he can rationally cooperate with them. He would talk only about practical constraints, and any philosophy based on positive thinking would only represent a childish theory and nothing more. If he could only learn to benefit from the contents of his wise consciousness, we would have a world without problems.

To denounce political thinking as life-negating provokes a pure lack of understanding in our society. Give it a thought. If you as an individual would feel better physically and mentally as a result of your own strength, then the so-called representatives of the public would see all their hopes dashed. You would not be so easily manipulated anymore! You should determine what you want and what makes you feel good. Do not let yourself be assigned anything that someone else has decided for you.

To participate in politics means to suffer under the blind direction of the intellect. I know some politicians who do try to make ethics and harmony a part of their party politics. The result is that they are laughed at as being "esoteric" and are mostly found in the lower ranks.

Surrender to a future with inner freedom, harmony, and love in your life. Harmony and success in life will come to you in great abundance if you start trusting your wisdom. The physics law of the balance of forces is valid even at the level of spirituality. Pressure produces counter-pressure. Love creates requited love and harmony creates harmony. What do you create?

No one will ever give you any compensation for a single minute of unnecessary suffering and fear.

Who would think about nuclear holocaust or the arms race while searching for harmony? All those who stir up fears are wasting their life. Think of Mahatma Gandhi, who successfully opposed a foreign power in his country with the majority of the population on the Indian subcontinent. Non- violence coming from the consciousness of the inner strength and harmony saved a nation from exploitation and unpleasant despotism. Love of his own country overcame all outside powers and the weaponry of this world.

An Exercise for Calmness of Thoughts

Do not let yourself be infected by your noisy and hectic surroundings. Free yourself from fears by beginning to believe in your ability and becoming the way you were meant to be.

Carry out a short exercise. Sit in a comfortable chair. Close your eyes and relax. Now give yourself the affirmation: *"My head is free of thoughts. All useless ideas fly away. I let them go. There is perfect stillness within me."*

Perhaps it will not be so easy to reach stillness at the first attempt. Try, without desiring it too much, not to have any thoughts for 30 seconds. Try to be empty. You will find that it is possible, although you are not used to it. If you repeat this exercise a few times daily as a short relaxation exercise, sticking to it a while, you will be more and more successful. Finally, you will really reach the level of having stillness of thoughts for 30 seconds. That will be a huge step in the right direction and you will recognize its usefulness by being generally calmer.

It is crazy to refuse to see the light shining on those who have seriously dealt with it simply because of your prejudice against the eternal philosophy.

RE-CHARGING THE BATTERIES OF LIFE

If the soul suffers, it loses its joy of life. If fear has its "home" within you, it will influence all areas of your life. We give up our autonomy too easily to the dangerous energy of thought, in such a way cultivating our worries. Is this not contrary to our scientific way of thinking?

Do not let yourself be convinced by any traditional medical practitioner that the cause of your illness is exclusively your proneness to it, or a virus etc. This is the purely physical basis of an illness. It overlooks the subtle mentality within you. Your fears and negative thoughts discharge your batteries, making you prone to all types of infections. Immunity against a severe lack of hygiene, attributable to the Hindus on the Ganges or Indian village communities under the worst conditions, is seen by Indians as a consequence of their spiritual stability. According to their holistic philosophy, nothing can harm them if it has not been predetermined.

When it comes to the inner world, put your will out of the game. To wish to help yourself with your will is tantamount to trying to calm yourself down with a sledgehammer. The will, controlled by the intellect, cannot cope with mental confusion. Our inexhaustible fountain of infinite vitality is hidden more deeply. Everyone can reach it if they use the strength in their inner world. The subconscious mind follows statements of the consciousness and not the desired ideas.

I sometimes have the experience that a patient brings in a whole list of their ailments. These ailments seem so important that they even write them down in order to be able to report on them in detail. Stop worrying about your illnesses. Take care of your health! Stop concentrating on your problems. Instead, start caring about all that is desirable and that you have always longed for!

A middle-aged female teacher from an elementary school once applied for therapy with just such a list from the last decade of her life. After listening to a detailed report, I tried to tell her that it was top-heavy. She had got used "to being" in the head too much. She had not noticed that she was being terrorized by her own thoughts, blocking access to her center.

I told her that she could help herself only by becoming a seeker. She should not accept the dictate of her intellect anymore, constantly seeing her negative mental state confirmed by new thoughts. First, I let her realize over the course of long conversations why she had ended up how she was. Up to that moment she had only followed her own view of life, which had led to all these non-desired events.

If you learn to really let go, harmonizing your inner life, then you are on the best path to finally putting your catalog of illnesses back on the shelf. It is even better to burn that catalog in order to prevent you from once again returning to the memories of the past. Someday you may be tempted to see whether some of them can eventually be used again. Many negative events and thoughts from a time now behind you would be better left "forgotten" than memorized.

The tired out female teacher did actually succeed, although she had to fight against her rationalism more than some others have had to. After a few weeks of therapy, she told me that she had finally gained control over her class and not the other way round, which had previously been the case. She even began integrating a part of her suggestion therapy into her lectures, thus amazing her pupils with new communication techniques that she had learned at my seminars.

AN END TO AN INFERIORITY COMPLEX

A business consultant who I had freed from an inferiority complex shook his head over and over again during our final conversation. His voice would falter whenever he tried to sum up what he was trying to say. He could not understand that he could have reached the age of 48 before accidentally (accidentally!) finding out through positive thinking the connection between suffering and negative ideas.

"Could two thousand years of science not have brought more light into the darkness of the soul to prevent us from having to constantly make the same mistakes?" he asked me.

He was also surprised about my simple explanation. Thought is the energy that induces experiences such as happiness or failure, illness or health. It is the breeding ground for inferiority complexes and timidity, for fears and frustrations of all kinds, but, if positively reversed, simultaneously the source of strength to enjoy your life. There is only one controlling power in the universe. It is within you. You can feel connected with it since it is your own higher Self.

This is, to begin with, a particularly great mystery to the over-pressurized professional. Have you created this state yourself? The top manager of a huge company gave me an explanation of his nervous tension and the diversity of his illnesses over the last few years. He was also aware that too much pressure at work and too many meetings had had an effect on his condition. In reality, he was afraid that at the age of 54 he could not keep up with the demands of his position, the demands for performance by society and the pressure exerted by the ambitions of younger rivals. He was afraid that he would simply be outstripped and that he would suffer another heart attack if he did not calm down.

The interconnections of his stressful situation were soon explained. I reminded him of the "Harzburger model" that he had once studied. This model recommends you delegate more responsibility. That may include employing a collaborator in order to reduce some of the burden. Generally, he understood the problem, although he did not see a necessity for any assistance at work. He had simply been blinded by routine and scared. He had lost the ability to overview his life, losing all insight.

He experienced hypnosis as a real success. During the therapy, first his stomach ulcers disappeared. He lost the "inner readiness" to give in to an especially acute form of migraine which often leads to neuralgia. This outside suffering is often described as suicide pain because it is among the most intensive and painful alarm signals that show us we are really in the "red zone." A migraine is almost literally translatable as "I'm racking my brain about something."

My patient threw himself into non-stop activity on the subject of the interconnections of positive thinking as any intellectual would. It became his salvation. Within a few weeks, he was blooming, having found a way back to his outer framework through inner harmony. I gave him a tip to take with him. I told him to avoid, as much as possible, his diverse social obligations. One who makes themselves rare becomes more valuable in society. Nothing can sap energy and frustrate more than the circus of thoughts arising from constant gossip at parties.

BECOME A DETERMINED PRACTITIONER OF OLD WISDOM

Be aware that your intellect can never resolve your problems. Mental suffering is created by conflicts suppressed in the subconscious mind or by ideas and experiences that are followed by strong and mostly alarming emotions that are then suppressed into the bottom of the unconscious mind. If you were once scared to death or you failed in an important situation, the conscious memory of that may have faded away long ago. However, your subconscious mind will make you feel that long-ago- experienced fear over and over again in an unrecognizable form and in a completely different situation. If our society is constantly discussing fear-inducing issues, these fears will inevitably exert their influence on more and more areas of our everyday life. Never-ending BSE [bovine spongiform encephalitis] scandals, AIDS, pension problems and environmental issues do not just stop there with their alarming effect. They have further impact, affecting us detrimentally.

Positive thinking has the effect of a ray of light during a mental experience that at once brightens one who is experiencing it. We live here and now. One who concentrates on the moment, positively shaping almost every action and thought, will immediately experience a freedom from worries and burdens.

If you are frank with yourself and others, half your troubles will melt away. A good personality is appreciated for its straightforwardness and sincerity. Discard all tricks in your thinking. "Make that which gives you pleasure," once explained the Indian teacher of wisdom Yesudian. One who reaches their inner freedom is always stronger, more genuine, and only they really live their life.

"I can feel the smell of flowers and my world is again full of color," I was told by a student who had left the gray area of her fears and outside worries after treatment. During numerous sessions, we awakened a series of her complexes from their "exile." She was the one who had to explain and thus process her strong accumulated emotions, which were released in wild, symbolic scenes.

Even a change for the better sometimes includes healing pains. Before reaching a harmonious mental state, accumulated emotions may well emerge. The therapist is like a spiritual assistant keeping a close eye on events and giving the patient at every moment essential help. What is mystical about this is that the cause, be it fear, a trauma or something else, can finally be eliminated if the patient really wants it to happen. They are deprived of its energy, not allowing it to harm the subconscious mind.

I consider catathymic image perception, as recommended by the Ministry of Health and taught to parents and teachers at elementary schools, a mild way of releasing mental blocks and neurotic features. One cannot easily generalize which is the right method. It depends on the mental and spiritual constitution of the individual which way and which form of therapy will best be chosen.

Every moment of happiness is a gift to this world.

POSITIVE HELP IN AVOIDING FORCED SITUATIONS

A 54-year-old man whom doctors had given up on because his fear of life and his more and more pressing compulsions in everyday life had (medically) caused incurable cancer, experienced in the clinic a strange version of enlightenment. After being carefully informed about his condition by the doctors, he burst out laughing about the absurdity of human life. He went home with the intention of laughing till the break of day at all he had taken seriously and considered really important in his life. Now he had driven himself mad. He had been pushed out from his old frame. Only humor interested him now. He collected jokes, steadily trying to establish contact with humorists and cabaret artists, laughing throughout the day. He could be royally entertained by any human folly. Later, the doctors were afraid that their patient would further lose his mind, but he had actually forgotten his illness long ago.

Today, after more than two years, he is completely healthy and living proof of the intensity of the joy of life. The biggest shock in his life, the allegedly "deadly" illness, helped him to attain this mental and physical freedom. I have also described my own case of cancer and its healing in one of my books.

Not everyone experiences such a wonderful salvation, but all of us stand on the threshold of positive change at every moment of our lives. Let us open our eyes to look over the barriers that limit our own view of life so that we can see that the path to freedom is right before us. Whether or not we follow it is up to us.

Some fears that find no outlet can create extreme behavioral disorders. Twenty-five-year-old married Marie Ann tried to withdraw from her self-induced compulsive situations through fantastic lies. Depression and aggression interchanged and under their influence she would hurl plates in her kitchen at the walls instead of washing them. Worse for her were her nightmares, which deprived her of a good night's sleep, making her get up exhausted in the morning. Fear of being a loser in bed, fear of being beaten by her husband, and fear of not doing her job properly all had their origins in traumas from her hard and frustrating childhood, where she had lacked love.

The cause of her new fears was her husband. He himself was present at the treatment. Marie Ann was open and capable of allowing the strength of her positive thoughts to have an effect. Constant suggestions built up her feelings of self-worth. She realized that she was a free and responsible person who could look for "her" own way. She relearned to live and strongly oppose her husband if she had the feeling of needing to defend herself. Her steadily growing patience and her understanding sometimes left her husband speechless. He was no match for her in his put-on role of ruler. Through Mrs. Marie Ann's positive change, their marriage entered again into a calmer phase.

Freedom is an internal matter.

Extracting Power from Natural Deep Breathing

Many of our petty fears are part of our everyday life, often making our existence appear difficult. Such fears can really be eliminated right away because they exist only in our perception, having little to do with reality.

"All very well and good," some would say, "as if my boss doesn't frighten me enough!" Or as one female patient expressed it, "You have to be worried. The newspapers are always full of new and terrible stories! You simply can't switch off, pretending that everything is all right!"

Here we have examples of the impersonal word "you." Why does one cede so much power to a term that anything can be hidden behind? Whatever happens, you are unassailable and safe if you rest within yourself, keeping your inner harmony by means of creativity and not allowing any disturbance. A harmonious person calmly accepts what they cannot change and changes what they can change. They accumulate a lot of strength within themselves in order to deal with the unexpected. They radiate so much security that criminal elements do not even notice them. Harmony has the effect of a tranquilizer, both in one's personal life and in one's surroundings.

The effect of fears is mirrored in certain everyday expressions, for example, in "It took my breath away," "I nearly choked on that," "That knocked the wind out of my sails," "That made my heart jump." These expressions show that breathing, or our "autonomous life support system," is very often impaired by danger.

You only need to observe anxious people. With hunched shoulders as if they would like to sink into themselves, they breathe flatly through the upper area of their lungs. In such a tense posture, they cannot breathe in any different way. We can live sixty days without food. We can live six days without water, but not six minutes without breathing. To breathe badly or falsely means to live falsely.

"First aid" in alarming situations can be given through breathing. Do not let it come to tension at all. Keep your head up and relax your shoulders. A deep breath up to the stomach area will bring you primary relief and soon you will feel again like the master of your situation.

People with naturally deep breathing live more healthily and are calmer. They are balanced and relaxed both physically and mentally. According to the Hindi view, not only more oxygen penetrates our lungs through deeper breathing, but also the subtle Prana, which mentally strengthens us. Modern physics recently included this ancient knowledge in its research. Deeper and calmer breathing up into the stomach, as is taught in yoga, is therefore one pre-disposition for our well- being. During relaxation exercises, as part of hypnotherapy, the therapist pays attention to deep breathing from the stomach. Without this letting go, relaxation is impossible.

Wherever you are, adopt the following exercise. It is more important than a mid-morning snack or a coffee break:

1. Leave your work for a few minutes. Even in a huge office, the boss will soon notice that this break can be more tolerable than "work by the books."

2. Position yourself close to an open window, or better still, in the open air; breathing slowly, lift your arms at the side above your head. While breathing out, let them slowly fall by your side until they again fully hang by the side of the body.

3. Slow down your breathing so that exhaling lasts 10-20 seconds, as it is pleasant to you. Imagine the air flowing through your whole body up to the pelvis. The stomach should also be relaxed.

4. Keep your breath for a few beats of the pulse, pushing air out again through the mouth while exhaling with a kind of hissing sound. Then wait for four pulse beats to pass until you inhale again.

5. Five to ten breaths are enough. You will feel rejuvenated, having more energy and joy to continue the work. One who has to perform a monotonous or sedentary job should repeat this exercise once a day.

What will others think when they see you? Do not pay attention to that. Your health and inner calmness are far more important. Others will soon get used to such behavior and might even join in. In Japan and China, teams from all the working rooms interrupt their work for a common physical exercise period twice a day.

Sarah, a young and single mother who wanted to take her final exam and graduate from school at the age of 27 was typical proof. As with many other women, she also had very shallow breathing. Her intellect did not allow her to express her feelings. Mental blocks, frustrations, and now fear of her exams were the direct causes of her temporarily strong headaches.

In only 14 days, the lines on her face were more relaxed and her headache had disappeared. After relaxation training and suggestions of harmony and love, the whole upper part of her body relaxed. Her thin lips became fuller. Before that she had a tired, depressed posture. She soon came to us as well rested as after a week's vacation.

When I bid her farewell, she caused me to experience one of the most beautiful feelings of success. With a single sentence, she made me realize that positive thinking had opened up her deeper being. "Fear is not worth it anymore," she explained. "I cannot understand at all why I had so little self- confidence in my own strength!"

8

Is Happiness a Matter of Thinking?
Thought as a Cause of Mental Disorder

Miracles do not happen
in contradiction to nature,
but only in contradiction
to what we know about nature.

TEST YOUR PLAY ON THOUGHTS

"Any bad luck that we impose on ourselves cannot ever be stopped," says a Chinese proverb.

The truthfulness of this proverb still remains intact if we remove the adjective before the word "luck." Thus we get the following positive directive for our future life: "any good luck that we attract cannot ever be stopped. "

Print out this proverb to put it on the wall. It will become a monument to your greatest life successes.

Erhard F. Freitag

Immediately start taking care of your health rather than your illnesses. Attract luck through positive thinking. Good luck and bad luck differ on a spiritual level only through the quality of their vibration. You are not forced to stay in an energy field you dislike. Through your thoughts only, you can realize the miracle of desired improvement.

Test your intellect to determine how and when it is cooperating with you. Mark your calendar in red every week when you withdraw for five minutes, two to three times a day in order to keep what you have thought of in the previous five minutes.

For example, decide in the morning that you will examine yourself at 9:50, 1:10 and 4:05. This time can be found in any job. The results will surprise you. Remain sincere! Sink back with full concentration in these moments.

In every consideration break, make notes on literally every thought that preoccupies you at the time. Small intimate thoughts are often the most important ones. After this week, systematically evaluate your notes. Write on a big piece of paper one after the other the main point of each thought. For example, a quarrel with a female neighbor; longing for physical love; happiness because of nice weather; speculation for profit; ambitious objectives at work; longing for change; furious thoughts about your boss; looking for tools and so on.

Whenever the same thought crops up in your notes, which might be attributed to striving for profit or the eternal search for an ardent longing, make a note in the vicinity of that point. At the end, you will notice that 60-70 percent of your thoughts keep repeating themselves. These thoughts contain the substance of the strongest suggestions that you are exposed to while you are thinking. Your well-being, health, and success depend on these prevailing words. If you succeed through positive thinking in having mostly positive thoughts dedicated to your well-being and your longings, then you are not only perfectly happy, but also at the peak of your life.

Comfort yourself with the fact that this would not be easy even for a priest. Absolute control over our train of thoughts in our inner world really would make us supermen. People with such abilities would appear unreal. The most important thing in this small experiment with thoughts is the fact that a path lies here! There also lies the cause of my suffering and my weaknesses. The strength to rise above everything that burdens me at every moment of my life is within me. At every moment of awareness in my life, I am thinking and my future depends on the quality of my thoughts!

Misleading Negative Thoughts

If we now observe in more detail the effects of false ideas, it will be more and more clear how much power we have at our disposal. One who sticks to a fear transforms their created images full of fantasy directly into a negative quality of life. The subconscious mind "listens with you," giving your thoughts form, function and experience. In this sense, we are whatever we think of. Our subconscious mind is the executor. Our subconscious decides, our subconscious mind carries it out!

A suggestion based on a fear becomes a reflex for seeing only bad and negative moments and alternatives in everything. People who think in this way are simply cutting off the positive half of their life for no good reason. Give them this book as a present if you meet them. They should also be made to realize that they create their own worries and that they are the masters of their own fate.

A harsh sentence, often used in a legal context, can be applied: "Ignorance does not protect you from punishment." You can now protect yourself from suffering by not turning the energy of your thoughts into dark clouds, but into the sun of your being that keeps on shining.

There is no other way but to direct your ideas. Positive thinking eliminates your hard-headedness, behind which you often "narrow-mindedly" defend your position. The vernacular very creatively describes mental events that can figuratively characterize well one entrapped in false patterns of thinking. This entrapment by narrow-minded patterns of thought can be felt as a lack of awareness of our relationships with others. Sometimes we all look for guilt in others and the whole world is our rival. Our excuse is that we do not wish to be in conflict with our destiny.

Generally, our feelings of guilt pile up in overwhelming quantities. This was the case with a depressed female patient who at the age of fifty still felt sorry for not having said yes to a man thirty years before. In reality, her stresses had their roots in an abortion from that period, which nonetheless could not keep the man around. Her strongest maxim was to now help herself follow the spiritual law of living here and now and eliminate the issue of her unresolved past.

"Your past thoughts have formed your present, what you are now thinking shapes your future," I told her. "As long as you rehash your past, you will live in the shadow of your old ideas that wear out your vitality. Live and act now. Live and act positively and you will immediately rest freely and without burden within your divine core of being, like at the moment of your birth."

Can you see through the charade that we have created by our negative thoughts? Everyone has sun in their heart and we only need to pull across the dark curtain of our thoughts to live in the light of a new creative realization. Your soul will again be bright and warm and your body will be freed from undesirable patterns of thoughts.

The more sensitive you are, the lower the quantity of suffering you will experience. Insensitivity leads to unnecessary resistance, creating unnecessary suffering.

WHAT IS CRAZY, WHAT IS NORMAL?

Neurosis, depression, and many other psychosomatic disorders all have similar causes. They are reactions to too much pressure imposed on our psyche by a negative and stressful strategy to life and the fear arising out of this. As long as you are not anchored in positive thinking, I would advise you to take down the following list on a spare piece of paper.

Seducers to negative thinking:
1. Narrow-mindedness, intolerance
2. Fanatical views

3. Suspect rules of life that appear reasonable
4. Feelings of guilt
5. Doubts about the sense of life

Do you remember that medical practitioners consider 95 percent of humanity to be neurotic? You and I surely belong to this group. Knowing how and why, what choice do we have other than to day by day take greater steps toward getting closer to our longings and real concerns of life, sincere in our efforts? One or other of us will perhaps succeed in this very soon.

Dedicate yourself daily to your mental hygiene. At least once in the evening before falling asleep you should call up the spirit within you, being in contact with it by way of this "conversation." Also use the quotation that I recommended for daily consideration break: "God's love fills my soul, God's peace is in my heart and my mind. There is perfect harmony within me. I radiate love, peace and good will to all people who I come into contact with."

If you act like this, you will never be one of those who pushes others into feelings of guilt and fear. Our mental institutions are full of patients who have been pushed into hopelessness by the harshness of others. Their paranoia often has its origin in a lack of love and affection in their surroundings during the most deciding phase of their life.

The dividing line between an adapted and isolated person is not all that thick. A psychologist humorously described three iterative levels between spiritual clarity and confusion in the following way: "a neurotic person is one who builds a castle in the clouds, a psychopath is one who lives in it, and the psychotherapist is one who rents it out."

A psychotic person demonstrates the real power of thoughts. The magic of their own ideas limits them and they sit in the most secure prison in the world. Behind the walls of their illusions they live their life with visions of horror and with a feeling that they are a victim of some kind of conspiracy. Such people should be fed love and patience and not pharmaceutical drugs.

The wife of a 38-year-old schizophrenic, in whose case hypnotherapy could not be used, asked me to meet her husband at least once. In a session using catathymic image perception, he immediately pictured himself in an air raid on Dresden. It is highly probable that he is still suffering from a trauma from that time. The conversation with him gave me an extremely interesting insight into his spiritual attitude. He felt he was misunderstood by people, claiming that in all his interactions he had to go a few levels lower in order to even be understood at all. Like a psychedelic on the best of LSD trips, he parted from us and from my therapist with the words: "This conversation has helped me! You have a lot of crystals around you" (that was how he "saw" my words). To my secretary he said: "Goodbye. Oh, by the way, your left eye is on the right!"

Who could give a precise judgment on this man's statements? One who has read about experiences with LSD will have found out about the incomprehensible diversity of colors and forms that the human sensory perception can produce under the influence of drugs. In the case of a schizophrenic patient, this is a normal state. The richness of symbols while on a trip (drugs) has been less well researched. Levels of perception that our five senses do not have access to are opened up.

LOVE & HARMONY AS A SUBSTITUTE FOR NEUROSIS

I was once invited to a trial of a runaway drug addict as an expert witness. The accused, an apprentice without any support from his family, looked within drug circles for what he could not find at home. He was from a well-to-do family and was given, as many rich parents' children are, everything that he desired, except, that is, for the love that he needed for his development. As is the case with many drug addicts, he also had an extremely strong impulse to escape from a normal level of consciousness. Face to face, he once told me: "I can't stand it any more!" At least sometimes he wanted to be able to forget his so far dissatisfying earthly destiny, finding escape in a more blissful state of consciousness. It is really astonishing how much has been written and discussed about drug addicts' upbringing and family problems, but nothing effective is ever done to change this. Love and affection, interest in another person's inner life, this simplest and greatest strength cannot be institutionalized, perhaps because of a lack of initiative on the part of the individual. We still have to take our inner life into our own hands and as a rule, without a competent person's guidance. Every young generation is only ever as good as adults deserve with respect to their attitude to life.

Alcoholics are in a very similar situation to drug addicts. However, they have the big advantage of being able to ruin themselves by a socially acceptable means. The alcoholic is in my view not an ill person, but a person who urgently needs mental support and care.

An excess of mental pressure almost always affects the body in such a way. A lack of love for oneself or in one's surroundings always drives people to acts of desperation.

It can start already if a child has to grow up in an orphanage without parental guidance. If you can see through the terrible loneliness that many people are pushed into in their earliest childhood, then you will also be able to see the negative substitute for a lack of positive contact with one's fellow man in a police officer's actions when he is cuffing a convicted criminal. A thief, whose trial I was attending, was released on probation under the condition that he go for therapy. He explained to me in a conversation: "Generally, no one really cares about me! In prison, I am top dog for at least three days, that is, until the next one is brought in!"

Many desperate souls with their deep troubles see the only solution as withdrawing from normal life. They believe that in such a way they will forever bring down the curtain that will hopefully separate them from all experienced suffering. If they only knew what awaits the soul outside the body, then the suicide rate would plunge. Is it not the conclusion of the hundreds of reports from clinically dead people who have been reanimated that "over there" is the same as living here and now on Earth?

Here or in the next world, with or without our body, we can now resolve our life's task realizing why we are here.

To some people this might seem quite speculative. However, it is a fact that every problem that might burden the human heart comes from a misleading one-dimensional thought that we have chosen. All lovesickness, the cruelest fate and the worst illnesses can be seen from a narrow-minded and egotistic point of view.

Is our heart not open to the wisdom of our center? Perhaps we do not know anymore why we have ended up in our current situation, or maybe we do not want to know.

Together with the strength within us we can reach a union with our being which is above all problems.

I could lead every tired-of-life person who has surrendered to my therapeutic guidance out of the blind alley of their narrow-minded ideas back to their holy center. The state of having apparently insoluble problems is a state of not being conscious. Only looking up to your highest Self can help you to get out of this blind alley. One who returns to their all-reaching Self will find the harmony of the mental strength within him. A peace that does not seem to be from this world will come back to them.

The Natural Function of Sexuality

It would be a fascinating study to uncover all the complications caused in the world by frustrations in our sex life. The natural function of sex in our society occupies such a negative place that a whole chain of illnesses have been created. Even in these times of free "love," we should not be mistaken into believing that we do not have among us a host of frustrated sexual deviants. In many conversations with my patients, I have found that an unfulfilled sexuality and sexual aberrations are very often the cause of their problems.

Young, pleasant and married Martin N. paid me a visit. He could not achieve an orgasm in his marital sex life if his wife did not "lend a hand." Since he had used coitus interruptus in the past in order to avoid pregnancy, the subconscious mind had tuned this into a reflex, not being able to differentiate between procreative and non-procreative sexual intercourse. His worry of conceiving a child while he was a bachelor now prevented him having an orgasm even when it was desired.

Martin N. needed only a corresponding short treatment in order to get rid of his old fear. Soon he was free with his feelings, able to "let his strength turn to joy."

Every month, impotent patients find their way to me. In some exceptional cases the frustration and inability to have a normal relationship with a partner turns into aggressive brutality.

It was quite difficult to explain to one of my patients, who liked to stub out his cigarettes on his wife's sexual organs, that there are more pleasant things in this world than enjoying the suffering of others. Perversion and sex crimes have their causes in a diversity of unresolved conflicts. One who is estranged from their deep and natural being is not harmonious and within their center. They are egocentric in their feelings and actions. Nowadays, a more and more "obvious" sexual imbalance demonstrates a growing frustration which is in turn resulting in growing aggression in our society. I have met men and women who look for their sexual pleasure in group sex. I know women who try to get rid of their frustration through sexual intercourse with as many men at the same time as possible. Men want two or three playmates in order to get their money's worth.

The job of opening up not only physically, but also emotionally, has unfortunately remained a dead letter in our culture.

One grows up with a life-long fear of the opposite sex, another cannot understand their inner blocks, and the Don Juan type or nymphomaniac takes physical love as being fulfilling work of self-affirmation, changing partners very often.

One of the greatest frustrations can be experienced in the violation of life imposed by faith. There cannot exist a more negative suggestion than the fairy tale of original sin. If we are searching for reasons for the various forms of dysfunction, then this is one of the main causes.

God does not take revenge, he does not punish, and he does not let those that he loves suffer. He is God who provides everything and is the expression of the infinite cosmic strength to the very last atom of matter. God is the love that fills every soul. To reasonably use all we were given on this earthly world is our task and duty. Sexuality forms a part of that task and should increase our happiness.

What remains is the path to inner harmony. It is the path to sexual passion and joy that stands for life. In this sense, I wish you a lot of pleasure while enjoying the gifts of heaven on Earth!

SLEEP AS A SOURCE OF STRENGTH: A RENDEZVOUS WITH THE UNCONSCIOUS

The almost overwhelming stream of sensory impressions that influence us from the moment of waking up to falling asleep represents an enormous challenge, if we have to process it all. Through sleep, nature has provided an essential regenerative balance if we are tired or too much under nervous strain, also showing us our limits. Under immersion, during sleep we find a natural and direct contact with the wisdom of our unconscious. What we sometimes try to produce in vain through a suggestive technique in daily consciousness can naturally be achieved in a few hours of good sleep.

The increasing prevalence of insomnia is one of the greatest "signs" of our times. Technology and entertainment have turned night into day. A successful businessman, who lit a cigarette with trembling hands every couple of minutes, told me that his head was like a bunch of drunken monkeys in a tree. "When I go to bed at night," he told me, "all daily problems pass in review in front of my eyes. Often fantastic ideas occur to me, but I get no real sleep. Only large quantities of pills can help."

A frail-appearing 83-year-old lady reported to me that she could not survive without "her" sleeping pills at night. "Otherwise I would never reach my eight to nine hours of restful sleep," she opined. She did not know that at that her age she would have been better off with five hours of nightly rest. She probably owed her physical weakness to the side effects of her sleeping pills.

In one case, worries, in another, physical pain, drives away sleep. The grabbing of pills has become a regular habit to many people. Stop undermining your health with this harmful behavior of sinking into a deadened state that paralyzes your unconscious layers. If your thoughts do not want to leave you, then you should leave them. Before falling asleep give your highest instance everything that it needs to resolve problems and tomorrow the proverb will not have to be applied: Good morning dear worries, are you still here?

You should use a personal suggestion for the exercise that I recommend. It should be about your greatest concern. You should ask your higher Self to resolve what needs to be resolved.

Preparation for a good rejuvenating sleep:

1. If possible, I have dinner before 7:00 p.m. The body finds it more difficult to digest meals that are taken later, because the digestive system switches to a nightly period of rest.

2. In the evening I eat only easily digestible meals, low in fat and only small portions of meat. Alcohol should only ever be drunk with meals.

3. A quarter of an hour before I go to bed I will have finished all my activities, reading or mulling over. I go on a short meditative trip, i.e. I dedicate myself to my momentary feelings. I am fully here and now.

4. In bed I do not read or think anymore. I lie stretched out according to my personal preference for the five to ten minutes of the relaxation exercise period. I let go of all daily events, immersing fully into my center. All outside events are now irrelevant. The head is free, clear and without thoughts.

5. In this state I can feel my selected suggestion which I then place into the workshop of my subconscious mind with full confidence. I know that I will get an answer through my dreams, next morning or

very soon. I rely on my higher Self. I will surely understand the answer given to me by my intuitive intelligence and I will follow it with faith.

6. After this, I thank my Creator, letting myself go into restful sleep.

Tasks Given to a Higher Self

You can give your subconscious mind direct orders and your higher spiritual strength should adjust to them. This can be a desire to set your internal alarm clock to wake you up in the morning at the desired time or to know in the morning where to find an object lost long ago. Your inner wisdom will even take out from your unconscious memory a name forgotten decades ago, which will perhaps help you to find the key to a serious problem.

Many people experience through their dreams what their higher consciousness wants to tell them. A woman told me about her divorce that she had decided upon overnight. For twelve years, she had martyred herself to a quarrelsome egoist who saw himself as the center of the world. Her highly ethical view of marriage for a long time had made her believe that it was her task to help her husband.

Suddenly, in the thirteenth year of her marriage, she had a dream about a dark power which darkened her life and finally fully switched off her life light. Wherever she set foot in her dream, the black shadows of that dark power were immediately cast over her. Then suddenly she sprouted wings and she was able to free herself from all her burdens through a glorious flight into eternal light. She was aware that she only had to use her wings, i.e. her mind. Over the following days she handed over a petition for divorce. She had for the first time in her life left her husband speechless by her explanations regarding her intentions.

One who makes a habit out of the evening task to his higher Self will free themselves from fear-inducing ideas, soon experiencing restful sleep.

If all these measures do not help, there can be only two reasons for this. One of them is doubt. "I will of course try, but will it help me to cure my chronic disorders? A pill here and there cannot be that harmful!" You cannot document your lack of self-confidence in a better way. Up to this chapter, you may have already learned how to eliminate your negative ideas through exercises. Do you want to remain weak or do you want to change? You should recall again the already well-known demand: "Choose who you want to serve."

The other reason you do not want to get out of the old monotonous routine is the unconscious background effect that has been based on old accepted patterns of thinking. This pattern crops up time and time again in conversations with patients. One woman told me after the first week of treatment: "I can do what I want and I have really truly followed your advice using my suggestive formula before falling asleep, but as I lie down in bed, I already know that I will not fall asleep."

Of course, the formula is useless if you believe it to be useless in advance. First I had to make this woman understand that she had undermined in advance her preparations for sleep by her negative attitude of expectancy. One who gives their desires the powerful negative package of old habits should not wonder if they fail.

If you have difficulty falling asleep you should use the following preliminary exercise. Tell your subconscious mind before falling asleep: "Now let me really sleep or now tell me what is preventing me sleeping!" The answer is often given overnight. Either in a dream or in the form of an intuitive feeling, you will know over the course of the following day what is the cause of your sleepless nights.

In such a way the strangest reasons often come up. In the case of a young widow, the reason was a promise to marry, given to a man whom she subconsciously could not accept as a good father of her eleven-year-old daughter. An older woman could not sleep because of her feelings of guilt for not having supported her dead son enough during his illness. A company accountant was deprived of sleep for fear of incorrectly using the company computer, causing it to malfunction.

Do not think that you will gain any advantage by suppressing sleep. An exhausted driver who unconditionally wants to reach their destination will enter a zone in which his over-pressurized brain will simply stop functioning and will find peace only in an early grave. One who deprives himself of essential sleep becomes nervous, moody, aggressive and finally depressive. No will can eliminate our need to sleep for a long time. The autonomous nervous system is stronger, being able to switch off in cases of emergency. Here is abject proof that we consist of more than just will and intellect. When these two become conceited in the belief that they are the highest authority, thus torturing the body, the real center of strength within us will unexpectedly express its scorn. Do not let this result in a nervous breakdown. A positive thinker is aware of the interconnections, sticking to the right side of their being, to the basis of health and harmony.

9

Overcoming Illness
Thought as a Cause of Mental
Disorder

Only the mind is ill,
the body becomes ill through the mind.

CREATING A BASIS FOR HEALTH

Above the temple of Delphi stands written "realize yourself." It is a demand that we either follow every once in a while or we do not follow at all. We mostly only want to explain to others what we think and what we want. If our desires offend the rules of society, or if we are stopped in our ambitions or demands for power, we end up feeling frustrated. Soon illness that starts to develop from thereon replaces that frustration. Since we cannot stand outside pressure anymore, we often stand on the verge of a period full of suffering. If you keep convincing yourself of not being good enough and "capable" for a certain period of time, your subconscious mind will show you the influence of this negative idea in the experience of reality.

Medicine treats illnesses symptomatically to a large degree. However, what the outer appearance of the body reveals is only a mirror of our mental condition. The number of doctors who take into account the psychosomatic view of an illness in their diagnosis and therapy is still small.

Most illnesses represent the independent courses of energetic events within the body. Simply put, this means that falsely directed mental energy has become independent and is thus called an illness. Unexpressed and suppressed feelings come to the surface, "telling" us through certain symptoms if something is not in order.

Among many people, you are privileged to know that the energy of your thoughts pushes forward to realization, determining your everyday life and experiences. If we are ill, it means that we have accumulated a pool of negative thoughts, bringing them to light again, either quickly or slowly. Physical pain is a pain that we have not experienced in the domain of our feelings. It is an ache that we have left unexpressed and suppressed. An illness becomes the warning sign of our false behavior. To become aware means to correctly interpret the signs of your fate in order to change what is to be changed and to accept what cannot be changed. We lack the maturity to avoid illness or suffering. One who still does not respect the cosmic law of harmony and love creates a problem that they have to deal with.

A proud man who has based his life too much on the strength of his intellect will be alarmed in his "midlife crisis" to find that by his subconscious mind, he can finally grasp the meaning of life, returning to a union of the mind, body, and soul. Instead of constantly exposing yourself to more and more demands, there are far more important things to experience, such as self-realization and self-fulfillment. These interconnections are not taught in any school. I wrote these pages because it is high time you transferred this knowledge to the world.

Alarm in the subconscious mind is often experienced in the form of a strong hint. For example, heart attacks, kidney damage, stomach and intestinal disorders or chronic headaches are among the signals that our body sends us in order to bring us to reason and deeper insight. Do not let it come to that anymore. It is now in your hands. You now think in a positive way, not having any problems in your mind. Even if you had cancer or tuberculosis, surrender to the power of your subconscious mind, which makes everything turn out for the best. Follow Dr. Murphy, who used the following method in his book *The Power of Your Subconscious Mind*. He writes: "When I had cancer, I made sure I had full spiritual and physical relaxation a few times daily. As in autogenic training, I relaxed, suggesting to myself: "My heart and lungs are relaxed, my head is relaxed, my whole being and existence are fully loosened up. God's perfection now finds its expression through my body. The image of complete health now fills my subconscious mind. God created me according to his perfect picture. My subconscious mind now creates my body again in full accordance with the picture in God's spirit." In approximately five minutes, he would, as usual, fall into a sleep-like state. He would wake up after an hour feeling rejuvenated.

His subconscious mind succeeded in manifesting the idea of his health. He became healthy again. You too have the strength to act this way if you ever find it necessary to do so. I am convinced that spiritual strength can heal. I witnessed it on my own body. I have experienced so many cases of "spiritual" healing that I would like to entrust you with the belief that miracles do happen if you need them.

THE PATH TO FREEDOM

From now on, you are on the path to inner harmony, already being protected from physical affliction to a large degree. Since you started studying at this "University of Life," your inner voice will surely send you warning. If in spite of this, you someday get a serious illness, tell yourself: "I chose happiness, I am healthy, resting perfectly harmonious in my center."

If you need the healing power of your subconscious mind, use the desired number of affirmations. Repeat the suggestions full of devotion, "seeing" yourself in a state of perfect health.

Many illnesses are an escape from everyday life, or self-punishment if our feelings of guilt have become immense. Statisticians have calculated that eighty percent of all incidents at work are caused by only twenty percent of employees. It verges on the masochistic how, in this way, some people unconsciously take out their personal worries or dislikes on themselves.

I have an acquaintance who always tests our friendship through her negativity. Whenever I call her,

I immediately find out that some flu or intestine virus is afflicting her again. There is always some illness that is ruling over her and she is always ill. However, she does not want to hear it that she has caused her own suffering.

Office illnesses such as flu or sneezing fits are a typical expression of unwillingness in our civilization. Dissatisfaction with your job, boyfriend, wife or whole everyday routine creates collective escapes into illness. One who is ill must be pitied. Perhaps they can even stay in bed or have the chance to go for a walk over to the doctor's for a change instead of going to the office. We are mostly unaware of the lengths our ego goes to in order to avoid the non-stop strain coming from society, conjuring up various ailments, both big and small.

One who dedicates themselves to their mental and physical health will soon be aware that they have to jump over fences in order to get closer to their longing for happiness and satisfaction. Your child is also like this if they suddenly wake up with a sore throat because they perhaps have a mathematics test that morning. In such a situation, love is needed and fear-inducing school should not be avoided using this illness. Do not violently force your child to go to school, but carefully pay attention to the loss of self-confidence that your child is demonstrating that day. Try to immediately spread harmony and love, letting them grow in your child. It does not just seem difficult. It is in fact difficult because with a backdrop of a stressful lifestyle, this implies having to change our way of acting impatiently and without love toward other members of our family.

Psychosomatic Disorders

I would rather write about health than discuss the vagaries of the psychosomatic domain. If you are expecting real individual help in your personal life, then the next paragraphs will provide answers to many of your questions.

The psychosomatic domain represents the science of mentally caused physical illness. We have witnessed a large upsurge of this over the latest decades.

If a person, becomes blinded (in the metaphorical sense) to a certain extent, this narrow-mindedness will affect their physical functions, depriving them of energy to that same extent. Many small incidents, from a sprained joint to a fall on the street during winter can be avoided if our thoughts are not somewhere else, but in our consciousness.

The Eastern view of interpreting illness as a sign or a task that we have to accomplish in order to mature is more and more to be found in Western thinking. A friend of mine, a doctor in one of the big clinics in Munich, told me that after a difficult operation many people decide to start a new life, really sticking to what they say they are going to do. Many feel that they have followed flawed routines and that their painful physical experiences have made them more perceptive and sensitive to the real sense of life.

To anyone who has "survived" their life crises, it means that the consequent transformation of their realizations coupled with the decision to live a healthier life are not to be forgotten if they want to leave the hospital. If it concerns you or one of your relatives, then read this book over and over again, marking the places that personally refer to your concern.

Start replacing your old ideas with positive thoughts today. At first do not discuss your plans and intentions with anyone. Even your life partner has a rigid view of you. We sometimes grab too quickly at preconceived opinions. As long as your metamorphosis is incomplete, keep it a secret. Let members of your family be astonished by your transformed being once it has become fully official.

If you desire it, live as a perfect being in your new consciousness and strength from now on. Avoid situations where you are unnecessarily exposed to criticism. Even advice given with the best of intentions can disturb you if your inner picture is still not complete.

Now you have realized what makes you suffer. You have also discovered the strength in your being to "rise above," making all positive power of the universe come to help you.

Recognizing Insanity in Normality

You will notice that in many cases the official norm is actually, in all reality, insanity. In the USA, a husband is supposed to earn money. In the strictly religious Spain, a mistress with a paid-for apartment in the city presents a solvent businessman with a secret obligation. On the other hand, if one actually "stays" with his own wife, this will be met with the comment: "His wife must be pretty hot if he does not see the need to go elsewhere!" Here is another example. In our society, no one is ever disturbed when offered a poison of the nerves known as alcohol at every visit or business meeting.

Whatever you do in the course of your positive change, at first it will be difficult. Be persistent and gentle with yourself. With this book, I am standing by your side assuring you that your surroundings will very quickly get used to your personality profile once it realizes that you have transformed yourself to your own advantage. It will profit from your change to a significant extent because you will strengthen the sunny side of your life. You will also increase your inner harmony, making the positive power of the cosmos present.

It is not at all easy to become aware of the mental causes of your suffering. An employee in a high position came to my office complaining about the depression that was depriving him of any joy in life. He had just been released from the hospital, where they had tried to remove his stomach ulcers through surgery. One-third of his stomach had been removed and he wanted to understand what was going on in his inner secret "workshop."

Over the last couple of years, he had never been asked about the cause of his disorders or mental state. Only rolling treatment, tablets and diet were prescribed for the treatment of his symptoms. However, what could medication achieve against stress and a dried-up vitality? In conversations full of understanding, I could convey to him that his family problems and professional difficulties would in the future destroy the rest of his stomach if he continued to follow his old pattern of behavior.

Two months of suggestive therapy made him a free and healthy person who could now activate the positive strength within him in order to resolve his problems. The suggestions that he used at home after the therapy concentrated on inner harmony, self-love and his surroundings.

"If I had only visited you earlier," he told me at one of the meetings of the Friends of Positive Thinking. "The self-confidence that I have acquired has made some of my problems resolve themselves."

A heart attack is the most intensive warning of being in the "red zone." Its origins and effects have become common knowledge, having been spread by the media over the last decade or so. However, it is strange that the number of heart attacks has hardly dropped.

Many people's favorite habit is still, unfortunately, smoking and in many cases it has already taken a life-endangering form. Statistics show that people are smoking more than ever and a prognosis says that in the next decades a further alarming growth can be counted on.

These words should put you into a state of alarm. Use this minute to have a look at your present behavior in your life.

Take a piece of paper, draw two vertical lines and note on the left-hand side everything that you want to realize. In the middle put everything you should do in order to reach your goals and on the right what you should let go of in order to reach your goal. Finally, estimate from the quantity of notes on the right, in the middle and on the left hand side how much of your time and strength is required. Avoid things that create the highest pressure and require too much time. Lean back and think of the following: "Do I really want what I have written down? Is it worth it to do that? Will I really be able to enjoy my success?" If the answer is yes, then do what has to be done. Act with love and you will fly toward your goal carried along by the creative omnipotence.

If you are not fully convinced, at least go into a lower gear. Your body will thank you for it because it was not built for the pace of life we attain in today's technological age. You will also find out that your enjoyment in participating in worldly events will enormously increase at this more moderate tempo. And the heart attack? You can forget about it since the warning has been acknowledged.

The Pathway to Psychosomatic Health

It is rarely too late to turn back. A life in harmony and love can result in real miracles transforming the shadowy sides of being into joy, harmony, and love. From now on you do not need to experience any suffering in order to grow spiritually. There is no house doctor, preacher, or psychologist who can do more for you than you can do for yourself.

To ease your workload, test yourself to determine which type you belong to.

Type 1
Charges into walls head first if their idea has ordered it.

Type 2
Takes into consideration the obvious benefits as well as the risks of a good idea.

Type 3

Completely follows his intuition. Thinks and acts based on feeling.

The first person does not learn much from his experiences, the second becomes more careful, the third is the only one who succeeds in overcoming all consequences of their flawed behavior. A collapse of the circulatory system or a heart attack does not force them to fear. It is a misconception to believe that you have to put the body into overdrive after such an illness. There is a sanatorium in the Schwarzwald for patients who have had a heart attack. The first day begins with a short physical exercise period for patients who have just been released from the hospital. The next day, they are asked to run very briefly in the forest and this is every day prolonged by a minute. Four weeks later, all heart patients between the ages of 30 and 80 go for a daily half-hour run through the forest. One who frees their subconscious mind from negative images through positive thinking and in future lets their thoughts be directed by the wisdom of their high spirit will soon lead a much healthier life.

Positive thinking asks for persistence. All talk of illness, bankruptcy, bad luck or slip-ups etc, are to be put into the spiritual waste-disposal unit. Handle it the way I do with my constantly ill acquaintances. Do not call them anymore, do not listen to them anymore! You will only get negative energy foisted on you and disaster will befall you.

Positive thinkers are not indifferent. They only have deaf ears for thoughts of weakness and denial, because they know how destructive a story of illness is. No one can accuse you of lacking sympathy or of emotional coldness. Would you expect a healthy partner to drink poison that you have given them? In the same way, you would also not expect them to accept the spiritual poison of negative thoughts that is created by talking about illness. No one has the right to influence another person through their negative view of the world. You have to protect yourself. As for me, I distance myself from such conversation partners, both inwardly and outwardly.

PROTECTION & SECURITY UNDER SPIRITUAL LAW

A fear of death can be eliminated only by confidence in life. With older people, the greatest spiritual help is to be found in their infinite inner wisdom, knowing that life has no end and that at the end of their days, they only have to take off the garments they are wearing.

Love toward all events in life is surely more effective than any tranquilizer. Fear of death will always be connected with physical disorders that come up. Not only because we are getting older, but also because it makes our life spirit slowly and surely dry up, thus encouraging illness.

We had an especially interesting experience with one young man. A mother brought her 20-year-old son for a first consultation. Because of his shortness, at first I thought I had a 14-year-old boy in front of me. The young man was apparently not capable of doing anything in his life because he was full of fears. He steadily fell from one illness to another. In order not to have to leave the house and to keep his mother caring for him, he was almost constantly ill in some way or other. For seven years he had been suffering from diabetes (increased level of sugar in the blood).

The beginning of the therapy turned out to be difficult. It was not easy to calm him down. After approximately four weeks, a therapy break had to be introduced because he had to go for clinical treatment for strong kidney pains. What came to light during these examinations was not an atrophy of the kidneys or anything similar, but an indication of healing. The doctors determined the first significant decline in the level of sugar with no clear reason. After a detailed discussion with my colleagues, we reached a conclusion. The four weeks of suggestions for the general improvement of his health had significantly improved the functioning of his lower kidneys. The cell groups in charge of this had resumed their job of producing insulin. We were all delighted with this speedy change of Peter S. It was once again visible that no illness is safe from a massive attack of positive spiritual energy.

When some parents brought me a cerebral palsy sufferer, I had to give up on hypnosis. Cerebral palsy sufferers can only to a limited extent, or even not at all, be influenced by suggestions because of their uncontrollable movements. However, I was able to persuade the parents to take the young man for dynamic meditation at an Osho Centre in Munich. This special type of meditation, in which the body is put into strong vibration, provokes an intense discharge of physical pressure within a quarter of an hour. It turned out that the spastic cramping movements could be treated on one's own initiative. The young man shook off his accumulated energy. His spastic twitches were undoubtedly only half as strong after only one session of this meditation.

We had an especially successful experience with Mrs. Charlotte P., who had an intestinal disorder. For four and half years she had been suffering from depression, thyroid gland disorders, headaches and ulcerous colitis. At the beginning of hypnotherapy, my associates and I had the impression that she was a really tormented person who desperately needed help.

First, we asked Mrs. P. to come to one of my seminars. The experiences she had there almost brought about instant enlightenment, and she then wanted to include the doctor within her in her treatment to a much greater extent.

After the first 14 days, on the basis of my notes, she made up a number of her own suggestions. Here I shall give you a small excerpt of her evening meditation texts. As a devout Catholic, she noted down the following suggestions:

⚜ Peace, harmony and balance rule my heart and my mind.

⚜ The infinite healing power of my subconscious mind beams through my whole being. It takes on a visible form of harmony, health, peace and joy.

⚜ God's perfection now finds wonderful expression in my body. An image of complete health now fills my subconscious mind, making me healthy again.

⚜ I have found the Lord, who then listens to me, freeing me from all my fears. Nothing can happen to me, because he leads me to still waters and green pastures.

Twenty double sessions of therapy turned her into a calm person who had learned to handle her suffering and get rid of it. Her headaches had already disappeared during therapy. In the summer, I heard at one of the events that her intestinal and thyroid gland disorders had also disappeared.

Cancer—Our Most Difficult Task

The efforts of medicine to put under control the unapproachable illness called cancer are among the most important preoccupations of this decade. Over and over again, the ill are given fresh hope by new miracle drugs or therapy, which finally prove to be flawed or only useful to a small number of people. Trying to give reasons for the appearance of cancer, scientists often point to toxic substances in our so polluted environment or genetically inherited characteristics. Numerous details playing a role in the cancer are pieced together. Up until today, these efforts have been in vain. Only two percent more become healthy today compared to fifty or even hundred years ago. Is this to be the final conclusion regarding this apparently incomprehensible illness?

The reason why medicine faces this illness so helplessly is because it still sees patients as physical objects whose mechanisms are out of control. This unreasonableness on the part of the medical profession sometimes leaves alternative practitioners breathless. Since the status quo that supports the edict "it cannot be what it is not allowed to be" has been maintained and consequently a large number of people continue to die of cancer unnecessarily.

Professor Dr. Douves bases his cancer clinic on a new holistic treatment. He was able to help me when I got cancer. He confirmed to visitors of a seminar some years ago that for a long time he has been giving spiritual help according to Dr. Murphy's method to his cancer patients, who had mostly been pronounced incurable.

In his introductory speech, he said: "If you know Dr. Murphy, you know that we are all falsely programmed, that especially cancer patients are falsely programmed because it is said from all sides: you cannot be cured, you cannot be helped. Based on Dr. Murphy's teaching of positive thinking, we know that we finally have to throw out this scratched record. We have to follow new paths to attain spiritual freedom and openly face a treatment of the mind.

Our medicine is in most cases still very primitive. We treat our patients somatically (physically) believing that we have done everything possible. In the last decade the psyche has far more been taken into account. Now we partially treat patients psychosomatically. That already represents significant progress, but we still cannot fully understand what the person is in their deepest core.

We have apparently forgotten that the mind is above the body and that it can offer help.

Our attitude to spirituality and to God is decisive. Whether we live in harmony with our Self is of similar importance. We exactly know that spirituality is the active principle of the soul and the body and that we have been paying it too little attention."

His orthodox colleagues for a long time could not forgive this doctor his farsightedness regarding new treatment methods. However, he is not the only one convinced that the solution to the cancer problem should be looked for in the area of spirituality. The medical practitioner and head of the Centre for Individual and Social Therapy, Dr. Rolf Büntig, holds lectures in Munich on the topic "Suicide Cancer." Even he gives priority to mental stimulus over intervention on a physiological level. In such a way, he has adopted the view of Eastern holistic science. If you swallow problems, conflicts and negative ideas, for years distancing yourself from the strength of your divine being and enrapturing the wholeness of the divine order, the effect can be eventually seen in the physical alterations that are called cancer.

All searching for outside causes is superficial. The attempts of orthodox medicine to find a physical and material cause of cancer are inadequate. However, do not allow my remarks to take away any faith you might have put in this type of treatment. As I have showed you, every positive idea is helpful in resolving a problem. All that I have told you up to now should only serve to strengthen your hope. You should know that you have already made a further step, rising above treatment with medication only.

Dr. Carl Simonton from Texas/USA really persistently follows this spiritual path in treating cancer. In his Cancer Counseling and Research Center, the emotional needs of his patients are from the beginning taken into account. As one of the top specialists, he found out during research that it is mostly stress that induces depression. This depression very probably leads to a physical "depression." In such a way, the accompanying weakness of the immune system encourages the spreading of illness. Dr. Simonton systematically rebuilds his cancer patients' mental state, helping them to become aware of their body, be more motivated to live and build their feelings of self-worth again. Thus, from the position of "helpless victim in their illness" a patient becomes the doctor's most devoted associate.

Many elements of Dr. Simonton's attempt to reach a higher consciousness and spiritual meaning of an illness have become an important component of my seminars.

One who changes the negative aspects of their stressful life situation through positive motivation and action leaves the vicious circle to which they were drawn into. Positive thinking, relaxation, suggestion techniques and meditation activate a segment of that 90 percent of our unconscious potential which we rarely fall back on in our everyday life. Here lie the reserves of ability to change the picture of yourself and your possibilities in order to better understand the symbolism of your illness.

THERE IS NO SUCH THING AS A HOPELESS CAUSE

Not even the weakest body, not even one who is "incurable" is a hopeless cause. It is incurable only if the patient gives up, surrendering to their negative energy and therefore letting it freely influence their body. Their downfall lies in the doubt that has been allowed to reach their infinite strength, finally killing them.

Possessing this knowledge, can you feel the responsibility that you have toward other ill people? Can you feel the strength of the comfort that you can give them in order to open their ears, eyes, and hearts? The story that life describes is without a final end. At any time and in (almost) every situation we can be directors influencing a process, and cancer is no exception.

In the meantime, I have met numerous men and women in whose cases healing was possible even in the most hopeless of situations. In Munich I know many patients who were given up for dead by their doctors. Years after being given a death sentence by their doctors, they approached me radiating happiness after a positive clinical health test. The metastases toward which medical practitioners sometimes feel hopeless then disappeared. What actually happened?

The salvation of these patients took a very similar course. Almost all of them experienced the cancer after a life full of worries, frustrations and exposure to high mental pressure. Even at the climax of their illness, no one was concerned about their mental and spiritual state. Surgery and radiation treatments were the final alternatives and even that was unable to end their suffering. An Eastern sage would say that one who has fallen into the ocean of ignorance cannot be saved if only their outside garments i.e. their gross material body, is saved.

Many people get in touch with positive thinking in the period of their greatest suffering. It was sent to them at the right moment. One reads Dr. Murphy's or my books, another pays me a visit after an operation etc. The realization that they have accumulated too much negative energy in their life has the effect of enlightenment in all cases. From the moment of that realization, they fully dedicate themselves to the harmonization of their inner life. Some use prayer, others self-made suggestion texts.

Humbly they accept the divine order. They have said and meant it: "Let your will happen!" By following the spiritual laws of harmony and love, this inner attitude brings them salvation. They do not desire anything more. They no longer quarrel with their destiny, but they accept it without reservation. This way of letting it happen helps them to recover using the strongest and holiest strength within their Self.

It is the final break with their false ideas and their misconceptions about God and the world. Pressure has induced an expansion of consciousness that schools of meditation and yoga centers are trying to bring closer to the pure rationalists in our society. Everyone can become such a "blessed" person. Everyone can make the infinite intelligence of their higher Self flow into their earthly reality. "Heaven is within you," said Jesus. No one will ever find it outside themselves.

"A wise person is like a white cloud that drifts in the sky, not knowing where it is going, but full of confidence. Wherever the wind blows will be its goal. We only have to let it happen!"

If you are informed about the presence of cancer by those closest to you, you should not desperately twiddle your thumbs if the ill person still does not know that they can use their inner strength to heal themselves. Send the ill person love and strength so they may find themselves. Unite all your strength with a group of like-minded people. Every extra participant will make the effect stronger. A whole family that sends its energy to an ill person in prayer or group meditation develops a strong healing power that can change a great deal if the ill person wants to accept it. Not sympathy, but participation can help an ill person. Everyone should imagine them healthy and radiating happiness. As a result of spiritual laws, we can transfer any positive idea over any earthly distance.

A colleague reported that he had suggested using this possible way of transferring vitality to a family with a very rational father with incurable lung cancer. In February of that year, the doctors gave him only fourteen days. According to the latest information, he was still alive in winter four years after that prediction. His family reported on the father's unbelievable spiritual change and doctors spoke of an unexplainable "spontaneous remission."

THE FINAL POSITIVE STROKE

There is no trouble that cannot be helped and where nothing can be done. There is also no trouble and problem that does not carry a gift in itself. Osho once said: "You are looking for problems because you need presents!"

Problems can give us important insights. They want to help us to realize what would not occur without them, i.e. without a good reason. Every problem at the same time contains its own solution. The time that has to pass between the appearance of a problem and its eventual solution serves to make us spiritually more mature in the real senses of the word. Sometimes death is part of this. Do we humans dare to ask why?

Once you realize that you are your spiritual savior, then this book will be a connecting thread and will serve you well.

Use all that you need for your concerns from this book. Leave the rest aside until you can make use of it. Surely you will perceive many things in a different way when you read this book for the second time. Do not always take me literally. Some things can be different to how I have presented them. Accept the fact that what I have described does not have to be your truth, but that it can lead you to truth if you ask for it.

There are as many paths to a higher state of consciousness and to a perfect life as there are people on this Earth. Make your life in this beautiful world a unique joy. Receive the spirit that I would like to give you to extend your consciousness. All roads lead to Rome. Therefore follow your road to Rome because it is your road and because enlightenment does not care how it is achieved!

You will find your own path if you get rid of the common thinking patterns which you have been forced into by your up-bringing and school knowledge. I only represent a passing state to an infinitely deeper knowledge whose experience is flowing toward you from now on. Perhaps its final meaning will transcend your ability to understand, but soon "a new heaven and a new earth" will be opened within you. As long as we have an earthly body, we are well on the way and in the process of development. Who would be so conceited as to believe that they have gone further than the person next to them?

Your personal life happiness is the only experience in this world that you cannot get from another person. In order to experience it you have to create it yourself. Thus do not hold your hand out waiting for the generosity of your destiny. Do not put this book aside. Underline all the places that are of personal importance to you as long as you are not living as God desired it. When you learned to read, you had to deal with reading every day. Now do the same thing by starting a fertile relationship with your subconscious mind. Also use this greatest wisdom and newly acquired realization in small areas of your everyday life. In such a way, you will become a new person within a short period of time.

If the highlighted interconnections of mind, body, and soul seem plausible to you, help to change the orthodox scientific spirit, which still thinks too "physically." With positive thinking, prepare access to the core of your being, to health, and all happiness of this world.

The path to spiritual freedom can either be long or short, depending on how intensively you dedicate yourself to it. The more unwaveringly you go down that path, the more you will feel connected with your life. I know some people who, having cancer, did not want to be operated on. They realized the powerlessness of outside intervention, being aware of the warning that lies within the illness itself. At this point, only absolute subordination to spiritual guidance can help and the outcome depends on the non-material powers.

If you share my opinion in this, generally go only to an alternative practitioner or a doctor who uses such methods. Do not allow yourself anymore to be prescribed a quick medication that will only put off your symptoms. In the future, first try to clear up as to whether the doctor in your confidence is also treating your mental causes. In cases of doubt, turn to the American Association of Naturopathic Physicians, the National Center for Homeopathy or similar oranizations.

If you have a critical spirit, then test your feigned surroundings. Do not subject yourself to every commercial offer or magazine article and do not believe that you have to try every new product designed for your well-being.

Treat the state of well-being as a desire and you will first sink into your own Self. Now you have learned about the possibilities to trace the causes of mental and physical disorders. Correct relaxation and suggestive thoughts will help you to regain your inner harmony.

You will soon realize that harmony and love will grant you everything that you have longed for in your life. They will also provide health, success, and even reconciliation with some of my thoughts that you have not yet completely accepted. Remain a person like me. Together we want to strive not to wander down the winding paths of that part of the soul that is egotistical. Remember that we have chosen happiness!

I thank you for following the same path as me through these pages. Perhaps our destinies will touch again. If we meet, simply smile at me. The fruits of our work will make us recognize one another.

Yours,

Erhard F. Freitag

Visit my Web Site:
http://www.efreitag.com

A Short Biography of
ERHARD F. FREITAG

Erhard F. Freitag, born 1940 in Memel East Prussia, first trained as a professional craftsman and then completed an education in commerce. But his leanings were at that time more toward the extensive field of alternative medicine. He then took the decision to make this subject his chosen profession. So he studied at the alternative medical practitioners' school to attain his own professional objectives.

Soon the young alternative medical practitioner discovered that a person's physical illness is often only part of their trouble. Much more drastic are psychological problems, which are frequently the cause of the physical illness itself. Because of this realization, Erhard F. Freitag increasingly turned his attentions toward hypnotherapy. In 1974, he founded his own Institute for Hypnosis Research in Munich, and turned it into one of the most successful Institutes in its field together with his colleagues. His meeting the legendary Dr. Joseph Murphy influenced his work further. He put Dr. Murphy's teachings and therapy of "positive thinking" at the hub of his work. Erhard F. Freitag is recognized today in Germany as a mentor for a holistic way of life. In the meantime, a dangerous illness, which he overcame partially thanks to his spiritual attitude, induced him to shorten his working life. He decided to hand over his Hypnosis Institute to his therapist colleagues whom he had in fact trained. From this time onwards, he decided to focus more on his writing, his training sessions and lectures.

Today he is one of the most read authors of esoteric and psychological literature with millions of copies sold.

He is able to convey the positive experiences of his life to others, and is able to listen and fill with enthusiasm, to provoke and compensate. He is an author and a therapist with charisma. Erhard F. Freitag considers himself to be a normal man who has the simple aim of making known one's own power to bring about personal success as well as having the interests of humanity at heart.